ACKNOWLEr ~~~~~~

Every journey of transformation is sh
along the way. This book would no
profound influence of several i
principles discussed in these pages.

First and foremost, I want to acknowledge my family's deep literary roots and unwavering support. My grandfather's cousin, Simpi Linganna, president of the 62nd Kannada Sahitya Sammelana, and my grandfather, Virupakshi Simpi, whose international publications demonstrated the power of written word, laid the foundation for this work long before it began. Their legacy echoes through these pages, particularly in how we can forge our own paths while honoring tradition.

This book owes its existence to my parents, Channaveer Simpi and Shanta Simpi, whose sacrifice and dedication to education embodied the principles of ikigai discussed in Part VI—finding purpose through meaningful contribution. Their unwavering commitment to their children's future demonstrates the kind of purposeful living this book advocates.

The transformation of this book from concept to reality would not have been possible without my immediate family. My wife, Sheela Simpi, has been my anchor throughout this journey. My daughter, Rashi Simpi, deserves special recognition for bringing these ideas to life through her invaluable work in crafting the manuscript. My son, Hrishikesh Simpi, has taken on the crucial role of ensuring this message reaches its intended audience through his work in publishing and marketing.

The refined quality of this manuscript owes much to the meticulous attention of Uma Bagalkoti, Disha Bagalkoti, and Vaibhavi Awaradi, whose careful editing and thoughtful feedback helped shape each chapter's message with clarity and purpose. Their contributions reflect the principle of kaizen—continuous improvement—discussed in Part IV of this book.

I am deeply indebted to my Japanese friends and cultural guides—Keiko San, Hirasawa San, and Murata San—whose generous sharing of Buddhist wisdom and Japanese traditions provided the authentic cultural foundation for this book. Their patient explanations and lived examples of concepts like shikata ga nai, omoiyari, and ikigai were instrumental in shaping my understanding of these transformative principles discussed throughout these pages.

I am deeply grateful to Hideyuki Hanaoka, whose lived demonstration of *shikata ga nai* during a challenging project recovery fundamentally shaped my understanding of acceptance and resilience, as explored in Part II of this book.

The principles of Kaizen and continuous improvement discussed in Part IV were profoundly influenced by the leadership of Rajkumar Rajagobalan and Suraj Venkataraman, whose unwavering support during critical moments in Japan exemplified the power of persistent, incremental progress.

My understanding of compassionate leadership, detailed in Chapter Fifteen, was deeply enriched by Bruno Coelho, whose approach to leadership demonstrated how empathy and effectiveness can coexist and reinforce each other.

The concept of finding and nurturing one's ikigai, explored in Part VI, owes much to Induraj Nadarajan, whose guidance helped me discover new dimensions of professional growth and purpose.

THE
KATANA
MINDSET

Ravindra Simpi | Rashi Simpi

I am indebted to Anup Mishra, Pankaj Kumar, and Alex Loiseau, whose mentorship during challenging times embodied the principles of resilience discussed throughout this book. Their influence particularly resonates in the chapters on accepting adversity and finding strength in letting go.

The transformative power of authentic leadership, discussed in Chapter Fourteen, was demonstrated daily by Mukul Talwar, Karan Kashyap, Saurabh Ranchan and Abhinav Arya, whose actions showed how genuine connections foster growth and development.

The success stories of Mahesh Pawar and Akesh Kuwar have been instrumental in shaping my understanding of how the principles in this book can catalyze personal transformation and achievement.

Special thanks to Flora Langel De Kock, whose enthusiasm and engagement with these concepts helped validate their universal relevance beyond cultural boundaries.

Together, these individuals have not only contributed to this book but have also demonstrated how the principles of transformation, when applied with dedication and authenticity, can create lasting positive change in our lives and the lives of others.

About the Author

The author's journey bridges Eastern and Western perspectives on personal transformation, shaped by deep cultural immersion in Japan and a rich family legacy of literary and educational achievement. Born into a family of writers and educators—his grandfather's cousin was Simpi Linganna, president of the 62nd Kannada Sahitya Sammelana, and his grandfather Virupakshi Simpi was an internationally published author—the author's path to writing was perhaps inevitable, though the direction it would take was unexpected.

A transformative accident and subsequent recovery in Japan became the catalyst for deep exploration of Japanese principles of personal growth and resilience. Through extended time spent in Japanese hospitals and communities, the author gained intimate insights into concepts like kaizen (continuous improvement), shikata ga nai (acceptance), and ikigai (purpose)—insights that would later form the foundation of The Katana Mindset.

Working extensively with Japanese mentors including Keiko San, Hirasawa San, and Murata San, the author developed a unique understanding of how traditional Japanese wisdom can be applied to modern challenges. His professional experience in Japan, particularly during challenging project recoveries with leaders like Hideyuki Hanaoka, provided practical applications of these philosophical principles.

The author's work has been deeply influenced by both his cultural experiences in Japan and his professional background, allowing him to bridge philosophical concepts with practical application. Through his writing, speaking, and mentoring, he helps others discover how ancient wisdom can guide modern transformation.

Today, the author continues to explore and share these principles of personal transformation, working with individuals and organizations to apply the lessons of The Katana Mindset in their own journeys of growth and development.

His approach to writing, like the principles he teaches, emphasizes authenticity, resilience, and purposeful action. The Katana Mindset represents the culmination of his experiences, observations, and insights, offering readers a pathway to their own transformation through the lens of Japanese wisdom and practice.

TABLE OF CONTENTS

Introduction 1

The Hospital As A Turning Point 3

Meeting Kenji Tanaka: The Swordsmith As A Mentor 6

Discovering The Six Stages Through Japanese Encounters 10

The Katana As A Metaphor For Transformation 14

The Journey Ahead 17

Part One: 23

Chapter One: The Illusion Of Stability 24

Surface Genki Vs. Authentic Genki (Visible Happiness Vs. Inner Stability). 25

Why Humans Crave Stability And The Danger Of Stagnation 30

How Are Habits Formed: Modelling Habit Formation In The Real World 34

Social Relationships And Mortality Risk: A Meta-Analytic Review 37

Chapter Two: Building True Genki 40

Cultural Contrasts: Tatemae Vs. Honne And Their Influence On Stability 43

Tools For Building Authentic Stability 46

Exercises: Crafting A "Stability Blueprint" For Health, Relationships, And Work 51

Guided Pathways: Navigating The Genki Stage 57

Chapter Three: The Foundation For Change 61

A Japanese Craftsman's Obsession With Perfecting The Base Of A Blade 61

Stability Isn't The Endpoint But The Foundation: Resilience As The Key To Handling Instability *64*

Action Steps: Create A "Resilience Inventory" *67*

Part II: Acceptance – Shikata Ga Nai **74**

Chapter Four: The Fire Of Adversity **75**

Witnessing A Hospital Patient's Acceptance Of Their Terminal Illness In Japan *75*

Shikata Ga Nai: "It Cannot Be Helped" – The Cultural Nuances Of Surrendering Control *79*

The Science Of Acceptance: The Difference Between Resignation And Healthy Acceptance *84*

Reflection Questions: What Challenges Have You Been Resisting? *89*

Acceptance And Commitment Therapy: Model, Processes And Outcomes *95*

Embracing What Cannot Be Changed: The Shikata Ga Nai ... *97*

Chapter Five: Surrendering To Growth **104**

A Moment Of Personal Failure That Led To Unexpected Clarity *104*

How Japanese Acceptance Fosters Adaptability *107*

Tools: Guided Journaling To Process Loss, Failure, Or Change *112*

Exercises: Practice Reframing Setbacks With A "Growth Lens" *116*

Chapter Six: Strength In Letting Go **123**

The Japanese Wisdom Of Letting Go *126*

Neural Correlates Of Acceptance And Commitment Therapy *130*

Practical Steps: Simplifying One Area Of Your Life *132*

The Fire Doesn't Destroy—It Transforms 138

Part III: Reflection – Naikan **144**

Chapter Seven: The Mirror Within **145**

*What Is Naikan? A Structured Self-Reflection
Tool Based On Three Questions* *149*

*The Science Of Introspection: How Reflection
Rewires The Brain* *154*

*Exercises: Guided Naikan Practice Focusing
On Gratitude And Accountability* *159*

The Role Of Self-Reflection In Personal Growth *165*

Deep Self-Reflection: The Naikan Stage *167*

Chapter Eight: Confronting Your Shadows **173**

Confronting Your Shadows: A Personal Regret *173*

*Cultural Contrasts: Japanese Vs. Western
Approaches To Shame And Accountability* *177*

*Tools: Shadow Journaling—Acknowledging
And Embracing Your Flaws* *182*

*Action Steps: Create A "Forgiveness Letter"
For Yourself Or Others* *187*

*Mindfulness Practice Leads To Increases
In Regional Brain Gray Matter Density* *192*

Chapter Nine: The Gift Of Rock Bottom **195**

Why Hitting Bottom Is A Starting Point *198*

Practical Steps: Creating A "Rock-Bottom Toolkit" *201*

Part IV: Improvement – Kaizen **207**

Chapter Ten: The Power Of Small Changes **208**

*What Is Kaizen? The Science And Art
Of Incremental Improvement* *210*

*Exercises: Create A 1% Improvement Plan
For One Area Of Life* *213*

Small Steps To Significant Change *219*

Continuous Improvement: The Kaizen Stage *221*

Chapter Eleven: Discipline Over Motivation **226**

Why Discipline Outlasts Motivation *230*

*Practical Tips: Habit Stacking,
Accountability Systems, And Removing Barriers* *235*

Action Steps: Design A "Discipline Calendar" *239*

Chapter Twelve: Momentum Through Mastery **245**

The Japanese Appreciation Of Slow Progress *249*

*Tools: Building A "Momentum Map"
To Track Your Progress* *254*

Implementation Intentions And Goal Achievement *259*

Part V: Compassion – Omoiyari **262**

Chapter Thirteen: The Heart Of Growth **263**

What Is Omoiyari? The Science Of Compassion *266*

*Tools: Daily Compassion Practices—Acts Of Kindness,
Gratitude Letters* *271*

*Compassion Training Alters Altruism And Neural Responses
To Suffering* *277*

Chapter Fourteen: Healing Connection **280**

*Cultural Contrasts: Japanese Collective Thinking Vs. Western
Individualism* *284*

*Exercises: Strengthen One Key Relationship Through
Intentional Communication* *289*

Chapter Fifteen: Compassionate Leadership......................295

*How Compassion Creates Stronger
Teams And Communities*..298

*Practical Tips: Applying Omoiyari In Professional And
Personal Relationships*..302

The Role Of Compassion In Leadership Effectiveness 307

Cultivating Compassion: The Omoiyari Stage 309

Part VI: Purpose – Ikigai 315

Chapter Sixteen: Discovering Your Ikigai..................316

What Is Ikigai? 317

Exercises: Mapping Your Own Ikigai................................320

Discovering Purpose: The Ikigai Stage 324

Chapter Seventeen: Living With Alignment 330

Tools For Aligning Daily Actions With Long-Term Purpose 332

*Action Steps: Developing A "Purpose Compass"
For Decision-Making*...337

*Purpose In Life And Reduced Risk
Of Myocardial Infarction* 341

Chapter Eighteen: The Legacy Of A Well-Forged Blade....343

*How To Leave A Legacy Rooted In Authenticity, Resilience,
And Compassion*...346

The Role Of Purpose In Life Course Development...............347

Exercises: Define Your Legacy Statement 348

Conclusion...351

INTRODUCTION

The morning air was crisp, the kind of brisk chill that nudges you awake as you pedal through it. I was on my way to pick up groceries, taking the same route I had cycled countless times before. The streets were calm, dotted with early risers bustling about their routines. I had just approached the crosswalk when it happened.

It wasn't cinematic—a blur of motion and screeching tires. It was more surreal, the kind of slow-motion disaster where reality bends and the world narrows to a single moment. I remember the thud of metal against my bike and the sensation of my body being flung sideways, as if gravity itself had betrayed me. My helmet cracked against the pavement, a jarring sound that seemed to echo forever. Then silence, broken only by the faint hum of a car engine and the hurried voices of strangers rushing to help.

Pain followed swiftly, sharp and electric, radiating through my lower back and legs. I tried to move, but my body refused, as if pinned under the weight of something invisible. A passerby knelt beside me, her voice calm but urgent. "Daijoubu desu ka?" she asked—Are you okay? I couldn't answer. Words felt slippery, unreachable in the haze of pain and confusion.

The ambulance ride was a blur. Sirens wailed faintly in the background as paramedics worked efficiently, their faces focused but calm. I remember looking at the ceiling of the vehicle, counting the fluorescent lights above me, trying to anchor myself to something, anything.

At the hospital, the diagnosis hit like a second collision: severe spinal fractures, herniated discs, and a recovery that would be measured not in weeks but months. "You're lucky," the doctor said, though it didn't feel that way. I was alive, yes, but the road ahead seemed impossibly long.

Confined to a hospital bed, the world shrank to a sterile room with pale walls and the rhythmic beeping of machines. Days stretched into nights without distinction, a monotony that dulled even the edges of pain. At first, I tried to focus on small victories—wiggling my toes, sitting up for a few minutes—but the enormity of what I had lost overshadowed them. I couldn't walk, couldn't work, couldn't even cycle, which had always been my sanctuary.

Despair crept in like a shadow, slow but unrelenting. The physical pain was a constant hum, but the emotional weight was crushing. I felt like a prisoner in my own body, a spectator to my life rather than a participant. Memories of freedom—the wind on my face as I cycled, the ease of moving without thought—became bittersweet taunts.

Worst of all was the fear of stagnation. Before the accident, I had always been in motion, chasing goals, solving problems, moving forward. Now, forward felt impossible. Each day was a battle against the creeping thought that this was my new normal, that I might never reclaim the life I once had.

There were moments of light, though faint and fleeting. The hospital staff moved with a kind of quiet efficiency that fascinated me. Their demeanor was steady, almost serene, even under pressure. I began to notice their small acts of care—a nurse adjusting my blanket without being asked, a doctor explaining my condition with patience and empathy. These gestures stood in stark contrast to the chaos swirling in my mind, offering glimpses of stability.

As the weeks dragged on, I started to reflect, not by choice but by necessity. Immobilized and isolated, there was little else to do. Questions surfaced, unbidden and relentless. What did it mean to be strong? To endure? To rebuild? I didn't have answers, but the questions themselves felt like a lifeline, a tether to something larger than the pain.

Recovery was not linear. Progress came in frustratingly small increments, each step forward met with setbacks. Learning to sit up without assistance felt monumental, but the effort left me exhausted and sore for days. Physical therapy sessions were grueling, each exercise a painful reminder of my limitations. Yet, amidst the struggle, a thought began to take root: maybe strength wasn't about avoiding hardship but facing it, about finding stability even when the ground beneath you shifted.

It was during one of those restless nights, staring at the ceiling and feeling the weight of it all, that I first thought about transformation— not as a destination, but as a process. The idea was nebulous, unformed, but it offered a flicker of hope. Perhaps this wasn't the end but the beginning of something new, a chance to forge a version of myself shaped by adversity rather than broken by it.

Little did I know that this thought would lead me to a swordsmith in Tsukuba, a man whose craft would teach me lessons far beyond metal and fire. But at that moment, in the quiet stillness of a hospital room, all I could do was breathe and wait, hoping that the act of enduring was, in itself, enough to start again.

The Hospital as a Turning Point

Life in the hospital felt both static and transformative, a paradox I would come to appreciate only much later. At first, I thought of it as a place where time stood still—a world removed from the bustle of daily life, suspended in fluorescent light and the soft hum of machines. But beneath that stillness, I began to notice an intricate rhythm, a quiet choreography in the way the staff moved, spoke, and cared for their patients.

Each morning began the same way: the crisp swish of curtains being drawn, the muted clatter of trays, the polite but firm voice of the nurse announcing her arrival. Her movements were precise, her tone calm but never cold. "Ohayou gozaimasu," she would say, her eyes meeting mine with a brief but genuine smile. It struck me how deliberate everything was. No wasted motions, no rushed explanations. Even as she tended to my injuries—painful work that required pressing and stretching muscles that felt like fire—there was a steady rhythm to her care that put me at ease.

I remember one particular nurse, Matsuda-san. She was a small woman in her fifties, her hair neatly tied back, her demeanor quiet but unshakably confident. She had a way of speaking that softened even the harshest truths. One day, as she helped me practice sitting upright, she noticed my frustration. My body felt heavy, unwieldy, and the smallest effort left me breathless. I must have let out a groan of defeat because she paused, resting her hand lightly on my shoulder.

"Yukkuri, yukkuri," she said softly. Slowly, slowly.

It wasn't just the words but the way she said them, with a patience that seemed infinite. There was no urgency in her voice, no expectation that I should be doing more or better. Instead, she seemed to understand that the process was enough—that the act of trying, however imperfect, was progress in itself.

That moment stayed with me. I began to notice how this ethos—this sense of patience and quiet persistence—permeated the hospital. The staff never seemed hurried, even though I knew they were busy. There was an underlying trust in the process, a belief that healing couldn't be rushed. It was so different from what I was used to, where

4

efficiency often trumped empathy, and progress was measured in milestones rather than effort.

Visitors, too, left an impression. In Japan, hospital visits are often brief but deeply intentional. Friends or family would arrive with small, thoughtful gifts—fruit neatly wrapped, a thermos of tea, a handwritten note. They would bow politely, exchange a few warm words, and leave without lingering too long, as if understanding that rest was as important as company.

One day, an elderly man visited the patient in the bed next to mine. He must have been in his seventies, his back slightly stooped but his movements deliberate. He placed a small vase of fresh flowers on the bedside table, adjusting it until it was just so. Then he sat, hands folded neatly on his lap, speaking in a low, steady voice. He didn't stay long—perhaps fifteen minutes—but in that short time, he conveyed a depth of care that was unmistakable. It was in his tone, his posture, the way he placed the flowers as if they carried a message of their own.

Watching him, I felt a pang of longing. Not for flowers or visitors—I had my share of both—but for the kind of quiet strength he embodied. It was as if he carried the weight of life's challenges not with resistance but with grace, bending without breaking.

These moments sparked something in me. At first, it was just a flicker of curiosity. How did they do it? How did they move through difficulty with such steadiness, such quiet resolve? I began to see parallels between the hospital environment and the Japanese culture I had observed more broadly. There was a kind of resilience here, not flashy or dramatic but deeply rooted. It wasn't about avoiding struggle but about facing it with composure, finding balance in the midst of chaos.

In those early days, as I lay immobilized and grappling with my own frustrations, these observations planted seeds of reflection. The structured care, the deliberate kindness, the unspoken trust in the healing process—all of it challenged my assumptions about strength and progress.

Perhaps the most profound realization was this: stability wasn't the absence of hardship but the ability to endure it with grace. It wasn't about being unshaken but about finding your footing again and again, no matter how many times the ground shifts beneath you.

Looking back, I can see how these early days in the hospital became a turning point. They forced me to confront my own restlessness, my need for control, and my fear of stillness. And they introduced me to an idea that would shape the rest of my journey: that transformation begins not in moments of triumph but in the quiet, often painful spaces where we are forced to pause and reflect.

Meeting Kenji Tanaka: The Swordsmith as a Mentor

My first meeting with Kenji Tanaka was not planned, at least not by me. It was a suggestion from Matsuda-san, my nurse, who had become an unofficial guide to my slow recovery. One afternoon, as she adjusted my pillows with her trademark precision, she casually mentioned a family friend who forged katanas.

"It might be good for you to see," she said. "He believes the forging process is much like healing. Maybe it will help you understand your own."

At first, I was skeptical. What could swords possibly teach me about recovery? But the thought lingered, nudging at my curiosity. Matsuda-san arranged the visit, and a few weeks later, when I could manage short walks with a cane, I found myself on a train to Tsukuba.

Kenji's workshop was nestled on the edge of town, surrounded by trees that swayed gently in the late autumn breeze. The building itself was modest, almost understated, with a wooden sign at the entrance bearing his family name in elegant kanji. Inside, the air was warm and heavy with the faint tang of iron and ash.

Kenji Tanaka greeted me with a small bow, his hands rough but steady, the hands of a craftsman. He was 69 but moved with a deliberate grace, his posture upright, his eyes sharp. His demeanor was calm, almost meditative, as if every gesture was intentional.

"You are the friend Matsuda-san spoke of," he said, his voice low and even. "Welcome."

Kenji was the fourth-generation swordsmith in his family, a legacy that began in the late Edo period. His tools—hammers, anvils, and furnaces—had been passed down for decades, their surfaces worn smooth by the hands of his ancestors. But Kenji's story extended far beyond the workshop.

In the 1980s, during Japan's economic boom, Kenji had left Tsukuba to study metallurgy in the United Kingdom. He became a professor at a prestigious university, where he spent years teaching the science of metal to eager students. Yet, even as he built a career abroad, he felt a pull toward home. The art of katana forging was dying out, and Kenji knew that if he didn't return, his family's tradition might fade into obscurity.

"I realized that knowledge without roots is like a blade without a hilt," he told me. "Strong but unanchored."

His time in the UK had given him a unique perspective. He understood the katana not only as an artifact of tradition but also as a marvel of engineering. The folding of the steel, the careful tempering, the balance between hardness and flexibility—it all had parallels in human resilience.

When we first met, I had expected Kenji to be a figure steeped entirely in old-world tradition, someone who might dismiss modernity as an intrusion. Instead, I found a man who bridged worlds. He spoke with equal reverence for the ancient techniques of his craft and the scientific principles that underpinned them.

As we sat in his workshop, surrounded by tools that looked both ancient and timeless, Kenji began to explain the process of forging a katana.

"The steel is heated until it glows," he said, gesturing to the furnace. "Then it is folded, hammered, and folded again—sometimes thousands of times. This removes impurities and aligns the structure of the metal. It is a process of refinement, not unlike life itself."

He reached for a half-finished blade resting on the anvil. "But the folding is not enough. The blade must also be tempered, quenched in water to harden it, and then polished. Each step shapes the steel, making it stronger and more resilient."

As he spoke, I found myself captivated not just by the process but by the way Kenji described it. There was a quiet poetry in his words, a sense that this ancient craft held lessons far beyond the workshop.

"It is not the fire that destroys the steel," he said, "but the fire that transforms it."

I watched as he carefully examined the blade in his hands, tilting it to catch the light. "Life is the same. We all face heat and pressure—challenges that test us. But these challenges can also shape us, if we let them."

That conversation stayed with me long after I left his workshop. Kenji's words felt like a key, unlocking a way of thinking about my own struggles. My accident, the months in the hospital, the slow, frustrating process of recovery—all of it began to take on a new meaning. I started to see my challenges not as obstacles but as opportunities for transformation, much like the steel that passed through Kenji's forge.

Over the following weeks, I visited Kenji several more times, each visit revealing new layers of his craft and philosophy. He spoke of balance—the need for the blade to be both hard enough to cut and flexible enough to withstand impact. He explained how even imperfections in the steel could be worked into the design, becoming part of the blade's unique character.

"Perfection is not the goal," he told me once. "The goal is harmony. A blade must have balance, just as a person must find balance in life."

Kenji's insights became the framework for this book. The six stages I describe—stability, acceptance, reflection, improvement, compassion, and purpose—are all rooted in the lessons I learned from him. They mirror the stages of forging a katana, each one building on the last, creating a foundation for growth and resilience.

Kenji Tanaka was more than a craftsman. He was a teacher, a guide, and a living embodiment of the principles he shared. His workshop became a space of learning and reflection, a place where I began to see my own journey through a different lens.

Looking back, I realize that meeting Kenji was not just a turning point in my recovery but a catalyst for transformation. Through his words and his work, he helped me understand that life, like the forging of a katana, is a process—a series of trials that shape us into something stronger, sharper, and more resilient.

Discovering the Six Stages Through Japanese Encounters

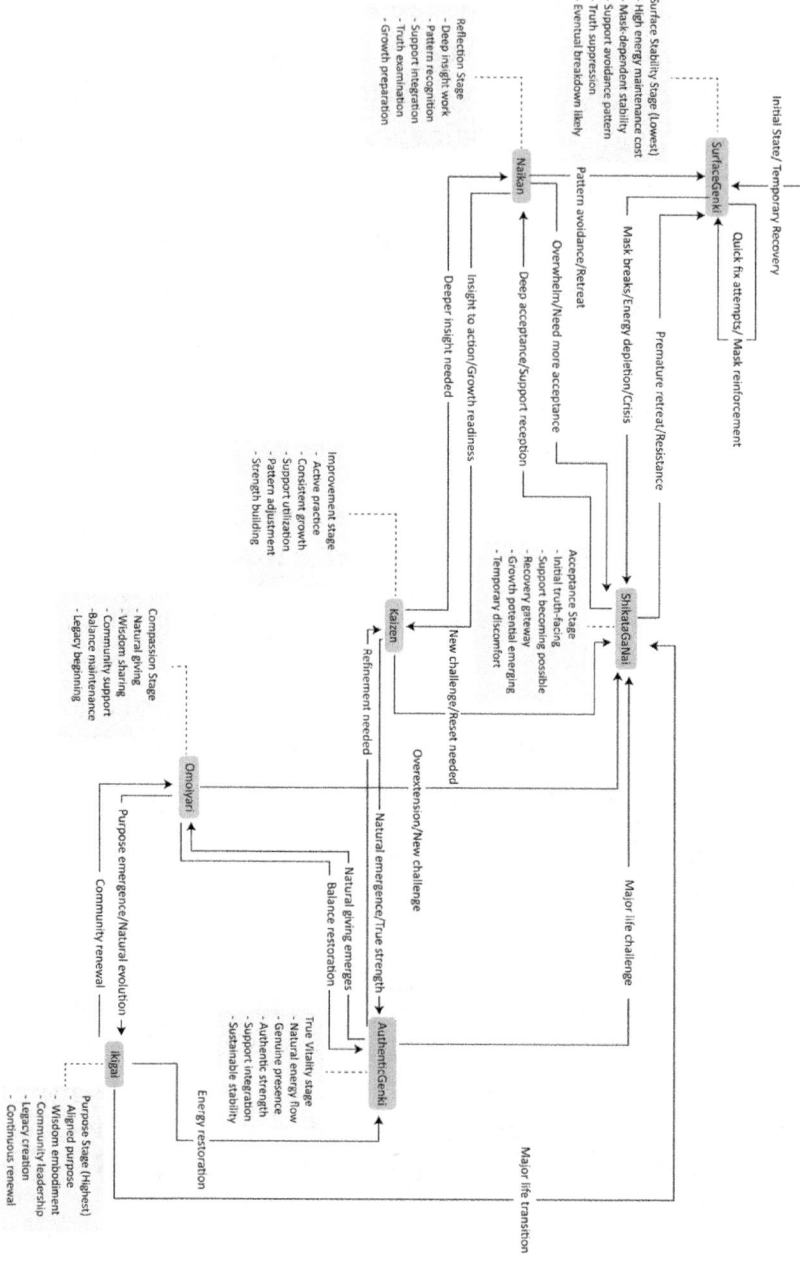

Recovery, as I quickly learned, was as much about the mind as the body. During my months in the hospital, I became a quiet observer of the rhythm of Japanese life. Confined to a small ward, I was surrounded by the steady hum of daily routines, where every act seemed infused with intention and care. It was here, in these quiet moments, that I began to uncover the seeds of the six stages that would later shape this book.

One of the first lessons came from an older nurse named Michiko, whose approach to care struck me immediately. She would arrive each morning with a calm presence, her movements precise and deliberate. Even the way she adjusted my blankets seemed to carry a certain grace.

One particularly difficult day, I was frustrated by the pace of my recovery. My body, once so reliable, felt like a betrayal. Michiko noticed my tension and sat beside me for a moment.

"Shikata ga nai," she said softly.

The phrase was unfamiliar, so she explained. "It means, 'It cannot be helped.' Sometimes, we must accept what is beyond our control."

Her words lingered, not as a dismissal of my frustration but as an invitation to let go of the resistance that was adding to my suffering. I started noticing how often this phrase was echoed in the hospital— the doctors, the other patients, even the visitors seemed to carry an unspoken understanding of it. In this acceptance, I began to find the first glimmers of stability amidst my chaos.

During my second month of recovery, a visiting chaplain introduced me to the practice of *Naikan*, a form of structured reflection that asked three simple but profound questions:

1. What have I received from others?

2. What have I given to others?

3. What troubles or difficulties have I caused others?

At first, these questions unsettled me. My natural instinct was to focus on my own pain and struggles, but *Naikan* shifted my perspective. When I thought of Michiko's patience, the meals brought by kind hospital staff, and even the encouragement from strangers, I realized how much I had been supported. This practice became a daily ritual, one that offered clarity and gratitude, and eventually became the foundation for the stage of *Reflection*.

Another pivotal moment came during a conversation with my physical therapist, Hiroshi. He had an almost stubborn optimism, even when my progress felt excruciatingly slow. "Small steps," he would remind me, "are still steps forward."

Hiroshi's philosophy was rooted in *Kaizen*, the Japanese principle of continuous improvement through small, incremental changes. He shared stories of factories that transformed operations by making one tiny adjustment at a time, and he challenged me to find my own *Kaizen* in recovery. At his suggestion, I set micro-goals for myself: a longer walk each day, an extra repetition of an exercise. These incremental victories began to accumulate, building momentum where there had once been despair.

Compassion, or *Omoiyari*, revealed itself in countless small acts. One day, a visitor I didn't recognize—a friend of a fellow patient—left a handwritten note on my bedside table. It was a simple message of encouragement, written in neat kanji, with an English translation beneath it: *"Even in winter, the plum blossom waits to bloom."*

That anonymous kindness reminded me of what I had seen so often during my stay: the Japanese ability to extend empathy without expectation. From the orderly way visitors brought gifts to patients, to the quiet smiles exchanged in hallways, compassion here was not performative; it was woven into the fabric of daily life.

Toward the end of my hospital stay, I met a retired professor named Takashi, who often visited patients to share stories of his life after retirement. One afternoon, he spoke about *Ikigai*, the Japanese concept of a life aligned with purpose.

He described how he found his own *ikigai* in volunteering, using his knowledge to help others navigate aging with dignity. "It is not about finding happiness," he explained. "It is about finding meaning in what you do." His words resonated deeply, planting a seed that would grow into my exploration of purpose as the final stage in this book.

Not all moments were transformative in the same way. My conversations with non-Japanese patients often highlighted the stark differences in cultural approaches to hardship. For instance, a fellow expatriate—an engineer from Canada—spoke candidly about his frustration with what he saw as an overly resigned attitude in the hospital staff. "It feels like they're too accepting," he said one afternoon.

His perspective reminded me of how easy it is to misinterpret acceptance as passivity. But for the Japanese staff and patients, *Shikata ga nai* was not about giving up; it was about conserving energy for what could be changed. The contrast helped me appreciate the depth of the lessons I was learning here, lessons I might have overlooked without the broader context.

These anecdotes were not just fragments of my recovery; they became the threads that wove together a new understanding of resilience and transformation. Each principle—acceptance, reflection, improvement, compassion, and purpose—seemed to echo the stages of forging a katana. Through conversations, observations, and quiet moments of introspection, I began to see how these ideas could extend beyond my recovery to shape a broader philosophy for life.

When I finally left the hospital, I carried more than physical scars. I carried the beginnings of a mindset forged in fire—a way of seeing the world that was both uniquely Japanese and universally human. This mindset, shaped by the people and principles I encountered, became the foundation for what I now call *The Katana Mindset*.

The Katana as a Metaphor for Transformation

On my first visit to Kenji Tanaka's workshop, the air was heavy with the scent of heated metal and charred wood. The forge glowed like a living thing, its heat radiating across the room. Kenji stood by an anvil, his posture straight and deliberate, as though the act of forging demanded not just physical strength but spiritual focus.

"Do you know why the katana is considered a masterpiece of Japanese craftsmanship?" he asked, breaking the silence with his deep, steady voice.

I shook my head.

He picked up a raw piece of steel, its dull, unremarkable surface a stark contrast to the polished swords displayed behind him. "This," he said, holding it up, "is how it begins. Just steel. Unformed, impure. But inside, there is potential."

Kenji explained how forging a katana mirrors life itself—a process of transformation through intense challenges. The blade begins as an ordinary piece of tamahagane steel, mined and smelted in a way that leaves it strong but filled with imperfections.

"This steel is like us," he said, his eyes meeting mine. "Strong in some ways, flawed in others. Life's trials are the fire that reveals what is within."

He plunged the steel into the forge, the metal quickly glowing orange, then red. With each hammer strike, sparks flew like tiny stars scattering into the air. The steel was shaped not in one decisive blow but through relentless, repetitive hammering.

"This is how we begin to grow," Kenji said, pausing to wipe the sweat from his brow. "The fire is our adversity—the moments that test us to our core. The hammering is the discipline, the repeated effort to shape ourselves into something better."

I couldn't help but think of my own journey: the accident that had broken my body and the slow, grueling recovery that followed. Each physical therapy session, each struggle to reclaim my independence, felt like its own hammer strike—relentless, sometimes painful, but undeniably shaping me into someone stronger.

Kenji continued, folding the steel over itself and hammering it again. He explained how the process of folding was not merely symbolic but essential to the katana's strength. Each fold aligned the steel's imperfections, distributing its weaknesses evenly throughout the blade.

"Imperfections are part of the process," he said. "When you fold steel, you don't eliminate them—you align them. In life, this is reflection. When you face your flaws, your mistakes, and your pain, you don't erase them. You integrate them. They become part of your strength."

His words resonated deeply. In the hospital, I had begun to reflect on my life in ways I never had before. Through practices like *Naikan*, I confronted not only the challenges I had faced but the ways I had caused difficulties for others. That reflection was uncomfortable, yet it gave me clarity and balance. Like the folded steel, I was beginning to align the imperfections within myself.

After the folding came tempering, a process that seemed almost paradoxical. The blade, heated to an extreme temperature, was plunged into water to cool rapidly. This sudden shock gave the katana its signature balance—a hardened edge for cutting and a softer spine for flexibility.

"This," Kenji said, holding the blade in the light, "is refinement. The tempering teaches the blade to withstand pressure without breaking. In life, refinement is learning balance. Too much hardness, and you become brittle. Too much softness, and you lose your edge."

His words brought to mind the moments of doubt and resilience I had experienced during recovery. There were days when I pushed myself too hard, driven by a stubborn need to reclaim my old life, only to collapse in frustration. And there were days when I leaned too far into self-pity, losing sight of my goals entirely. Slowly, I began to find a middle ground—a rhythm that balanced persistence with patience.

Kenji's process was not rushed. Each stage of forging demanded time and care, and there was no shortcut to perfection. As I watched him work, I realized that the katana's beauty and strength were not just the result of skill but of endurance. The swordsmith had to embrace the imperfections of the steel, the heat of the fire, and the resistance of the hammer.

"It's not just about making a weapon," Kenji said, as he ran a whetstone along the blade's edge, honing it to razor sharpness. "It's about transformation. The blade begins as nothing special. But through fire, folding, and tempering, it becomes something extraordinary. And so can we."

Standing in that workshop, I saw my own journey reflected in the blade. The accident had been my fire, the breaking point that exposed my vulnerabilities. Recovery was the hammering, the relentless effort to rebuild myself. Reflection was the folding, aligning my imperfections rather than denying them. And tempering was the balance I found between pushing forward and embracing patience.

Kenji handed me the unfinished blade to hold. It felt heavy but purposeful, as though it carried not just strength but a story.

"Remember," he said, "the fire does not destroy the steel. It transforms it."

His words stayed with me long after I left the workshop, becoming a mantra as I navigated the challenges of recovery and the journey of self-discovery that followed. The katana, I realized, was more than a weapon or a tool. It was a metaphor for resilience, growth, and the beauty of transformation—a reminder that our greatest challenges can shape us into our most extraordinary selves.

The Journey Ahead

As I lay in that hospital bed, staring at the muted gray ceiling, I often wondered how my life had come to such a sudden, unyielding stop. The once-familiar rhythm of my days—biking through bustling streets, meeting friends, chasing deadlines—had been replaced by a slower, quieter existence. My body was broken, and for a time, my spirit felt broken, too. But in those still moments, I began to ask myself questions I had never dared to before: *What truly gives life its strength? What kind of person do I want to become when I walk out of here?*

These questions weren't just for me. If you've picked up this book, it's likely because you, too, have faced moments of stagnation, loss, or uncertainty. Maybe it's a job that no longer fulfills you, a relationship that feels fractured, or a dream you've put on hold for too long. Life has a way of halting us in our tracks, forcing us to confront our vulnerabilities, whether we're ready or not.

What I've come to realize, through the guidance of people like Kenji Tanaka and the wisdom I encountered in Japan, is that these moments of difficulty are not the end. They are a beginning. Much like the katana, life's trials are not meant to break us; they are meant to forge us into something stronger, sharper, and more aligned with our true purpose.

This book is not just a recounting of my journey—it's an invitation for you to embark on your own. It's a roadmap, rooted in six stages of transformation that I came to understand during my time in recovery. Each stage reflects a principle of Japanese wisdom, each one building on the last to create a foundation for authentic strength and purpose.

Let me briefly introduce you to these stages, as they will form the framework for our journey together:

1. Genki: Establishing True Stability

Before a katana can take shape, the raw steel must first be purified and stabilized. In life, too, we cannot begin to grow until we have a foundation of balance and clarity. Genki is about finding that stability—not the fleeting kind that depends on external circumstances, but the kind that arises from within. It's about distinguishing between what is real and lasting versus what is merely a distraction.

2. Shikata ga nai: Accepting What Cannot Be Changed

One of the most profound lessons I learned in Japan is embodied in the phrase *shikata ga nai*, which loosely translates to "it cannot be helped." This stage is about surrendering to the inevitable—embracing the things we cannot control and finding strength in acceptance. Just as a swordsmith cannot control the nature of the steel, we must learn to work with life as it is, not as we wish it to be.

3. Naikan: Reflecting Deeply to Understand Oneself\

The folding of steel during the forging process is a powerful metaphor for self-reflection. Each fold strengthens the blade by aligning its imperfections, just as introspection helps us integrate our experiences, both good and bad. In this stage, we explore Naikan, a Japanese practice of structured reflection that helps us understand ourselves and our relationships with others.

4. Kaizen: Embracing Small, Continuous Improvements

The art of kaizen teaches that progress is not about monumental leaps but about small, consistent steps. Whether it's sharpening a blade or refining our habits, the path to mastery lies in persistence. This stage is about identifying the micro-changes that lead to lasting transformation and embracing the discipline required to implement them.

5. Omoiyari: Cultivating Compassion for Oneself and Others

A katana is more than a weapon; it's a symbol of honor and responsibility. Likewise, true strength is not about power over others but about compassion. *Omoiyari* is the Japanese practice of putting oneself in another's shoes, fostering empathy and kindness. This stage is about extending that compassion not only to others but also to ourselves.

6. Ikigai: Aligning with Purpose

At the heart of every forged blade is its purpose—to cut, to defend, to endure. In life, too, we are at our best when we align with a purpose that feels both meaningful and authentic. Ikigai is about discovering the intersection of what you love, what you're good at, what the world needs, and what sustains you. It's the ultimate stage in living a life of intention and fulfillment.

Each of these stages represents a step in the forging process—not just of a katana, but of a well-lived life. Through Kenji's guidance, the lessons I absorbed from Japanese culture, and the trials of my own recovery, I came to see how these principles could be applied universally. They are not quick fixes or surface-level hacks; they are deep, enduring truths that require patience, effort, and introspection.

As you move through this book, you'll encounter stories, tools, and exercises designed to help you navigate each stage. Some may resonate immediately; others may challenge you to think differently about your life and your choices. Wherever you are on your journey, I encourage you to approach these pages with curiosity and an open mind.

Kenji once told me, "A well-forged blade isn't made overnight—it's forged through patience, precision, and perseverance." The same is true of transformation. Whether you're facing a moment of crisis or simply seeking to grow into your fullest potential, know that the process will take time. But with each step, you'll begin to see the blade taking shape—the person you're meant to become, stronger and sharper than before.

A Note on the Journey

While this book presents transformation through six distinct stages, real growth rarely follows a straight line. You might:

- Experience multiple stages simultaneously

- Move back and forth between stages

- Spend varying amounts of time in each stage

- Find certain stages more relevant than others

- Revisit stages as you face new challenges

Think of these stages not as a rigid sequence, but as a map of possibilities. Some days you'll focus on building stability (Genki), while others might call for deep reflection (Naikan). This is natural and expected.

The Katana Mindset is a framework, not a formula. Just as each sword emerges from the forge with its unique characteristics, your journey will have its own rhythm and pace. Trust this process. There is no "falling behind" or "doing it wrong" - there is only your authentic path of growth.

Remember:

- Progress isn't always visible

- Setbacks are part of the journey

- Growth often happens in spirals rather than straight lines

- Each person's timeline is different

- You can return to any practice at any time

In these pages you are about to uncover, you'll discover:

- Why stability isn't about avoiding chaos but building an unshakeable core.

- How Japanese concepts like *kaizen*, *ikigai*, and *omoiyari* can transform your approach to growth.

- Practical techniques for developing mental strength and emotional resilience.

- The six stages of transformation, modeled after the ancient art of sword making.

My journey from that broken moment on the pavement to discovering these principles wasn't just about physical healing. It was about understanding that our greatest challenges can become our greatest teachers. Through the wisdom of Japanese culture—from seasoned craftsmen to compassionate nurses, from ancient traditions to modern insights—I learned that true strength isn't about being unbreakable. It's about how we forge ourselves anew when life breaks us apart.

Whether you're facing a crisis, seeking personal growth, or simply wanting to build greater resilience, the principles in this book offer a pathway forward. Like the master craftsmen who forge ordinary steel into extraordinary blades, you too can transform your challenges into strength. The journey begins here.

PART ONE:

CHAPTER ONE

THE ILLUSION OF STABILITY

S tability is a seductive illusion. On the surface, it appears calm, predictable, and safe—a solid foundation on which to build our lives. But beneath this facade often lies a fragile reality, vulnerable to the slightest disturbance. The illusion of stability can lull us into complacency, masking the effort and resilience required to sustain it.

****

It was a crisp spring morning in Kyoto, the kind where the air felt soft, carrying the faintest hint of cherry blossoms. I was a guest at a traditional tea ceremony, held in a small, unassuming tearoom tucked away in a quiet garden. The host, a master of the art, greeted me with a polite bow before inviting me to step inside.

The room itself was minimalist, almost austere. Tatami mats covered the floor, and a simple scroll hung on the wall alongside a small flower arrangement. There were no distractions—no clutter, no noise, just the hum of stillness that seemed to envelop the space. As the ceremony began, every movement the host made was deliberate, almost hypnotic. The way she folded the cloth to clean the bowl, the precise angle at which she poured the water, the gentle turn of the cup before offering it—all of it was a study in grace and control.

To an observer, the ceremony might seem effortless, as if it unfolded naturally without any strain. The atmosphere exuded calm, and yet, there was an undercurrent of something deeper—an unspoken discipline that brought this calm into being. This wasn't just a casual act of making tea; it was a ritual honed over years of practice.

But it wasn't until later, during a conversation with the tea master, that I truly understood what I had witnessed.

"Many people see the tea ceremony as simply beautiful and peaceful," she said, her voice soft but steady. "But beauty is not born from ease. Every gesture you saw today took years of training. Every detail—how the water boils, the weight of the whisk in my hand, the placement of the utensils—must be learned, repeated, and refined. What looks effortless is the result of countless hours of effort."

Her words struck me. What appeared as serene stability on the surface was, in truth, the product of immense effort and discipline. The tea ceremony wasn't stable because it was easy—it was stable because it had been forged through intentional practice.

This revelation mirrored so many aspects of life. Whether in relationships, careers, or even our inner peace, stability often seems like a natural state. But in reality, authentic stability requires constant cultivation. It's not about maintaining a perfect surface but about developing the inner resilience and discipline to keep going when things become turbulent.

As I left the tearoom that day, I couldn't shake the lesson I had learned. The tea ceremony wasn't just about tea—it was a metaphor for life. True stability isn't effortless; it's intentional. It's about building something enduring, even as the world around us remains unpredictable. This experience opened my eyes to the concept of authentic stability.

Surface genki vs. Authentic genki (visible happiness vs. Inner stability).

In Japanese, *genki* broadly translates to "healthy," "energetic," or "full of vitality." It's a word you hear often in Japan, whether it's a casual

25

greeting (*Genki desu ka?*—"Are you well?") or an observation about someone's demeanor. On the surface, *genki* appears simple, a cheerful state of being. But as with many elements of Japanese culture, there's a deeper layer beneath this seemingly straightforward concept—a distinction between *surface genki* and *authentic genki*.

What Is Surface Genki?

Surface *genki* is the energy or happiness that's visible to others. It's the smile you wear even when you're stressed, the cheerfulness you project to avoid worrying those around you, and the optimism that masks inner struggles. In Japanese society, this kind of visible *genki* is deeply ingrained, partly as a reflection of cultural values like harmony (*wa*) and the avoidance of burdening others (*meiwaku*).

Take, for example, the salaryman who greets his coworkers with a boisterous "Ohayo gozaimasu!" despite running on only three hours of sleep. Or the young mother who volunteers enthusiastically at her child's school even though she's juggling countless other responsibilities. On the surface, they embody *genki*—outgoing, capable, and cheerful. But beneath that exterior may lie exhaustion, anxiety, or even burnout.

Surface *genki* serves a purpose. It allows people to maintain social harmony and navigate daily interactions without exposing their vulnerabilities. However, it's also fragile. Because it's often disconnected from inner well-being, it can falter under pressure, leaving individuals feeling hollow or overwhelmed.

What Is Authentic Genki?

In contrast, authentic *genki* goes beyond appearances. It's a state of inner stability and vitality that doesn't depend on external validation or superficial optimism. Authentic *genki* is rooted in emotional resilience, self-awareness, and a deep connection to one's values and purpose.

Imagine a bamboo tree swaying in the wind. Its surface may bend and move, but its roots are firmly anchored in the earth. This is authentic *genki*. It's not about maintaining a façade of happiness at all times; it's about cultivating a sense of balance that allows you to endure life's inevitable challenges.

Unlike surface *genki*, which is often reactive—responding to social expectations or immediate circumstances—authentic *genki* is proactive. It comes from within and is nurtured through practices that foster mental, emotional, and physical well-being.

The Cost of Surface Genki

Surface *genki* may seem harmless, even helpful, but relying on it exclusively can take a toll over time. When we prioritize appearances over genuine stability, we risk:

1. **Emotional Exhaustion**: Constantly projecting energy and happiness can be draining, especially if it's masking underlying struggles.

2. **Loss of Authenticity**: Over time, the disconnect between how you feel and how you present yourself can lead to a sense of alienation from your true self.

3. **Vulnerability to Stress**: Because surface *genki* isn't grounded in inner resilience, it's more likely to crumble when faced with adversity.

4. **Erosion of Trust**: In close relationships, maintaining a façade can prevent meaningful connections and open communication.

One poignant example comes from my own experience while living in Japan. A coworker, known for his cheerful demeanor and willingness to help others, shocked everyone by resigning abruptly. When we finally had a candid conversation, he admitted he'd been struggling for months but felt he couldn't show weakness. His *genki* had been a performance, one he could no longer sustain.

Building Authentic Genki

Authentic *genki* requires a shift in mindset. It's not about denying difficulties or striving for constant positivity; it's about creating a foundation that supports your well-being, no matter the circumstances. Here's how to cultivate it:

1. **Develop Self-Awareness**: Take time to reflect on your emotions, values, and needs. Practices like journaling or mindfulness can help you tune in to your inner state.

2. **Prioritize Rest and Recovery**: Authentic *genki* thrives when you honor your body's need for rest. Sleep, proper nutrition, and moments of stillness are essential.

3. **Cultivate Emotional Resilience**: Learn to navigate negative emotions without suppressing them. Therapy, meditation, or simply talking with trusted friends can help.

4. **Align Actions with Values**: Authentic *genki* comes from living in alignment with what truly matters to you. Identify your core values and let them guide your decisions.

5. **Practice Acceptance**: Embrace imperfection, both in yourself and in life. Accepting that struggles are part of the journey can make you more adaptable and less reactive.

Cultural Lessons: Finding Balance Between the Two

Japanese culture often highlights the tension between surface *genki* and authentic *genki*. On the one hand, there is immense value in maintaining harmony and showing consideration for others, even if it means putting on a brave face. On the other hand, there's a growing awareness of the need for self-care and authenticity, particularly among younger generations.

For instance, movements like *honne to tatemae* (true feelings vs. public façade) have sparked discussions about the importance of balancing societal expectations with personal truth. Similarly, practices like *Naikan* (self-reflection) and *shinrin-yoku* (forest bathing) encourage individuals to reconnect with their inner selves, fostering authentic *genki*.

Real-Life Example: Surface vs. Authentic Genki in Action

Consider two individuals navigating the same stressful situation— losing a job.

- **Surface Genki**: Emily immediately reassures her friends and family that she's fine, even joking about her situation. She dives into job applications and networking events with a smile, but privately, she's overwhelmed and struggling to sleep. Her outward energy masks her inner turmoil, and over time, the pressure begins to wear her down.

- **Authentic Genki**: Sarah, on the other hand, allows herself to process the loss. She confides in a close friend about her fears and takes a few days to reflect on her next steps. She starts journaling to understand what kind of work aligns with her values and begins her job search with clarity and purpose. While she may not seem as outwardly "genki" as Emily, her inner stability allows her to navigate the challenge with greater resilience.

The Katana Connection

The distinction between surface *genki* and authentic *genki* mirrors the process of forging a katana. A blade that looks sharp but lacks proper tempering will break under pressure, just as surface *genki* falters when life becomes difficult. Authentic *genki*, like a well-forged katana, is resilient and enduring because it's been shaped by patience, effort, and inner strength.

The journey from surface *genki* to authentic *genki* is not always easy. It requires letting go of the need to appear perfect and embracing the messy, imperfect process of self-discovery. But in doing so, we create a foundation of true vitality—one that supports us not just in moments of calm but in the storms of life as well.

Let us strive for a *genki* that is more than just a smile or a polite "I'm fine." Let us aim for a *genki* that comes from within—a deep, unshakable sense of stability and purpose that sustains us through life's challenges. In this, we begin to forge the Katana Mindset, sharpening ourselves with each experience and emerging stronger and more authentic with every step.

Why humans crave stability and the danger of stagnation

At our core, humans are wired to seek stability. The predictability of routines, the comfort of familiar environments, and the reassurance of secure relationships all contribute to a sense of safety. From an evolutionary perspective, this craving for stability makes perfect sense. For our ancestors, a stable environment meant survival—a predictable food source, shelter from predators, and a cohesive social group increased the chances of staying alive.

Yet, in a world that is constantly changing, this hardwired preference for stability can become a double-edged sword. While it protects us from chaos, it can also tether us to stagnation, preventing growth and adaptation in the face of new challenges.

The Danger of Stagnation

While stability provides comfort and security, clinging to it too tightly can hinder personal and professional growth.

1. The Hedonic Treadmill

Behavioral scientists describe the *hedonic treadmill* as the tendency to adapt quickly to stable conditions, whether good or bad. For example, getting a promotion might make you happy initially, but over time, the new role becomes your "new normal." Similarly, a predictable routine can feel satisfying at first but eventually becomes monotonous.

This adaptation means that stability, while comforting, rarely leads to lasting fulfillment. Without new challenges or changes, our sense of satisfaction diminishes.

2. Fear of the Unknown

Our craving for stability often stems from a fear of the unknown. Behavioral studies have shown that humans are risk-averse by nature, preferring predictable discomfort over unpredictable possibilities. This is why people stay in unfulfilling jobs, relationships, or environments—they perceive the unknown as riskier than the dissatisfaction they currently endure.

But this aversion to change comes at a cost. By avoiding uncertainty, we miss opportunities for growth, creativity, and resilience.

Balancing Stability and Growth

To thrive, humans need both stability and growth. The key lies in striking a balance: maintaining a stable foundation while embracing change as a catalyst for personal and professional development.

1. **The Growth Zone**

Psychologists often refer to the "growth zone" as the space just outside your comfort zone. While stepping too far into the unknown can trigger anxiety, taking incremental steps outside your comfort zone fosters growth without overwhelming your sense of stability.

For example, learning a new skill, meeting new people, or taking on a challenging project can stimulate growth while keeping you anchored to familiar aspects of your life.

2. **The Role of Resilience**

Resilience is the psychological ability to adapt to change and bounce back from adversity. Building resilience allows you to navigate the tension between stability and growth. Techniques such as mindfulness, self-reflection, and cultivating supportive relationships can help you develop this adaptability.

3. **Embracing *Kaizen***

The Japanese philosophy of *kaizen*—continuous, incremental improvement—offers a practical way to balance stability and growth. Rather than seeking drastic changes that destabilize your life, *kaizen* encourages small, consistent steps toward improvement. Over time, these small changes accumulate, leading to significant transformation without overwhelming your sense of stability.

Real-Life Application: Stability and Stagnation in Modern Life

Consider two professionals, Alex and Maya, who both crave stability but respond to it differently.

• **Alex's Approach to Stability**

Alex has worked the same job for ten years. He performs his tasks competently but avoids taking on new challenges or pursuing promotions. While he appreciates the predictability of his role, he often feels bored and unmotivated. Alex's stability has turned into stagnation, leaving him disengaged and dissatisfied.

- **Maya's Approach to Stability**

Maya also values stability but seeks growth within her comfort zone. She regularly attends professional development workshops, volunteers for new projects, and reflects on her long-term career goals. By balancing stability with growth, Maya maintains a sense of security while continuing to evolve.

The difference lies in their willingness to embrace change. While Alex clings to stability as an end goal, Maya views it as a foundation for growth.

The Katana Mindset: Stability as a Forge, not a Prison

In the *Katana Mindset*, stability is not the end of the journey; it's the starting point. Like the forge where a katana begins its transformation, stability provides the foundation for growth, but the real strength comes from the fire and folding that follow.

By understanding our natural craving for stability, we can appreciate its role in providing security and balance. But to live authentically and meaningfully, we must also challenge ourselves to step beyond it, embracing the discomfort of change as a necessary part of the transformation process.

True strength lies not in clinging to the illusion of stability but in cultivating the resilience to grow and adapt within a dynamic and ever-changing world.

How are habits formed: Modelling habit formation in the real world

The study by Lally et al. (2010), *How are habits formed: Modelling habit formation in the real world*, offers profound insights into the mechanics of habit formation and sheds light on why some changes stick while others fall apart under pressure. It's a study that peels back the layers of human behavior, revealing the gap between surface-level changes and deeper, more enduring transformations. Reflecting on this research, I couldn't help but see parallels with the lessons I learned during my time in recovery and the forging process of the katana.

Lally and her colleagues tracked participants over a 12-week period as they attempted to integrate a new habit into their daily lives, whether it was drinking water with lunch or running for 15 minutes every morning. The researchers found that forming a habit wasn't about sheer willpower or sudden inspiration; instead, it was a gradual process that required consistent repetition in stable conditions. On average, it took participants 66 days for their new behavior to feel automatic, though the time varied depending on the complexity of the habit and individual differences. This discovery emphasized that meaningful change doesn't happen overnight—it's a slow burn, not a flash of light.

But the study also revealed a deeper truth: habits anchored in external motivations or superficial goals often failed to last. When participants relied solely on external rewards—like wanting to lose weight or impress someone—their efforts fizzled out once the initial motivation waned. By contrast, those who tied their habits to intrinsic values or long-term aspirations were far more successful in making lasting changes. This distinction is critical. Surface-level stability—the kind that comes from chasing quick fixes or temporary goals—can be easily shaken. True, deep-rooted stability, however, is built on internal alignment and resilience.

During my recovery, I often thought about this fragility. At first, I tried to motivate myself with superficial benchmarks: standing without assistance, walking unassisted, and eventually cycling again. While these goals were important, they didn't hold up during moments of discouragement. It was only when I reframed my approach, focusing on what kind of person I wanted to become—stronger, more patient, and more disciplined—that I found the strength to persevere. This shift from "what I need to do" to "who I want to be" mirrors what Lally's study uncovered: behavior tied to identity is far more resilient than behavior tied to outcomes.

Another striking finding from Lally's research was how lapses—moments of failure to maintain the habit—didn't necessarily derail long-term progress. Participants who viewed setbacks as part of the process were able to recover and stay on course. On the other hand, those who saw failures as proof of their inability to change often abandoned their efforts entirely. This reinforced an essential truth about transformation: perfection isn't the goal; persistence is. Just as a swordsmith doesn't discard a blade because of a single imperfection, we must learn to embrace our own flaws as part of the journey toward self-mastery.

Reflecting on the katana metaphor, it becomes clear why superficial approaches to change often fail. A blade that's hastily forged or poorly tempered will crack under pressure, just as habits built on weak foundations crumble in the face of adversity. True transformation, whether it's a habit or a sword, requires depth. It demands heat and pressure, repetition and refinement. The steel must be folded over and over, aligning its imperfections into a cohesive whole, just as we must repeatedly engage with our habits until they become part of who we are.

Lally's study also highlighted the importance of context in habit formation. Stable environments made it easier for participants to build habits, while chaotic or unpredictable settings often hindered their efforts. This resonated deeply with me as I thought about the structured, intentional environment of my hospital stay. The predictable routines, the calm demeanor of the staff, and the supportive atmosphere all played a role in helping me develop new ways of thinking and being. It was a reminder that creating conditions for stability—both external and internal—is a cornerstone of lasting change.

As I think back to the times when I tried to make surface-level changes in my life—whether it was attempting to adopt healthier routines or manage stress—it's clear why so many of those efforts failed. They lacked depth, patience, and alignment with my core values. It's easy to be drawn to quick fixes, but as Lally's research shows, the real work lies in the small, consistent actions repeated over time. This is how habits are forged—not with sudden bursts of effort, but with steady, deliberate practice.

Ultimately, the lessons from Lally's study echo the wisdom I encountered in Japan: meaningful transformation requires patience, perseverance, and a willingness to go beyond the surface. It's not just about what we do; it's about who we become in the process. Like the katana, we are shaped through fire and repetition, emerging stronger and more aligned with our true selves. The study serves as both a reminder and a challenge: if we want changes to last, we must go deeper, embracing the process as much as the outcome.

Social Relationships and Mortality Risk: A Meta-analytic Review

The study by Holt-Lunstad et al. (2010), *Social Relationships and Mortality Risk: A Meta-analytic Review*, offers an extraordinary lens through which we can view the impact of relationships on human life. Analyzing data from 148 studies involving over 300,000 participants, the authors made a striking discovery: individuals with strong social connections have a 50% increased likelihood of living longer than those who are socially isolated. This finding is profound, not just in its statistical significance, but in what it reveals about the core of our humanity—our need for authentic relationships.

I first encountered this study after my accident, during long, introspective hours in the hospital. It made me reflect deeply on the relationships in my own life and whether I had prioritized authenticity or simply maintained appearances. It's tempting to present ourselves as "fine" or "strong," wearing masks that protect us from vulnerability. But as the study shows, the quality of our relationships, not their quantity or surface-level harmony, plays the biggest role in our well-being.

The researchers emphasized that authentic connections—where trust, understanding, and emotional support are present—are the relationships that matter most. These bonds provide a buffer against the physical and emotional stresses of life. When we invest in maintaining appearances, whether in friendships, family, or work relationships, we lose the opportunity to build the kind of meaningful connections that truly sustain us. It's like building a house of cards: it may look impressive from the outside, but it lacks the strength to withstand even the slightest disruption.

During my recovery, I couldn't help but think about how many of my past relationships revolved around maintaining an image. I'd focus on being the dependable friend, the high achiever, or the person who always seemed in control. But in the process, I often neglected to share my own struggles or allow others to truly see me. The accident stripped me of that façade. I couldn't hide my vulnerability anymore, and to my surprise, the people who truly cared showed up—not out of obligation, but out of love. That experience taught me that letting people see you as you are, not as you think they want you to be, is the foundation of authentic connection.

Holt-Lunstad and her team also highlighted how social isolation increases the risk of early mortality to levels comparable with smoking or obesity. It's not just loneliness that's dangerous—it's the absence of genuine, fulfilling relationships. Superficial ties may fill our social calendars, but they don't nourish our souls. The human need for connection isn't a luxury; it's as fundamental as the air we breathe. And yet, we often sacrifice it for the sake of appearances, whether it's to fit into societal expectations or to protect ourselves from rejection.

I remember a nurse in the hospital who embodied the kind of authenticity this study champions. Her kindness was quiet but unwavering. She didn't try to cheer me up with platitudes or mask my pain with hollow reassurances. Instead, she listened—really listened—and offered small, thoughtful gestures that made me feel seen. In those moments, I realized that authenticity isn't about grand gestures; it's about presence, honesty, and the willingness to engage with someone as they are. It's these connections, not polished interactions, that strengthen us and ultimately prolong our lives.

The study also underscored the importance of reciprocity in relationships. Authentic bonds are a two-way street, requiring both giving and receiving. This was a hard lesson for me to learn. Before my accident, I was more comfortable being the one who gave—offering help, advice, or support—than being the one who needed it.

But in my most vulnerable moments, I realized that allowing others to help me didn't make me weak; it strengthened our connection. It reminded me of the Japanese concept of *omoiyari*, or compassionate empathy, which emphasizes mutual care and understanding as the foundation of meaningful relationships.

One of the most striking implications of the study is that the longevity benefits of authentic relationships extend beyond the individual. Strong social bonds ripple outward, creating healthier families, communities, and workplaces. When we prioritize authenticity, we not only enhance our own well-being but also contribute to a culture of genuine connection. This is the antidote to the hollow pursuit of appearances—a reminder that depth, not perfection, is what truly sustains us.

As I think back to the study's findings, they feel less like research and more like a mirror reflecting the truths I've experienced firsthand. Relationships built on appearances are brittle; they can't withstand the pressures of life's challenges. But authentic connections, like a well-forged katana, are strong and enduring. They don't just enrich our lives—they extend them, offering both a longer and a deeper experience of what it means to be human.

In the end, Holt-Lunstad's study is more than a statistic; it's a call to action. It challenges us to move beyond the surface, to let go of the masks, and to invest in the kind of relationships that truly matter. It's not easy—it requires vulnerability, effort, and courage—but the rewards are immeasurable. After all, what's the point of living longer if we aren't living authentically? As you embark on your own journey, remember that true vitality comes not from fleeting appearances but from the deep well of authentic Genki.

CHAPTER TWO
BUILDING TRUE GENKI

A few years ago, I hit a wall. At first, I didn't see it coming. My days were packed with tasks and commitments, and I was constantly on the move—work meetings, side projects, family obligations. On the outside, I looked like I had it all together: always busy, always productive, always smiling. But inside, something was cracking.

I still remember the morning it all caught up with me. I was sitting in my car, parked outside the office, gripping the steering wheel as if letting go would send me spinning out of control. My chest felt tight, my thoughts scattered. It wasn't one big crisis that brought me there— it was the slow, silent accumulation of pretending I was fine when I wasn't.

For weeks, I had ignored the signs. A constant, low-level exhaustion that even a weekend of sleep couldn't cure. Little moments of frustration that seemed to bubble over for no reason. But the real red flag was how disconnected I felt from everything, even the things I once loved. Instead of facing it, I doubled down. "Keep going," I told myself. "You're fine." After all, wasn't that what everyone else did?

The Cost of Pretending

In hindsight, what I was doing wasn't "fine" at all. It was survival mode. I thought that keeping up appearances—staying busy, staying "strong"—was a sign of stability. But the truth was, I was building my life on a shaky foundation. My version of stability was surface-level. I was putting on a show, for myself and others, but it lacked the depth and resilience I needed to thrive.

The car that morning became my turning point. I finally allowed myself to admit the truth: I wasn't okay. And that's when something shifted. Instead of pushing those feelings aside, I started to ask myself hard questions:

- Why did I feel the need to appear "fine" at all costs?

- What was I avoiding by staying busy?

- What would it look like to stop pretending and focus on building something real?

The Truth About Genki

In Japanese, the word *genki* is often translated as "healthy" or "energetic." If you ask someone, *Genki desu ka?* ("How are you?"), a typical response might be *Genki desu!*—a cheerful "I'm fine!" But the essence of *genki* goes deeper than just looking or feeling fine on the surface. True *genki* is about having a wellspring of inner strength, a sense of balance and vitality that sustains you even when life gets tough.

What I had been projecting—the busy, smiley, "I've got this" version of myself—was what I now call surface *genki*. It's the kind of energy that looks good from the outside but is fragile underneath. Authentic *genki*, on the other hand, is quiet and steady. It's not about always being "on" or perfect; it's about creating a foundation that supports you, even in moments of struggle.

The aftermath of that morning in the car was messy. I didn't suddenly become enlightened or figure everything out. But I started to make small shifts. I learned to recognize when I was slipping into surface *genki*—the urge to mask stress with busyness, to overcommit when I should step back, to power through instead of rest.

One of the most important lessons I learned was this: True *genki* begins with honesty. You can't build a strong foundation if you refuse to see the cracks. I had to get real about what I needed—rest, boundaries, connection—and let go of the idea that stability meant never asking for help.

Another key lesson was that resilience isn't something you perform; it's something you cultivate. It's in the way you take care of your body and mind, the way you handle setbacks, and the way you stay grounded in your values.

Rebuilding from Within

Looking back, I'm grateful for that moment of burnout—not because it was easy, but because it forced me to confront the difference between surface and authentic stability. The process of rebuilding wasn't glamorous, but it was transformative.

I started by making space for rest, which felt almost revolutionary after years of pushing myself. I also began to simplify my commitments, focusing on what truly mattered instead of trying to do everything. And perhaps most importantly, I allowed myself to slow down enough to really reflect: What kind of life did I want to build? What would it look like to live with authentic *genki*?

Today, I still catch myself falling into old patterns from time to time. But I've learned to recognize the signs early and course-correct. I no longer equate stability with perfection or busyness. Instead, I see it as an ongoing process—a commitment to building a life that feels solid and meaningful, from the inside out.

Cultural Contrasts: Tatemae vs. Honne and Their Influence on Stability

In Japanese culture, two fundamental concepts often guide social interactions and personal behavior: **tatemae** (建前) and **honne** (本音). These words represent two sides of a person's expression—**tatemae** being the public facade or socially appropriate behavior, and **honne** being one's true feelings or desires. Understanding how these concepts influence Japanese ideas of stability can reveal both the strengths and challenges of balancing surface-level appearances with inner authenticity.

The Role of Tatemae: Stability in Harmony

At its core, **tatemae** is about maintaining social harmony. In Japan, where communal values often outweigh individual expression, presenting a composed, agreeable front is seen as a virtue. This isn't about dishonesty but rather about prioritizing the group's needs over personal emotions.

Imagine you're at work, and a colleague suggests an idea you don't entirely agree with. In a tatemae-driven interaction, you might nod along, offering polite encouragement rather than direct criticism. Why? Because the goal isn't to assert your opinion but to preserve a sense of collaboration and respect.

This approach can create an external sense of stability. When everyone upholds tatemae, interactions flow smoothly, conflicts are minimized, and the group feels cohesive. It's a powerful tool for maintaining order, especially in contexts like workplaces, family gatherings, or public spaces.

However, tatemae has its limitations. While it helps preserve surface-level harmony, it can sometimes prevent people from addressing deeper issues. When tatemae dominates, unresolved tensions can simmer beneath the surface, creating cracks in what appears to be a stable system.

Honne: The Anchor of Authentic Stability

In contrast, **honne** represents a person's true thoughts and feelings—their authentic self. Honne doesn't concern itself with appearances or social expectations. It's the quiet voice that knows what you really want, even when you don't say it aloud.

Honne is crucial for authentic stability. While tatemae can smooth over day-to-day interactions, honne is what grounds you during life's more challenging moments. Without honne, it's easy to lose touch with your core values, desires, and boundaries.

For example, in relationships, expressing honne might mean admitting when you're hurt or setting boundaries when something feels wrong. In work, it might mean acknowledging when you're overwhelmed or dissatisfied, rather than continuing to "go with the flow" out of obligation.

But balancing honne and tatemae isn't always easy. Japanese culture doesn't encourage abandoning one for the other; instead, it seeks harmony between the two. The challenge is knowing when to lean on tatemae to maintain harmony and when to embrace honne to preserve authenticity.

Tatemae and Honne in Action

Let's look at a common scenario in Japan: the workplace. A team member might work late into the night without voicing their fatigue. On the surface (tatemae), they appear dedicated and hardworking, contributing to the team's stability. But inside (honne), they might feel exhausted or resentful.

If this cycle continues unchecked, the facade of stability can break down. Burnout, miscommunication, or hidden dissatisfaction can undermine the very harmony tatemae seeks to uphold.

On the other hand, honne can create a different kind of stability. If that same team member feels safe to express their honest feelings—"I'm feeling overwhelmed; can we redistribute tasks?"—it might create an awkward moment initially. But in the long run, addressing the truth leads to a more sustainable and authentic sense of stability for everyone involved.

Surface vs. Authentic Stability: A Cultural Lens

The interplay between tatemae and honne mirrors the tension between **surface-level stability** and **authentic stability**. Tatemae offers a veneer of stability, much like the polished exterior of a house that hasn't been inspected for structural issues. Honne, on the other hand, is about digging deeper, ensuring that the foundation is solid, even if it means exposing cracks.

In Japanese society, this duality is often navigated with remarkable skill. People understand the importance of presenting a united front, but they also recognize moments when expressing honne is essential—often in private spaces or close relationships where trust allows for vulnerability.

Lessons for the West

Western cultures, which tend to emphasize individual expression and directness, might initially view tatemae as inauthentic. But there's wisdom in this approach. In highly interconnected environments, the ability to prioritize group harmony can be a stabilizing force.

At the same time, Western readers can relate to the concept of tatemae through their own experiences with social facades. Think of a polite smile at a party when you'd rather be home, or agreeing to a project at work because it's easier than saying no. Tatemae isn't exclusive to Japan—it's a universal behavior shaped by cultural norms.

What Japanese culture highlights is the importance of balancing these facades with moments of authenticity. Without honne, stability becomes brittle. Without tatemae, interactions can become chaotic. The goal is to integrate the two, creating a life that's both harmonious and real.

Building Your Own Balance

How do you navigate your own tatemae and honne? Here are a few ways to reflect:

1. **Identify Your "Facades"**: When do you find yourself projecting a version of yourself that isn't fully aligned with your feelings?

2. **Create Safe Spaces for Honne**: Who are the people or environments where you feel comfortable expressing your true self?

3. **Strengthen Honne Practices**: Journaling, therapy, or mindfulness can help you reconnect with your inner truth.

4. **Practice Constructive Tatemae**: Use tatemae consciously, as a tool to navigate social dynamics rather than suppress your authenticity.

Tools for building authentic stability

Building authentic stability in our lives is a process of aligning our inner and outer worlds. It's not about pretending everything is fine or keeping up with external expectations, but about creating a solid foundation that supports us even when life gets chaotic. Authentic stability comes from understanding who you are, what you need, and how to balance life's demands with your personal truth. Here are a few tools to help you build that kind of stability—tools that go beyond surface appearances and dig into the roots of your well-being.

1. Mindful Awareness: Tuning Into Your Present Self

The first step toward authentic stability is **awareness**—being in tune with how you're feeling, both physically and emotionally, at any given moment. Too often, we ignore the signs of stress, burnout, or discomfort, telling ourselves that we'll deal with it later. This is where mindfulness comes in.

Mindfulness isn't just a buzzword; it's the practice of observing your thoughts and emotions without judgment. It's about becoming an objective observer of your own experience. When you're mindful, you can notice when you're leaning too much into surface-level stability—when you're overcommitting, overextending, or suppressing your feelings. It's about pausing and checking in with yourself.

Try this simple mindfulness exercise:

- **Pause for 1 minute**: Close your eyes, take a deep breath, and focus on your body. Where are you holding tension? How does your mind feel?

- **Reflect**: What is it telling you? Are you feeling overwhelmed, anxious, or disconnected?

By practicing mindfulness regularly, you'll be better equipped to recognize when your life feels out of balance and take steps to realign yourself.

2. Emotional Honesty: Naming What You Feel

We often mask our true feelings in the name of keeping things smooth or avoiding conflict. But suppressing emotions is a quick path to

47

instability. Emotional honesty is a tool for not only understanding yourself but also building connections with others.

The next time you feel discomfort, frustration, or even joy, take a moment to name the feeling. Is it anger, disappointment, anxiety, or something else? By putting words to what you're feeling, you are acknowledging it rather than letting it fester. This simple act of labeling your emotions helps you better understand what's going on inside you and why.

Try keeping a journal where you track your emotions daily. At the end of the day, write down:

- **What I felt today**: Be honest with yourself, even if it's difficult to admit.

- **Why I felt this way**: Trace the events, thoughts, or conversations that triggered the emotion.

- **How I responded**: Did you avoid, repress, or act on that feeling?

Emotional honesty lets you build a life that's grounded in reality, not in avoidance. It fosters deeper self-awareness and supports your growth.

3. Setting Boundaries: Protecting Your Inner Peace

Boundaries are the invisible lines that protect your emotional, mental, and physical space. Without clear boundaries, you'll find yourself constantly giving away your time, energy, and focus to things and people that drain you. Setting boundaries doesn't mean being selfish; it's a form of self-respect. It's recognizing that in order to build authentic stability, you need to protect your well-being.

One effective tool is to use **"I" statements** when communicating your needs. For example:

- **"I need some quiet time to recharge."**

- **"I can't take on that extra task right now, but I can help later."**

- **"I'm feeling overwhelmed and need to step back."**

These statements help you express your needs without feeling guilty or over-explaining yourself. They set clear, respectful boundaries without resentment.

Another tool is the **time audit**:

- Take a week to track how much time you spend on different activities.

- Are you spending more time pleasing others or keeping up with obligations than focusing on your own well-being?

- Reflect on where you might need to create stronger boundaries.

By honoring your own boundaries, you create space for authentic stability to flourish.

4. Creating Routines: The Power of Consistency

In a world that's constantly changing, routine may seem boring or restrictive. But the truth is, routines provide a sense of control and predictability, which are essential for authentic stability. The key is to create routines that nurture your body, mind, and spirit.

Think about it: How many times have you had a chaotic day because you didn't know what to expect from your schedule? A lack of structure often leads to stress. But when you build a daily routine, even if it's simple, it helps you regain focus and calm.

Start small:

- **Morning routine**: Wake up 10 minutes earlier to stretch, meditate, or journal before diving into your day.

- **Evening routine**: Disconnect from screens an hour before bed and spend time reading or reflecting.

These small routines help you start and end your day with intention, creating stability even in the midst of unpredictable moments.

5. Building Emotional Resilience: Embracing Life's Ups and Downs

Resilience is the ability to bounce back from setbacks, and it's an essential tool for authentic stability. Life is filled with challenges—unexpected job losses, health scares, relationship struggles. But your response to these challenges determines your stability.

To build resilience, it's important to **reframe your thinking**. When faced with adversity, ask yourself:

- What can I learn from this situation?

- How can I grow through this challenge?

- What small steps can I take to regain my balance?

Resilience also requires **self-compassion**—being kind to yourself when you make mistakes or face difficulties. Resilience isn't about avoiding hardship but about learning to weather it with grace.

One tool to build emotional resilience is **the gratitude practice**:

- Every day, write down three things you're grateful for. They don't have to be big; they could be as simple as a hot cup of coffee or a good conversation with a friend.

- This shifts your focus from what's going wrong to what's going right, helping you stay grounded during tough times.

6. Reflecting and Adapting: The Kaizen Mindset

In Japanese culture, the principle of **kaizen** refers to continuous, incremental improvement. It's the idea that small, consistent changes add up to big transformation over time. When it comes to building authentic stability, this mindset is invaluable.

Rather than aiming for perfection or massive life changes all at once, kaizen encourages you to make small improvements every day. This could mean setting aside five minutes for mindfulness, saying "no" more often, or investing in learning something new. The goal isn't to overhaul your life in one go, but to steadily move in the direction of your ideal self.

To apply this principle:

- Identify one area in your life where you'd like to build more stability.

- Break it down into small, manageable steps that you can tackle daily.

- Track your progress over time and celebrate even the smallest victories.

By approaching stability as a continuous process rather than a destination, you build resilience that can weather any storm.

Exercises: Crafting a "Stability Blueprint" for Health, Relationships, and Work

Creating an authentic, stable life is a process that requires intention and action. It's not something that can be built overnight, but by taking small, purposeful steps, you can begin to craft a **"stability blueprint"** for the three core areas of your life: health, relationships, and work. These are the foundations that shape your day-to-day experience, and when they are aligned with your values and authentic needs, they create a solid base from which to grow.

In this exercise, we'll focus on these three crucial areas. The goal is to help you **identify where you currently stand, what's working well**, and **where adjustments are needed**. This is a practical exercise that will guide you through reflection and action planning. Let's begin.

Step 1: Health - Building a Solid Foundation for Your Body and Mind

Health isn't just about eating well and exercising; it's about nurturing your body and mind in a way that provides lasting energy and resilience. When your health is stable, everything else in your life has a stronger foundation.

Reflecting on Your Health:

Take a moment to assess your current health situation. Be honest with yourself, acknowledging both the areas where you're doing well and those where you need to improve. Consider the following:

- **Physical Health**: How is your energy? Are you exercising regularly? Are you sleeping well?

- **Mental Health**: How are you handling stress? Do you take time for relaxation and self-care? Do you have coping strategies for difficult emotions?

- **Nutrition**: Are you nourishing your body with food that supports your well-being, or do you rely on quick fixes or unhealthy habits?

- **Work-Life Balance**: Are you overworking or neglecting rest and recreation?

Building Your Health Blueprint:

1. **Identify Your Health Goals**: What would authentic health look like for you? It could be having more energy, getting enough sleep, or learning to manage stress more effectively.

2. **Small Changes for Improvement**: Break these goals down into actionable steps. For example, if your goal is to have more energy, one step could be to introduce a 20-minute walk into your daily routine. If you're struggling with mental health, incorporating a 10-minute mindfulness practice could be a great start.

3. **Accountability**: Who can you share your health goals with? Maybe a friend or a professional who can help hold you accountable or just check in from time to time.

4. **Tracking Progress**: Start a health journal. Each day, reflect on what went well and what didn't. What habits are helping you feel more stable? What habits are hindering your growth?

Step 2: Relationships - Building Stability with the People Who Matter Most

The relationships we form are fundamental to our well-being and emotional stability. Healthy relationships provide us with a support network during challenging times and a source of joy during good times. But relationships can also be sources of stress and conflict if boundaries aren't respected, or communication breaks down. The goal is to foster authentic connections based on mutual respect, trust, and understanding.

Reflecting on Your Relationships:

Take a moment to reflect on the most important relationships in your life—family, friends, partners, and colleagues. Consider the following questions:

- **Are your relationships supportive, or do they drain you?**

- **Do you feel heard and understood by the people around you?**

- **Are you giving enough time and energy to the relationships that matter most?**

- **Are there boundaries that need to be strengthened in any relationship?**

- **Are you allowing space for honest, vulnerable communication, or are you suppressing emotions for the sake of peace?**

Building Your Relationship Blueprint:

1. **Prioritize Key Relationships**: Identify the relationships that matter most to you, whether it's with a significant other, family members, or close friends. These are the relationships you want to invest your time and energy into. Write down the names of these people.

2. **Set Boundaries**: Determine where boundaries need to be set. For instance, if a family member or friend is draining you, what boundaries can you establish to protect your energy? Maybe it's saying "no" more often or communicating your needs clearly.

3. **Communication Plan**: Are you being emotionally honest with the people who matter most to you? Are you listening

fully or waiting for your turn to speak? To foster deeper connections, create a plan for how you'll communicate more openly—whether that's setting aside time to talk with your partner or having weekly check-ins with a friend.

4. **Strengthening Your Support System**: Do you have a solid network of people to support you when times get tough? If not, how can you begin building these relationships? You might join a group, reach out to someone you've lost touch with, or initiate regular meetups with close friends.

Step 3: Work - Creating Stability Through Purpose and Productivity

Your career or daily work is a major aspect of your life and contributes significantly to your sense of stability. Work can be a source of fulfillment, or it can feel overwhelming and draining. The key to authentic stability in work is aligning your tasks with your values, setting boundaries, and maintaining a sustainable pace.

Reflecting on Your Work:

Consider your current work situation:

- **Are you feeling fulfilled by your work, or are you simply going through the motions?**

- **Do you feel your efforts are being recognized and valued?**

- **Is your work-life balance healthy, or are you constantly overworked?**

- **Do you feel aligned with your long-term career goals, or is there a disconnect?**

Building Your Work Blueprint:

1. **Clarify Your Career Goals**: What are your core values when it comes to your work? Is it creativity, financial stability, freedom, or helping others? Understanding this is key to ensuring your career aligns with your authentic self.

2. **Set Boundaries at Work**: Similar to your relationships, your work life needs boundaries. Do you need to stop checking emails after work hours? Do you need to delegate tasks or ask for help? Identify where you can draw a line to protect your personal time and mental health.

3. **Create a Productivity System**: Being productive doesn't mean being busy all the time. It's about working smart. Consider adopting a time management system like the **Pomodoro Technique** (working in focused 25-minute intervals with 5-minute breaks) or the **Two-Minute Rule** (if a task takes two minutes or less, do it immediately).

4. **Reflection and Adjustments**: At the end of each week, take time to reflect on how your workweek went. Did you feel like you made progress on your goals? Did you burn out? What adjustments can you make to avoid repeating unhealthy patterns?

Now that you've crafted your **stability blueprint** for health, relationships, and work, it's time to step back and look at the whole picture. Are the areas of your life aligned? Do they complement each other, or is there tension between your personal, professional, and relational worlds?

The key to true stability is balance. Authentic stability doesn't mean perfection in every area—it's about creating synergy between your internal needs and external actions. Once you've identified your goals and challenges in each area, revisit your blueprint regularly, track your progress, and adjust as needed. Stability isn't a fixed point; it's a dynamic process that evolves with you.

By building your stability blueprint and taking these steps, you're laying the groundwork for a more balanced, grounded life—one where you can face life's challenges with resilience, authenticity, and grace.

Guided Pathways: Navigating the Genki Stage

The **Genki Stage**—translated as "vitality" or "stability"—forms the foundation for personal transformation. In this stage, you focus on creating authentic stability, moving beyond surface-level resilience to cultivate a deeper, lasting equilibrium. This stability is not about projecting strength but finding alignment within yourself, even amid life's turbulence.

Stage Recognition

Recognizing you're in the Genki stage requires self-awareness. You might feel disconnected, as though your outward stability doesn't match your inner chaos. Here are common indicators:

- **Thoughts and Feelings:** Persistent self-doubt, difficulty trusting your inner voice, or the constant pursuit of external approval.

- **Behavioral Patterns:** Overcommitting, people-pleasing, or using distractions to mask discomfort.

- **Environmental Signs:** Chaotic relationships, a cluttered physical space, or an overwhelming workload.

- **Relationship Dynamics:** Struggling to set boundaries, often prioritizing others' needs over your own.

Self-Assessment Exercise:

- Reflect on whether your sense of stability is dependent on external factors. For instance, ask yourself: *If these were stripped away, would I still feel grounded?*

Stage Completion Markers

As you progress through the Genki stage, you'll notice shifts in your mindset and behaviors. These are signs you've internalized its lessons:

- **Mindset Shifts:** You trust your inner stability, regardless of external chaos. Emotional reactions become measured rather than impulsive.

- **Behavioral Changes:** Clearer boundaries, more deliberate decision-making, and a reduced need for validation.

- **Emotional Milestones:** A sense of calm that persists through challenges, signaling genuine resilience.

- **Relationship Developments:** Healthier connections, based on mutual respect rather than obligation.

Next Stage Preparation

Once stability feels authentic, the next step is preparing for the **Shikata ga nai** stage, where you'll embrace acceptance. Signs you're ready include:

- **Internal Signals:** A curiosity to face uncomfortable truths or explore unresolved patterns.

- **Transition Challenges:** Fear of letting go of control, as stability may feel fragile initially.

- **Preparation Exercises:**

1. **Journaling on Challenges:** Reflect on a recent difficulty. Did your stability waver? Why?

2. **Building a Support System:** Surround yourself with individuals who encourage vulnerability and growth.

Regression Warnings

Even with progress, it's easy to backslide. Here's what to watch for:

- **Early Warning Signs:** Falling back into over-committing or relying on external validation for confidence.

- **Common Triggers:** High-pressure situations, unresolved emotional conflicts, or criticism from others.

- **Stages to Avoid Regressing To:** If you lose your footing, it's easy to retreat to superficial stability or old habits.

- **Prevention Strategies:**

    1. Incorporate mindfulness practices like meditation to anchor yourself.

    2. Use grounding techniques, such as deep breathing, when overwhelmed.

- **Recovery Practices:** If regression occurs, revisit earlier exercises, focusing on internal versus external stability.

Stage Integration

Integrating the lessons of Genki is vital for long-term progress. Here's how to maintain your gains while moving forward:

- **Building on Stability:** Use your inner calm as a foundation for the acceptance required in the next stage.

- **Sustaining Practices:** Maintain habits that reinforce your sense of balance, like consistent routines or mindfulness exercises.

- **Balancing Progress:** Recognize that stability isn't a static destination—it's a dynamic state that adapts to challenges.

- **Integration Exercise:**

  - Create a personal "Stability Manifesto," listing the core principles that keep you grounded. Revisit this during moments of doubt.

The Genki stage is where transformation begins. It equips you with the strength to face life authentically and the resilience to navigate what lies ahead. By rooting yourself in true stability, you're not just preparing for the journey—you're creating the foundation for every stage that follows.

CHAPTER THREE

THE FOUNDATION FOR CHANGE

A Japanese Craftsman's Obsession with Perfecting the Base of a Blade

In a small workshop tucked away in the quiet alleys of Kanazawa, Japan, an elderly craftsman named Takumi spends his days laboring over the base of a katana. The rhythmic sound of his hammer striking steel is a constant companion in his workshop—a place where time seems to slow, and the outside world fades away. His face is etched with years of experience, yet his eyes still gleam with the intensity of someone who sees each piece of metal not just as raw material, but as a vessel of possibility.

Takumi is not just any craftsman; he is a master in the ancient art of katana forging, a process passed down through generations. For decades, he has dedicated himself to perfecting the sword, focusing not only on the final sharp edge but also on the often-overlooked foundation—the base of the blade. Most people are mesmerized by the blade's sharpness, its beauty, and its lethal precision. But Takumi knows something that most don't: the true strength of the katana comes from its base—the spine that holds the edge together and provides the sword with the balance and power it needs to cut through anything with precision.

As the hammer falls against the steel, sparks fly, but Takumi is not merely reacting to the metal's resistance. He is listening, feeling the vibration that travels through the handle and into his hands. He feels the rhythm of the blade, sensing if it is right, if the foundation is solid enough to hold what will come next. He focuses on every minute detail, carefully shaping the base of the katana with the utmost care, making small but significant adjustments as he goes. He's obsessed with perfection, not because it's an obsession with the outcome, but because it's an obsession with the process—the belief that a strong base will shape the final product.

For Takumi, this obsession is not just about craftsmanship; it's about honor. The katana he's forging is an embodiment of his entire life's work, a representation of the values and dedication he has put into perfecting his craft. Every curve, every indentation, and every fold of the steel is a mark of his years of learning, of striving for something deeper than mere aesthetics.

But the work is never easy. Sometimes, the metal doesn't bend the way he wants. Sometimes, it cracks, and he must start over. The base is the most challenging part of the process, for if it isn't done right, the blade will fail to live up to its full potential. The katana might look beautiful, but without a strong foundation, it will lack the strength to endure the test of time.

One day, after several hours of intense focus, Takumi steps back, his hands covered in sweat and soot. The base of the katana is nearly complete, and he knows that the true test of his work lies ahead. The rest of the forging process will refine the edges and shape the blade, but it is the foundation—the part that is unseen by most—that will determine whether this katana can withstand the forces it will face.

What Takumi has spent decades perfecting is the embodiment of a larger principle: **true strength** comes not from what is visible, but from what lies beneath the surface. In the world of katana forging, the most important work is often the least celebrated—the foundation that allows the rest of the blade to exist in harmony. And it is this very foundation that parallels the process of **personal transformation**. Just like the katana, we must first focus on building a strong base—

an authentic, stable foundation—before we can expect to grow and change in meaningful ways.

In the context of **personal transformation**, the foundation is what enables growth and change to endure. Just as the katana must have a solid base for the blade to hold its sharp edge, we, too, must establish a strong foundation of self-awareness, discipline, and authenticity in order to build meaningful change in our lives.

Takumi's obsessive attention to detail and dedication to creating a perfect base reminds us that change doesn't happen all at once. It requires **patience, precision,** and an understanding that the true power of transformation comes not from flashy outcomes, but from the inner work—the building of the unseen foundation.

This focus on building a solid base speaks directly to the **first stage of transformation**, Genki—the ability to find authentic stability. If we don't get the foundation right, everything else we try to build on top will be shaky, superficial, and ultimately unfulfilling. By following Takumi's example of obsession over the small, unseen details, we can create a life that isn't just built on surface-level stability, but on something far more enduring and resilient.

The Japanese craftsman's approach offers an important lesson for us: **Transformation isn't about achieving perfection quickly; it's about the patient work of creating a strong foundation from which growth can naturally unfold**. This foundation isn't just physical, like the metal of the katana, but mental and emotional as well. It's about building a life that's strong enough to weather the challenges and changes that inevitably come our way.

As we move forward in exploring the stages of authentic transformation, Takumi's work will serve as a reminder that the most powerful changes begin not with grand gestures, but with the quiet, careful work of laying a strong foundation. A stable base is not only the starting point for the katana; it is also the heart of the transformation process itself. The craftsman's dedication to the unseen foundation mirrors the importance of resilience in our own lives.

Stability Isn't the Endpoint but the Foundation: Resilience as the Key to Handling Instability

Stability is often seen as the ultimate goal—a state of being unshaken, unwavering, and serene. Many people spend their lives striving to reach a point where things feel "steady." But what if true strength doesn't lie in achieving this unchanging state? What if stability isn't the endpoint but rather the foundation upon which resilience is built? Stability, in its truest form, is not about being unmovable; it's about being stable enough to handle the inevitable turbulence of life.

In the world of personal transformation, the goal isn't to construct a life that is free from challenges, conflicts, or discomforts. Such a life doesn't exist. Instead, true strength comes from learning how to weather life's inevitable storms. Stability, in this sense, becomes the bedrock that supports resilience—the ability to remain grounded despite chaos and uncertainty.

The Illusion of Perfection: Why Stability Alone Isn't Enough

Let's begin by looking at how people often misunderstand stability. When we talk about being stable, many envision an unshakable, flawless existence. This is where the idea of **surface-level stability** comes in—an appearance of balance that hides the cracks beneath the surface. On social media, we see perfectly curated lives, families that seem to have it all together, and individuals who appear to be perpetually calm, composed, and unbothered by life's struggles. But this version of stability is, for the most part, an illusion.

Surface-level stability is what people project in an attempt to avoid the discomfort of vulnerability. It's the calm on the outside that often masks the turmoil or insecurity underneath. And while this façade might seem appealing or desirable, it doesn't prepare us for the challenges that life throws our way. It's not about being perfect—it's about being able to face the imperfection that life inevitably brings.

Authentic stability, on the other hand, is more than just maintaining appearances. It's about creating a solid core—a foundation—that can withstand the winds of change. It's a state of being **centered** enough that when life's inevitable disruptions occur, you are able to move through them, adjust to them, and grow stronger because of them. This is the foundation from which **resilience** emerges.

Resilience is the ability to adapt to adversity. It's not about avoiding hardship, but rather, learning how to stay grounded and find your balance when the world around you seems anything but stable. True resilience doesn't mean you're impervious to pain or hardship. It means you're capable of weathering those hardships, learning from them, and continuing to move forward.

The Art of Building Resilience: How Stability Prepares Us for the Storm

Imagine standing on the edge of a great ocean, waves crashing against the shore. A small boat might get tossed about by the force of the waves, but a large, well-built ship can ride those same waves with confidence. Why? Because the ship is constructed with resilience in mind. It has been built with the ability to withstand rough waters and return to calm seas once the storm has passed.

This is the essence of authentic stability. It's not about avoiding the storm, but about creating the inner strength that allows you to navigate it with grace. Stability, in this sense, is the vessel—resilience is the ability to ride the waves.

Just as a ship's construction includes the careful planning of its hull, sails, and rudder to ensure it can handle unpredictable waters, so too must we cultivate the mental, emotional, and physical resources to handle life's unpredictable nature. When we focus on authentic stability, we're focusing on developing the kind of strength that doesn't buckle when things go wrong but bends and adapts to meet the challenge.

Consider a person who has built a career only to experience a sudden job loss or economic downturn. For someone with **surface-level stability**, this might cause panic. The loss of a job could shatter their sense of security, leaving them feeling unmoored and vulnerable. On the other hand, someone who has cultivated **authentic stability** and resilience might face the same challenge with a different mindset. Instead of allowing the setback to define their sense of self-worth, they see it as an opportunity for growth. They rely on their foundational strengths—problem-solving skills, adaptability, a supportive network—to navigate the turbulence and move forward.

Take, for example, the story of a business leader who faced an economic crisis. During the 2008 financial crash, many companies crumbled under the weight of uncertainty. However, there were a few leaders who not only kept their businesses afloat but even emerged stronger. These leaders didn't have a perfect, unshakable foundation—they faced losses, difficult decisions, and challenges along the way. What set them apart was their ability to remain calm, assess the situation objectively, and make the necessary changes to adapt to the shifting landscape. They exhibited resilience by staying rooted in their purpose and vision, adjusting their strategies, and learning from their mistakes.

Similarly, on a personal level, someone who is resilient may lose a loved one or face a health crisis. While the grief and challenges are real, they are able to lean into their support systems, reflect on their values, and continue moving forward. They don't deny the pain but are equipped to endure it and emerge stronger.

The Link Between Stability and Growth: A Strong Foundation for Transformation

Resilience is built upon a foundation of authentic stability. We cannot expect to thrive in the midst of hardship if we haven't first cultivated a sense of groundedness. Stability isn't the end of the journey; it's the beginning. And just like Takumi's dedication to perfecting the foundation of a katana, it's the painstaking work of establishing this foundation that gives us the strength to face life's challenges head-on.

The process of transformation doesn't start when we're at rock-bottom—it starts long before we reach that point. Just like a craftsman ensures that the katana's base is perfectly aligned before moving on to more visible elements, we must take the time to build our internal foundation. And just as the katana's sharp edge only works because of the solid base that holds it, our ability to endure life's storms relies on the foundational stability we've built in our hearts and minds.

This kind of foundational work isn't something that can be done overnight. It requires reflection, discipline, and an understanding that growth is a long-term process. It's the ability to remain adaptable and flexible in the face of adversity and to stay grounded even as life changes around you. Resilience is not about returning to where you were before the storm—it's about building something stronger and more flexible in the face of change.

Action Steps: Create a "Resilience Inventory"

Building resilience isn't just a conceptual exercise—it's about putting the work into practice. A "resilience inventory" is a personalized toolkit, a roadmap of the skills, habits, and support systems that will help you withstand and grow through life's challenges. Just like a craftsman preparing the materials for the creation of a katana, you must identify the elements that will form the foundation of your resilience. This inventory will serve as your guide to navigating adversity with grace and strength.

Let's break down the components of your resilience inventory—skills, habits, and people—and how you can begin actively cultivating each one.

1. Skills: Your Resilience Toolbox

Your skills are the practical tools that you'll rely on when the going gets tough. These are the techniques and abilities that will help you navigate change and adversity. Building resilience requires self-awareness and a commitment to growing these foundational skills.

Identify Core Skills

Start by reflecting on the skills you already have that contribute to your resilience. These might include:

- **Problem-solving:** The ability to break down a situation into manageable parts and create a plan to address it.

- **Adaptability:** Being open to change and willing to adjust your course when necessary.

- **Emotional regulation:** The ability to manage your emotions and not let stress or panic dictate your actions.

- **Decision-making:** The skill to make decisions, even when faced with uncertainty.

- **Stress management:** Techniques for handling pressure without losing focus or energy.

Develop New Skills

Next, identify any skills you need to build in order to strengthen your resilience. These might include:

- **Conflict resolution:** Learning how to deal with conflicts in relationships or professional settings in a constructive way.

- **Communication:** Being able to articulate your thoughts and feelings, particularly in times of stress.

- **Mindfulness or meditation practices:** These can help ground you when things feel chaotic, improving your emotional regulation and mental clarity.

- **Time management:** When facing stress, managing your time effectively can help you stay focused and prevent burnout.

Action Step:

- Create a list of 5-10 core skills that you either already possess or want to develop. For each skill, identify an action you can take to improve or refine it. For example, you might decide to take a course on emotional intelligence or commit to learning stress-management techniques through mindfulness exercises. Keep this list accessible and review it regularly to track your progress.

2. Habits: Daily Practices That Build Resilience

Your daily habits are the foundation of your mental, emotional, and physical resilience. Habits are what you do every day—often unconsciously—that either build you up or break you down. Positive habits are essential for developing resilience because they lay the groundwork for stable, adaptive responses when challenges arise.

Identify Resilience-Building Habits

Begin by identifying the habits that are essential for your resilience. These habits help you remain centered in the face of adversity:

- **Self-care routines:** These include activities like exercise, getting adequate sleep, and eating well. Taking care of your body is essential for emotional regulation and mental clarity.

- **Mindfulness or meditation:** Starting your day with mindfulness practices can help you stay calm and grounded throughout.

- **Journaling or reflection:** Regularly reflecting on your thoughts and emotions can help you process challenges and maintain clarity.

- **Gratitude practice:** Focusing on what's going well, even in tough times, helps to reframe your mindset.

- **Goal setting:** Establishing clear, actionable goals allows you to focus on what's within your control, even when external circumstances are chaotic.

Create New Habits to Support Resilience

Just as skills are critical for resilience, so too are your daily habits. Identify where you're falling short and create new habits that will strengthen your ability to handle life's challenges:

- **Regular physical activity:** Even just a short daily walk or stretching routine can help release stress and improve mental clarity.

- **Time for recovery:** Schedule time in your day for mental rest and relaxation. This could be a hobby, reading, or even just sitting in silence for 10-15 minutes.

- **Mindful eating:** Pay attention to your diet and be intentional about what you put into your body. This impacts your energy levels and ability to stay focused.

- **Networking and support-building:** Regularly reaching out to friends, family, or mentors builds your social resilience.

Action Step

- Write down your top 3 resilience-building habits and commit to practicing each one every day for at least 30 days. Track your progress using a journal or app to stay consistent. After 30 days, evaluate the impact these habits have had on your resilience and make adjustments as needed.

3. People: Building Your Support System

No one can build resilience alone. One of the most powerful resources in your resilience inventory is the people around you—those who support you during difficult times and help you stay grounded in your values. Your support system includes not just family and friends, but also mentors, colleagues, and community members who can offer guidance, encouragement, and perspective.

Identify Key People Who Build Your Resilience

Think about the individuals who make you feel safe, understood, and supported. These are the people you lean on when times get tough. Consider the following categories:

- **Mentors or role models:** People who have been through tough times and emerged stronger can provide invaluable wisdom.

- **Friends and family:** These are your emotional anchors, the people who offer compassion, empathy, and perspective during difficult times.

- **Colleagues or professional networks:** Having a network of people who understand your professional challenges can be a source of strength during work-related adversity.

- **Community support:** This might include a support group, religious community, or online group that provides mutual encouragement and shared experiences.

Strengthen Your Relationships

While it's important to identify who your key supporters are, it's equally important to nurture those relationships. Resilience isn't just about turning to others in times of need; it's about consistently investing in and deepening these connections.

- **Be proactive in offering support:** Resilience-building is a two-way street. Check in on others in your life and offer support when they need it. This creates a mutual system of trust and care.

- **Set boundaries:** While it's important to lean on others, you also need to know when to say no or step back from relationships that are draining or toxic.

- **Seek professional support:** Consider working with a coach, therapist, or counselor to help you develop emotional resilience.

Action Step

- Create a list of the key people in your life who contribute to your resilience. For each person, note how they help you (e.g., offering emotional support, providing guidance, being a sounding board). Then, identify one relationship you want to strengthen and make a plan for doing so (e.g., setting up a weekly check-in or offering your support in return).

4. Finalizing Your Resilience Inventory

Once you've identified your skills, habits, and people, take some time to compile them into your full resilience inventory. Your resilience inventory is a living document—it should evolve as you grow and change. Return to it periodically and adjust it based on your current needs and challenges.

Action Step

- Create a physical or digital document where you can write down your resilience inventory. Break it down into three sections: Skills, Habits, and People. Regularly review and update it as you build new skills, habits, and relationships. Use it as a resource to turn to when you need to re-center yourself or face new challenges.

Building your resilience inventory is about taking a proactive, intentional approach to strengthening your ability to weather life's storms. The more tools you have in your kit—skills, habits, and support systems—the more prepared you'll be to adapt, grow, and thrive in the face of uncertainty. Building resilience isn't just about reacting to adversity; it's about preparing yourself so that when challenges arise, you can meet them with a sense of purpose, strength, and adaptability.

PART II:

ACCEPTANCE – SHIKATA GA NAI

CHAPTER FOUR
THE FIRE OF ADVERSITY

Witnessing a Hospital Patient's Acceptance of Their Terminal Illness in Japan

The fluorescent lights buzzed faintly as I sat in the sterile waiting room of the hospital, my mind racing in a haze of uncertainty. I had just come from my own appointment—a routine checkup that had me contemplating more than just my health—and was waiting for a friend who had been admitted. But in the moments between thoughts, I found myself observing the patients, the caregivers, and the subtle ways people interacted in the quiet corridors.

I was in Japan, in a hospital known for its excellence in both care and patient management, a place where respect for the process of life and death was seamlessly woven into the hospital culture. It was during one of these moments, sitting in the waiting room, that I witnessed something profound—a scene I will never forget.

In front of me was a woman, probably in her late 60s, sitting with her family. She looked serene, but her eyes told a different story. They were filled with a deep sorrow—yet also an acceptance that went beyond simple resignation. There was a calmness in her demeanor that I hadn't expected, considering the circumstances. I overheard snippets of conversation, the low, respectful tones of her children gently speaking with her, offering support. But there was no desperation in their voices—no frantic sense of trying to change what seemed unchangeable.

The woman, I later learned, had been diagnosed with terminal cancer. Her prognosis was grim, and while her family quietly discussed potential treatments, I noticed her face never wavered in its stoic composure. Her acceptance of the situation was palpable, and there was a sense that she had reached a place of peace that many others—myself included—would struggle to find.

What struck me, however, wasn't just her calm acceptance. It was the way she seemed to embrace this chapter of her life with a deep sense of gratitude, as though she were honoring the life she had lived rather than focusing on the inevitable end. The doctor had spoken to her softly about her options, but there was no confusion in her gaze, no desire to cling to false hope. She nodded slowly, acknowledging the reality, and as she sat back, she seemed almost liberated in her surrender.

I could see in her face that she had long ago made peace with the idea of death, a stark contrast to how many of us—myself included—might react in the same situation. She was not angry. She wasn't bitter. There were no tears or outbursts of grief. In a way, she seemed free—free from the fear that typically accompanies terminal diagnoses. There was grace in her acceptance, a quiet strength that radiated through her in that moment.

After a while, I overheard her family members speaking with the doctor about her wishes. There was a calm, methodical nature to their decisions. They had no questions about "fighting" her illness—no medical jargon about experimental treatments or desperate pleas for anything to buy more time. Instead, they focused on her comfort and dignity, understanding that the time they had left together was sacred. In a culture that prizes collective harmony and respect, this moment of acceptance seemed like the epitome of balance.

In Western hospitals, the approach is often much more interventionist. The emphasis is typically placed on extending life at all costs, often ignoring the quality of life in favor of quantity. The instinct is to fight, to push against the inevitable, even if it means sacrificing peace in the process. But here, I saw a different philosophy—one that intertwined acceptance with respect and grace. It wasn't about surrendering to the illness; it was about aligning with reality in a way that allowed for peace and closure.

The doctor's manner was also notably different from what I had experienced back home. His approach wasn't clinical and detached, but empathetic and considerate. He asked open-ended questions, allowing the family to guide the conversation, providing reassurance without trying to steer them toward a particular path. His presence was calm, and he gave the family the space to process their feelings, rather than rushing through the conversation to move on to the next patient.

Later, after the meeting had ended, I found myself lingering in the hallway, watching the family leave the room. The woman, who had earlier appeared so composed, now seemed even more peaceful, as though the weight of uncertainty had been lifted from her shoulders. It was in that moment that I realized what I had just witnessed was not simply the acceptance of an inevitable fate—it was a model of emotional resilience.

This experience changed my perspective on many things—on health, on suffering, on how we approach both the inevitable and the unknown. It made me realize that while we can't always control our circumstances, we can control our response to them. In the West, we are often taught to fight against adversity, to never give up. But in Japan, I saw a different form of resilience—the kind that accepts and adapts. This woman wasn't merely enduring her illness; she was living through it with a sense of calm that I could only hope to emulate.

That day, I left the hospital deeply moved. It wasn't just the woman's calm demeanor that left an impression—it was the culture surrounding her. It was the way her family supported her decisions without hesitation, the way the doctor respected her autonomy, and the profound peace that stemmed from accepting the truth of the situation.

There is a beauty in accepting what we cannot change. It's a form of strength that doesn't get enough recognition in cultures that emphasize pushing forward at all costs. The woman in that hospital didn't fight her illness; she honored it. And in doing so, she showed me that sometimes, the greatest strength comes from acceptance.

In the days that followed, I found myself reflecting on the idea of acceptance—not just in the context of death, but in every area of life. How often do we resist the natural flow of things? How often do we fight battles that we know deep down are not worth fighting? The hospital experience in Japan gave me an insight into what true resilience looks like—a balance between honoring reality and finding peace within it. It was a lesson I would carry with me for years to come, reminding me that sometimes, acceptance is not the end of strength; it is its beginning.

The story of the terminal patient's acceptance carries profound implications for anyone facing life's challenges. Her quiet dignity in the face of mortality wasn't just an isolated example of grace—it was a living demonstration of how acceptance can transform our relationship with life's most difficult moments. While few of us may face such stark circumstances, her example illuminates a universal truth: there is profound strength in surrendering to what we cannot change.

But how do we bridge the gap between witnessing such acceptance and embodying it ourselves? The answer lies in understanding that surrender isn't a single moment of letting go, but a continuous practice of growth through acceptance. Just as the hospital patient didn't arrive at her peace overnight, our own journey toward acceptance requires patience, practice, and a willingness to look beyond our instinctive resistance to change.

Shikata ga nai: "It Cannot Be Helped" – The Cultural Nuances of Surrendering Control

The phrase "shikata ga nai" is deeply ingrained in the Japanese cultural fabric. Often translated as "It cannot be helped" or "There is no way to do it," the expression speaks to the delicate balance between acceptance and surrender. In the Western world, the idea of surrendering control can sometimes be viewed as a weakness or a form of defeat. However, in Japan, "shikata ga nai" is not about giving up; rather, it represents a profound recognition of the limits of personal agency in the face of forces beyond one's control.

As I reflect on my own experiences in Japan and the lessons drawn from this phrase, it becomes clear how deeply the concept of shikata ga nai shapes people's response to hardship, failure, and even death. This quiet surrender to what cannot be changed is not passive resignation but an active, conscious choice to move forward with grace despite life's uncertainties. It challenges the Western idea that resilience always involves resistance or struggle.

The Historical and Cultural Roots of Shikata ga Nai

Shikata ga nai is rooted in Japan's long history of feudalism, natural disasters, and societal hierarchy. The idea of enduring hardship with dignity, without outward complaint, has been reinforced through centuries of cultural evolution. In Japan, there is an understanding that much of life is dictated by factors beyond individual control—be it fate, societal expectations, or the will of nature. The focus is not on changing what cannot be changed but on adapting gracefully to the circumstances.

This cultural outlook is particularly evident in the way Japanese people approach natural disasters, economic hardship, and even health crises. Whether facing an earthquake or the death of a loved one, there is an overarching sense that life is full of uncontrollable forces. Accepting them with composure and humility is seen not only as a practical necessity but also as a moral virtue. This acceptance is not about apathy or passivity; it is about preserving one's mental and emotional energy for the things that can be influenced.

In modern Japan, "shikata ga nai" serves as a reminder to not waste emotional or mental resources fighting the inevitable. It is a form of pragmatism that allows individuals to move forward in the face of adversity without succumbing to despair or anxiety. In fact, this acceptance often leads to remarkable resilience—the ability to endure suffering without being consumed by it.

The Role of Shikata ga Nai in Personal Adversity

I've had the privilege of witnessing "shikata ga nai" in action during difficult personal moments in Japan. One of the most profound instances occurred when I visited a Japanese friend who was grappling with a terminal illness. She was a woman of incredible strength, but unlike the aggressive "fighting spirit" often praised in the West, she showed a different kind of bravery. When I asked her how she was coping with her diagnosis, she simply said, "Shikata ga nai. It cannot be helped."

At first, I was confused by her response. In the West, we might expect someone to resist, to fight, or at least express anger or fear. But my friend wasn't resigning to her fate in a defeated way. She wasn't giving up on life, nor was she bitter about her situation. Instead, she embraced what she couldn't change and focused on the quality of the time she had left. It was not a denial of her illness but a profound act of surrender. This acceptance allowed her to enjoy each moment with greater clarity and purpose.

The simplicity and power of "shikata ga nai" became clearer as I watched her interact with her family and friends. There were no grand gestures of defiance or rebellion against her diagnosis. There was simply a quiet resolve to live with dignity, with the understanding that some things are beyond our control. It was not that she had stopped caring or stopped fighting for life; rather, she had prioritized what truly mattered—peace, relationships, and presence over resistance.

In this way, "shikata ga nai" can be a tool for emotional resilience. By accepting what we cannot control, we create space to focus on what we can influence: our actions, attitudes, and how we engage with the world around us. My friend's acceptance did not diminish her strength; it amplified it. She was not resigned in a way that led to bitterness but in a way that fostered greater compassion for herself and others.

The Paradox of Surrender

The Western world, steeped in the ideals of autonomy and self-determination, often struggles with the notion of surrender. To surrender control can feel like an abandonment of responsibility, a relinquishment of power. But in Japan, surrendering control is often viewed as an intelligent response to the limitations of human existence. It is not an act of weakness but one of wisdom.

Surrendering control through "shikata ga nai" does not mean disengaging from life or giving up on progress. Instead, it means choosing where to invest one's energy. It's a conscious recognition that not everything can be controlled or predicted. It's an understanding that there are forces at play—be it illness, fate, or environmental factors—that we simply cannot change. Accepting this allows us to move forward with purpose and without unnecessary stress.

This paradox—surrendering control to gain control—might seem contradictory at first, but it's central to the concept of resilience. When we stop resisting the uncontrollable, we free ourselves to engage fully with the aspects of life that are within our influence. It is a way of acknowledging that while we may not be able to control the circumstances, we can control our response to them.

Shikata Ga Nai and the Collective Good

Another dimension of "shikata ga nai" is its role in fostering social harmony. In Japan, this phrase often extends beyond the individual to the collective. The ability to accept the uncontrollable is seen as a means of maintaining group cohesion. By surrendering personal desires or frustrations in the face of shared hardship, individuals contribute to the overall stability and peace of the group. This collective attitude can be seen in various aspects of Japanese society, from the workplace to family dynamics.

For example, during times of national crisis, such as after natural disasters, Japanese citizens often exhibit a remarkable sense of unity. The phrase "shikata ga nai" becomes an expression of collective resilience—an acknowledgment that everyone is in this together, and while the situation may be difficult, the response should be one of cooperation, patience, and understanding. It is not the time for complaints or finger-pointing but for calm acceptance and constructive action.

This cultural emphasis on collective well-being can be seen in Japan's response to the aftermath of earthquakes, tsunamis, and other disasters. People line up for food, help one another in times of need, and maintain a sense of order and peace despite the chaos. This is the spirit of "shikata ga nai" in action—individuals surrendering their desire for immediate solutions for the sake of the greater good. In a world that often feels divided, this willingness to accept and adapt together is a profound reminder of the power of collective acceptance.

The Intersection of Shikata Ga Nai and Mental Health

In modern times, "shikata ga nai" also intersects with mental health. Japan has long struggled with the societal stigma surrounding mental illness, but the concept of "shikata ga nai" offers a gentle approach to managing life's emotional challenges. Rather than expecting individuals to overcome every obstacle or "fix" every problem, this cultural outlook offers a way of accepting emotional pain without becoming overwhelmed by it.

For example, when faced with overwhelming stress or anxiety, instead of battling against these emotions, "shikata ga nai" encourages individuals to acknowledge them without judgment. It allows people to recognize that sometimes, emotions like grief or frustration are a natural part of the human experience, not something to be immediately corrected or avoided. This mindset provides room for emotional growth, allowing individuals to accept their feelings without feeling that they need to constantly "fight" against them.

Shikata Ga Nai in Action: Embracing the Uncontrollable

At its core, "shikata ga nai" teaches us to distinguish between what is within our control and what is beyond it. It encourages us to focus on our responses, our attitudes, and our capacity to adapt. By surrendering control over the things we cannot change, we can move forward with peace of mind, knowing that we have done our best within the constraints of reality.

Ultimately, "shikata ga nai" is not about abandoning hope or giving up on life. It is about accepting the things we cannot control with grace and finding ways to continue moving forward in spite of them. It is a powerful tool for resilience, teaching us that true strength comes not from fighting against life's inevitable challenges but from accepting them and adapting in a way that preserves our peace and emotional well-being.

The Science of Acceptance: The Difference Between Resignation and Healthy Acceptance

In a world that constantly encourages us to push through adversity, succeed against all odds, and overcome every challenge, the concept of "acceptance" might seem counterintuitive. The idea of simply accepting what we cannot change may feel like a form of surrender or giving up. However, the science of acceptance tells a different story—one that reveals the profound benefits of embracing life as it comes, particularly in the face of adversity.

Acceptance does not mean passivity or resignation. Instead, healthy acceptance is an active process of acknowledging and coming to terms with situations, emotions, and challenges that are beyond our control. It is about learning how to respond to life's difficulties with a clear mind and a resilient spirit. To better understand this, it's important to distinguish between resignation, which can lead to stagnation and emotional distress, and healthy acceptance, which promotes well-being, resilience, and psychological growth.

Resignation vs. Healthy Acceptance: A Fine Line

At first glance, resignation and healthy acceptance might seem like two sides of the same coin. Both involve acknowledging a situation and not fighting it. However, the difference between the two is profound and lies in how we relate to the situation.

Resignation is a passive, often negative response to a challenging situation. When someone resigns, they give up without hope of change. It's a sense of defeat where the person feels helpless, as if nothing can be done to alter the circumstances. Resignation often stems from a sense of powerlessness, where a person believes their efforts are futile, and therefore, they withdraw emotionally or physically from the situation.

For example, if someone is faced with a difficult work situation, resignation might look like quitting without a fight, withdrawing from responsibilities, and feeling hopeless about the future. The individual may feel overwhelmed and unable to take action, believing that nothing they do will make a difference. As a result, resignation can lead to stagnation, apathy, and emotional burnout.

On the other hand, **healthy acceptance** is an active, mindful process that acknowledges the reality of a situation without giving up on oneself or the possibility of change. It involves coming to terms with the situation, but it does not mean that we are passive or indifferent. Healthy acceptance allows us to process our emotions, reduce unnecessary suffering, and move forward with a greater sense of clarity and purpose.

For example, in the same challenging work scenario, healthy acceptance would look like acknowledging the difficulty of the situation without allowing it to define your emotional state. It might mean recognizing that while the circumstances are challenging, you still have agency in how you respond. You might seek support, develop coping strategies, or find ways to manage your emotions while accepting the limits of the situation.

In short, **resignation** is about giving up in a way that leaves you stuck, while **healthy acceptance** is about acknowledging what is and finding the strength to move forward.

The Psychology Behind Healthy Acceptance

The science of acceptance is rooted in several psychological frameworks, most notably Acceptance and Commitment Therapy (ACT). ACT is based on the idea that psychological suffering arises not from the events themselves but from how we respond to them. When we resist unpleasant thoughts or feelings, we amplify their power and influence over our lives. In contrast, acceptance allows us to relate to those thoughts and feelings in a healthy way.

According to ACT, the goal is not to eliminate pain or distress—because that is not always possible—but to develop a healthier relationship with these experiences. Rather than fighting or avoiding difficult emotions, we learn to accept them, allowing them to come and go without over-identifying with them.

Research shows that accepting difficult emotions—whether they are anxiety, sadness, or frustration—can significantly reduce their impact. In fact, studies have found that people who practice acceptance tend to experience lower levels of stress and emotional reactivity. This is because acceptance allows us to process emotions more fully, rather than avoiding them, which can lead to greater psychological flexibility and emotional resilience.

A key component of acceptance is mindfulness. Mindfulness involves being present in the moment without judgment, allowing us to experience emotions and thoughts without becoming overwhelmed by them. By practicing mindfulness, we can develop greater self-awareness, which helps us respond to challenging situations in a calm and measured way, rather than reacting impulsively.

In healthy acceptance, we also acknowledge the limits of our control. We recognize that some things are simply out of our hands, and trying to force change in these areas is not only futile but also emotionally draining. This understanding gives us the space to focus on what we can control: our actions, our responses, and our attitudes. This shift in focus is crucial to building resilience in the face of adversity.

The Role of Self-Compassion in Acceptance

One of the key aspects of healthy acceptance is **self-compassion**. Self-compassion is about treating ourselves with the same kindness, understanding, and patience that we would offer to a close friend who is suffering. Instead of being self-critical or judgmental when we face difficulties, self-compassion allows us to acknowledge our struggles without shame or harshness.

When we practice self-compassion, we create a safe emotional space to experience our feelings without fear of judgment. This, in turn, makes it easier to accept difficult emotions, because we are not fighting against them or punishing ourselves for having them. Research has shown that people who practice self-compassion are better able to cope with stress, pain, and failure because they have a healthier, more supportive relationship with themselves.

In the context of acceptance, self-compassion means acknowledging that it is okay to feel upset, frustrated, or sad in the face of hardship. It means recognizing that you are human, and that all emotions, even the difficult ones, are part of the experience of being alive. Rather than judging ourselves for these emotions, we approach them with kindness and understanding, which allows us to move through them without becoming stuck in them.

Acceptance and Resilience

Healthy acceptance plays a crucial role in building **resilience**. Resilience is not about avoiding pain or challenges but about being able to withstand and recover from them. People who can accept difficult circumstances are more likely to adapt and bounce back, because they don't waste energy fighting against the inevitable.

One of the key ways that acceptance fosters resilience is by allowing us to **reframe** our challenges. When we stop resisting what is happening, we create mental space to assess the situation objectively. This shift in perspective allows us to focus on solutions and action, rather than dwelling on the problem.

For example, if someone loses their job, the first reaction might be fear, anger, or frustration. If the person fights against these emotions or denies the reality of the situation, they may remain stuck in those feelings for a longer time. However, if they practice acceptance, they can acknowledge their emotions without judgment, which opens the door to problem-solving and adaptation. Instead of getting bogged down by what is uncontrollable, they can start looking at what actions they can take to move forward—whether it's updating their resume, networking, or exploring new opportunities.

Acceptance also helps reduce **rumination**, which is when we obsess over negative thoughts and experiences. Rumination keeps us stuck in the past, preventing us from moving forward. By accepting that certain things cannot be changed, we free ourselves from the endless cycle of negative thinking and make room for growth and healing.

The Benefits of Healthy Acceptance

The benefits of healthy acceptance are numerous. By embracing what cannot be changed, we free ourselves from the emotional burden of resistance. Some of the key benefits include:

- **Reduced emotional suffering**: By accepting our emotions and experiences, we stop struggling against them and reduce the emotional turmoil they cause.

- **Greater emotional resilience**: Acceptance helps us build the mental and emotional flexibility needed to cope with future challenges.

- **Improved mental health**: People who practice acceptance tend to experience lower levels of anxiety, depression, and stress because they don't waste energy resisting their emotions.

- **Increased mindfulness**: Acceptance encourages us to stay present and aware, rather than getting caught up in past regrets or future worries.

- **Enhanced problem-solving ability**: By accepting a situation as it is, we can better assess the next steps and focus on what we can control.

The major key to cultivating healthy acceptance is to embrace the idea that it is not about giving up; rather, it is about making peace with what is beyond our control and finding strength in the process. Through acceptance, we can navigate life's challenges with grace, resilience, and emotional well-being. By letting go of resistance, we open ourselves to new possibilities and a deeper connection with ourselves and the world around us.

Reflection Questions: What Challenges Have You Been Resisting?

In our fast-paced world, it's all too easy to resist the challenges that life throws at us. Resistance often arises from our desire for comfort, control, or avoidance of pain. But what if we could reframe our relationship with challenges? What if, instead of fighting against them, we could acknowledge their presence and learn from them? This section is designed to help you reflect on the challenges you've been resisting and explore how to accept them, learn from them, and move forward with greater strength and clarity.

The Nature of Resistance

Before diving into the reflection questions, it's important to understand what resistance really is. Resistance is a natural human response to anything that feels uncomfortable, overwhelming, or threatening. It often manifests as a form of denial, avoidance, or defensiveness. We resist challenges because they demand change, growth, or discomfort, and our instinct is to preserve the status quo.

However, resistance often only prolongs our suffering. The longer we resist, the more energy we waste. Our emotions can become stuck, and the situation can feel more overwhelming. Accepting challenges, on the other hand, allows us to regain control over our responses. It frees us from the internal struggle and creates the space needed for growth and transformation.

The following reflection questions will help you examine the challenges in your life that you may be resisting and invite you to consider a new approach—one that is grounded in acceptance, awareness, and action.

1. What Challenge Have You Been Avoiding or Denying?

Think about the areas of your life where you've been trying to avoid difficult emotions or situations. Perhaps there's a conflict in your personal life, a career decision you've been putting off, or an uncomfortable conversation you've been avoiding. These are the challenges that you've been resisting, whether consciously or unconsciously. They might feel like a weight hanging over you, draining your energy and peace of mind.

Reflection: Write down at least one challenge you've been avoiding or denying. Why have you been resisting it? How does this resistance show up in your life (e.g., procrastination, anxiety, anger, avoidance)?

2. How Does Resistance Affect Your Emotional and Physical Well-Being?

Resistance doesn't just take a mental toll—it can affect our emotional and physical well-being as well. When we resist challenges, we often experience heightened stress, anxiety, or frustration. These negative emotions can manifest in our bodies as tension, fatigue, or even illness. The more we resist, the more our body and mind react, creating a vicious cycle.

Reflection: Take a moment to reflect on the physical and emotional symptoms you may experience when resisting challenges. Do you feel more anxious, tense, or exhausted? How does resistance affect your overall well-being? Can you notice any patterns in your thoughts or body when you avoid confronting challenges?

3. What Would Happen If You Accepted This Challenge Instead of Resisting It?

Acceptance doesn't mean giving up or resigning yourself to the situation—it means acknowledging the reality of the challenge without judgment. By accepting it, you free yourself from the internal struggle. Acceptance creates space for clarity, insight, and action. It allows you to approach the challenge with a calm and resilient mindset, rather than letting it overwhelm you.

Reflection: Imagine a scenario where you stop resisting the challenge you've been avoiding. What might happen if you allowed yourself to accept it fully, even if just for a moment? How might this shift in mindset change your emotional state? How might it open up possibilities for constructive action?

4. What Can You Learn from This Challenge?

Every challenge we face has something to teach us. Sometimes it's about developing new skills, other times it's about deepening our emotional resilience. If we resist a challenge, we miss out on these lessons. When we accept it, however, we open ourselves to personal growth.

Reflection: Take a step back and reflect on what you can learn from this challenge. What is it teaching you about yourself, your values, or your relationships? How can this challenge be an opportunity for growth or transformation? Write down your insights and look for ways to apply them in the future.

5. How Have You Grown After Facing Difficult Challenges in the Past?

Looking back on past challenges, you might realize that the moments when you stopped resisting and started accepting were the moments when you grew the most. These challenges were not only opportunities for learning, but they also showed you your own strength and resilience.

Reflection: Reflect on a past challenge that you eventually faced head-on, despite your initial resistance. How did you grow or change as a result of facing it? What strengths did you uncover within yourself? Write about how this experience shaped your current perspective on challenges.

6. What Would It Look Like If You Embraced This Challenge with Compassion Instead of Resistance?

In the face of difficult situations, we often turn to self-criticism or judgment. We may tell ourselves that we should have handled things differently or that we're not strong enough to deal with the situation. But self-compassion allows us to approach challenges with kindness, understanding, and patience. Instead of criticizing ourselves for the challenge, we can offer ourselves the same empathy we would extend to a friend in the same situation.

Reflection: How would your experience of this challenge change if you approached it with self-compassion? How can you offer yourself kindness, understanding, and patience in the face of difficulty? Write a compassionate message to yourself about the challenge you're facing.

7. How Do You Typically Respond to Challenges?

Our habitual responses to challenges often reveal a lot about our internal beliefs and coping mechanisms. Some people might react with anger, while others might withdraw or shut down. These automatic reactions can be helpful at times but can also prevent us from fully dealing with the situation.

Reflection: Think about your typical responses when faced with challenges. Are you someone who reacts impulsively, avoids the issue, or tries to control everything? How do these responses help or hinder your ability to move forward? What other responses might be more constructive in helping you face challenges head-on?

8. What Are the Benefits of Facing This Challenge Directly?

Every challenge, no matter how difficult, offers benefits when we face it with acceptance rather than resistance. By confronting challenges head-on, we gain the strength, insight, and clarity needed to move forward in our lives. The longer we resist, the more we limit our potential for growth and transformation.

Reflection: What specific benefits do you think you might gain by accepting and facing this challenge? How might this positively affect your personal growth, relationships, or sense of peace? Write down the potential rewards of tackling this challenge directly.

9. What Are Your Fears Around Confronting This Challenge?

Often, the reason we resist challenges is due to the fears or uncertainties associated with them. We fear failure, disappointment, judgment, or pain. These fears, while understandable, often prevent us from moving forward. Acknowledging these fears is the first step in overcoming them.

Reflection: What fears arise when you think about confronting this challenge? Are you afraid of failure, rejection, or something else? How can you reframe these fears in a way that empowers you to take action? Write down your fears and challenge their validity—are they based on facts, or are they projections of worst-case scenarios?

10. What Action Can You Take Today to Move Beyond Resistance?

Once you've reflected on the challenge and your relationship to it, the next step is to take action. Action doesn't need to be big or dramatic; it can be small and manageable. The key is to take a step, however small, in the direction of acceptance and forward movement.

Reflection: What is one small action you can take today to stop resisting and begin accepting this challenge? Whether it's having a difficult conversation, making a decision, or simply shifting your mindset, write down the action you can take. Commit to taking that step today.

Resistance is a natural human response, but it often holds us back from the growth and transformation that challenges can bring. By reflecting on the challenges you've been resisting, you can begin to shift your mindset and approach them with acceptance, self-compassion, and resilience. Through this process, you'll discover new strengths, gain valuable insights, and create space for personal growth. Remember, the challenges you face are not obstacles to avoid, but opportunities to evolve.

Acceptance and Commitment Therapy: Model, processes and outcomes\

The study, *Acceptance and Commitment Therapy: Model, Processes and Outcomes* (2006), explores the transformative power of acceptance-based strategies in reducing psychological distress. This work aligns closely with the Japanese concept of *shikata ga nai*, which translates to "it cannot be helped" or "what will be, will be." At first glance, this phrase might seem resigned or fatalistic, but my experience in Japan taught me its deeper meaning—one rooted in resilience, clarity, and moving forward despite challenges.

The authors of the study explain that Acceptance and Commitment Therapy (ACT) focuses on helping individuals make peace with difficult emotions rather than avoiding or fighting them. By fostering psychological flexibility, ACT encourages people to accept their experiences as they are, without judgment, while committing to actions aligned with their values. This perspective resonated profoundly with me, especially during my recovery from the accident, when the weight of physical pain and uncertainty felt insurmountable at times.

In the hospital, I often felt the urge to resist my situation, to wrestle against the pain and frustration. But the more I pushed back emotionally, the more overwhelming it became. I was introduced to the idea of *shikata ga nai* through a nurse whose calm acceptance of every situation seemed almost unshakable. When I asked her how she managed to remain so composed, she replied with a quiet smile, "We can't control everything. What we can do is face it and do our best with what's in front of us."

Reading the study much later, I realized how closely this aligns with the ACT model. One of its central principles is defusion—separating ourselves from our thoughts and feelings to reduce their power over us. For example, instead of thinking, "I am in unbearable pain," ACT encourages reframing: "I am noticing the sensation of pain." It's a small shift, but it transforms our relationship with discomfort, allowing us to coexist with it without being consumed by it. This mirrors the *shikata ga nai* mindset, where acknowledging reality becomes the first step toward reclaiming agency.

The authors highlight how avoidance strategies often amplify psychological distress. People expend so much energy avoiding uncomfortable emotions—fear, sadness, frustration—that they end up trapped by them. This hit close to home for me. Before the accident, I had a tendency to avoid acknowledging setbacks, convincing myself that sheer determination could overcome any obstacle. But lying in that hospital bed, I couldn't escape the reality of my condition. It was only when I began to accept my limitations, rather than resist them, that I found a sense of peace. Acceptance didn't mean giving up; it meant freeing myself from the futile struggle to control the uncontrollable.

ACT also emphasizes values-guided action, and this ties beautifully to *shikata ga nai*. Accepting what we cannot change doesn't mean surrendering; it means redirecting our energy toward what truly matters. I saw this reflected in the Japanese staff around me. Whether it was a nurse meticulously arranging supplies or a physical therapist guiding me through slow, painful exercises, there was a quiet focus on doing the best possible job with the circumstances at hand. They weren't fighting against reality—they were working within it to create positive outcomes.

The study underscores that acceptance-based strategies are not a passive coping mechanism; they are an active process of engagement. It's about making space for pain, fear, or disappointment while continuing to move forward. This aligns with one of the most important lessons I learned in Japan: strength doesn't come from avoiding life's difficulties but from meeting them with grace, adaptability, and a clear sense of purpose.

In those difficult hospital months, I began to see how *shikata ga nai* and the principles of ACT could coexist. Both invite us to release the struggle against life's inevitable hardships and instead focus on living meaningfully within the constraints we face. It's not about giving up hope or ambition—it's about making peace with the present moment, so we have the clarity and strength to shape what comes next.

Embracing What Cannot Be Changed: The Shikata ga nai

The **Shikata ga nai** stage, often translated as "it cannot be helped," is about acceptance—embracing the aspects of life that are beyond your control. This stage challenges you to move beyond resistance and denial, fostering a mindset of peace and resilience in the face of inevitabilities. Shikata ga nai is not about passive surrender; it's about finding strength in acceptance and focusing on what you *can* influence.

Stage Recognition

Recognizing when you're in the Shikata ga nai stage begins with awareness of your internal struggles against uncontrollable circumstances.

- **Key Indicators:**

- Feelings of frustration, helplessness, or anger when faced with challenges that cannot be changed.

- A tendency to overanalyze or ruminate on "what if" scenarios.

- Resistance to letting go of outcomes you hoped to control.

- **Behavioral Patterns:**

  - Attempts to fix unfixable problems or taking on more responsibility than you can manage.

  - Avoidance of situations or emotions that feel overwhelming.

- **Relationship Dynamics:**

  - Conflict stemming from unrealistic expectations of others or yourself.

  - Difficulty forgiving past grievances or accepting others' limitations.

Self-Assessment Exercise:

- Reflect on a recent frustration or disappointment. Ask yourself: *Was this within my control? If not, why am I holding onto it?*

Stage Completion Markers

As you progress in the Shikata ga nai stage, you'll notice significant shifts in your mindset and approach to challenges:

- **Mindset Shifts:**

- A calm acceptance of life's uncertainties and imperfections.

- Reduced emotional reactivity to situations beyond your control.

- **Behavioral Changes:**

  - Greater focus on actionable steps rather than dwelling on the uncontrollable.

  - The ability to let go of past regrets and future anxieties.

- **Emotional Milestones:**

  - Feeling a sense of peace, even when outcomes don't align with expectations.

  - Freedom from resentment or blame, both toward yourself and others.

- **Relationship Developments:**

  - Healthier dynamics with others, built on realistic expectations and mutual understanding.

Next Stage Preparation

Acceptance sets the stage for self-reflection in the **Naikan** stage. Signs you're ready to transition include:

- **Internal Signals:**

  - A growing curiosity about the deeper patterns behind your emotions and actions.

  - Readiness to explore personal accountability without judgment.

- **Transition Challenges:**

- Fear of confronting uncomfortable truths about yourself or your relationships.

- A tendency to remain overly passive, mistaking acceptance for inaction.

- **Preparation Exercises:**

  - **Mindful Reflection:** Spend time identifying what aspects of a recent difficulty were within your control versus outside it.

  - **Gratitude Practice:** Focus on appreciating what remains constant or positive in your life, even amid challenges.

Regression Warnings

The path to acceptance is not linear. Here are signs of potential regression:

- **Early Warning Signs:**

  - Falling back into rumination or obsessive problem-solving.

  - Resentment toward situations or people involved in uncontrollable outcomes.

- **Common Triggers:**

  - Unexpected challenges or reminders of unresolved past issues.

  - Social pressures that reinforce the need to "fix" everything.

- **Stages to Avoid Regressing To:**

- Returning to superficial stability (Genki) or relying on avoidance tactics instead of true acceptance.

- **Prevention Strategies:**

  - Regular mindfulness practice to maintain focus on the present.

  - Journaling exercises to process emotions rather than suppress them.

- **Recovery Practices:**

  - Revisit past moments where acceptance brought you peace, using them as anchors during new challenges.

Stage Integration

Integrating Shikata ga nai into your life is essential for sustaining the growth it fosters. Here's how to make its lessons part of your long-term mindset:

- **Building on Acceptance:**

  - Use acceptance as a springboard for self-exploration and growth.

  - Balance acceptance with action by focusing on areas within your control.

- **Sustaining Practices:**

  - Develop daily rituals, such as mindful breathing, to reinforce acceptance.

  - Create a mantra or affirmation (e.g., "I release what I cannot change") to remind yourself of this principle.

- **Balancing Progress:**

- Remember that acceptance doesn't mean complacency. It's about choosing where to direct your energy wisely.

- **Integration Exercise:**

  - Write a letter to your past self about a difficult experience you've now accepted. Reflect on how acceptance transformed your perspective and freed you to move forward.

Shikata ga nai is more than a coping mechanism—it's a philosophy that fosters resilience and clarity. By fully embracing this stage, you learn to let go of what you cannot control, allowing you to channel your energy into meaningful growth. It's not about giving up; it's about rising above, with the strength that comes from acceptance as your guide.

Consider how the patient's acceptance created space—not just for peace, but for deeper connections with her family, for meaningful conversations about what mattered most, for a different kind of healing that transcended physical cure. Her surrender wasn't an end point but a beginning, opening doors to growth that might have remained closed had she remained in resistance.

This is the paradox that connects acceptance to growth: when we stop fighting against what we cannot change, we free up enormous energy for transformation in areas where we can make a difference. The patient's story teaches us that acceptance isn't passive resignation—it's an active choice that creates space for new possibilities.

As we move forward to explore how surrender fosters growth, remember that the hospital patient's example isn't meant to be placed on a pedestal of impossible achievement. Instead, it serves as a compass pointing toward our own capacity for transformation through acceptance. Her story reminds us that even in life's most challenging moments, there is always potential for growth—if we're willing to first accept where we are.

The journey from witnessing acceptance to embodying it in our own lives begins with a simple truth: growth doesn't come from constantly fighting against reality, but from learning to work with it. In the following chapter, we'll explore practical ways to translate this wisdom into our own lives, discovering how surrender can become a powerful catalyst for personal transformation.

CHAPTER FIVE

SURRENDERING TO GROWTH

A Moment of Personal Failure that Led to Unexpected Clarity

I t was a cold winter evening, and I had just wrapped up a meeting with a client that had gone horribly wrong. I remember walking out of the building, my mind racing with a mix of frustration and disbelief. My heart was pounding, not just from the stress of the meeting, but from the realization that I had failed. Not just in a small way, but in a way that felt monumental at the time.

I had been working for weeks on this project, putting in long hours, crafting every detail with the precision of someone who thought they had everything under control. But as the client laid out their feedback, it was clear that I had missed the mark. What I thought would be an elegant solution turned out to be a mismatch to their needs. I'd built something that, in my eyes, was perfect, but it wasn't what they needed. That stark contrast between what I envisioned and what was actually wanted was a painful reminder of how far I had fallen from the mark.

At that moment, I wanted to turn around and quit—leave the meeting, walk away from the project entirely, or hide under the covers and pretend it never happened. I had never liked failure. I prided myself on being a perfectionist, and my entire identity was built around the idea that if I worked hard enough, I could control the outcome. I could avoid mistakes. But now, standing in the parking lot, I realized that in trying so hard to control everything, I had lost sight of what truly mattered: the ability to adapt, learn, and grow.

That failure—the sting of missing the mark so completely—set in motion something I hadn't expected: a moment of clarity. It wasn't an instant shift or a dramatic epiphany, but in the days that followed, I began to see the value of the experience. I found myself reflecting on what went wrong, not just in the project, but in my approach. I had been too focused on the external validation—on what others thought was right—rather than on understanding the deeper needs behind the task at hand. In trying to "perfect" everything, I had overlooked the core problem I was supposed to be solving.

I also began to recognize how deeply tied my identity was to my successes. If the project failed, it felt like I had failed. But that couldn't be further from the truth. I was learning. I was growing. That was the point. And it was in the humility of that realization that I began to accept failure not as a sign of defeat, but as a necessary part of my journey.

The real clarity came when I stopped looking at failure as something that needed to be avoided at all costs, and instead, I started to see it as a tool. I realized that my resistance to failure had been holding me back. I had been so afraid of not getting things perfect that I had missed the opportunities for growth in the messy, imperfect process of learning. What I thought was a personal failure was actually a pivotal moment in my transformation.

Looking back now, I can see how this experience fits into a broader pattern in my life. So often, we cling to stability and control, thinking that success is the key to happiness and fulfillment. But when we are too attached to success, we limit ourselves from learning the deeper lessons that come through trial, error, and ultimately, failure. When we let go of that attachment to perfection, we open ourselves to greater growth. In a way, this failure was the gift that kept giving.

It's funny how failure, something we often view as the opposite of success, can be one of the most powerful teachers in our lives. Through this experience, I learned that failure isn't the end of the road; it's the beginning of a new chapter. It teaches us to adapt, to question our assumptions, and to refine our approach. It's a teacher that forces us to dig deeper and find solutions that we would have never considered if everything had gone smoothly.

And so, this moment of failure became a defining moment in my life. Not because it was an easy or pleasant experience, but because it was the turning point where I began to truly understand what transformation meant. It wasn't about avoiding mistakes or seeking external validation; it was about embracing the messy, imperfect process of growth. It was about learning to face challenges head-on, without letting the fear of failure dictate my path.

In the days after that meeting, I started to reframe how I viewed my work, my success, and my failures. I began to understand that failure wasn't a reflection of my worth, but an integral part of my evolution. It became clear to me that personal growth doesn't happen in the absence of challenges or setbacks; it happens because of them. That realization was the key to unlocking a new approach to life and work, one that embraced change, allowed for imperfection, and welcomed the lessons that came with every failure.

Now, when I encounter setbacks—whether in my career or personal life—I try to remember that those moments aren't the end of the story. They are the beginning of a new chapter, one that offers me the chance to grow, learn, and become a better version of myself. Instead of fearing failure, I look for the lessons it holds. In fact, I've come to believe that failure is often the most direct path to clarity and transformation.

This story is just one example, but it encapsulates the essence of the process we all go through when we confront failure. It's not easy. It's not comfortable. But it's through these moments of personal failure that we often gain the most clarity and insight. And the clarity that comes from failure—especially when we embrace it with openness and humility—can lead us to a level of resilience and growth that we would have never thought possible. This realization resonated with the Japanese concept of Shikata ga nai – accepting what cannot be changed – which I had observed during my time in Japan.

How Japanese Acceptance Fosters Adaptability

In Japan, the concept of acceptance isn't merely a passive resignation; it's a proactive stance toward life's inevitable challenges. A perfect example of this can be seen in Japan's approach to natural disasters, especially earthquakes. Japan sits on the Pacific Ring of Fire, one of the most active seismic regions in the world. Earthquakes are a frequent and sometimes devastating occurrence, yet rather than living in fear or denial, the Japanese culture has developed a unique form of resilience and adaptability in response. This adaptability is deeply rooted in the Japanese approach to acceptance, which allows individuals and communities to face inevitable challenges with a mindset focused on preparation and constructive response, rather than resistance or panic.

1. Earthquake Preparedness: A Cultural Imperative

One of the most notable ways Japanese society embraces the inevitability of earthquakes is through its culture of preparedness. Unlike many other parts of the world where natural disasters are often met with a sense of disbelief or an attempt to avoid thinking about them, Japan has ingrained disaster readiness into the very fabric of everyday life. Earthquakes are accepted as a fundamental part of life in Japan, and the response is not one of resistance but one of readiness and resilience.

From a young age, children in Japan are taught how to respond to an earthquake. Schools conduct regular drills, ensuring that students know exactly what to do the moment the ground shakes. These drills aren't mere simulations; they're deeply embedded into the education system, often practiced multiple times a year. Students, teachers, and staff alike move through the drills with a sense of calm efficiency, reflecting the belief that preparedness is the best way to respond to the unpredictable. Rather than creating anxiety, these drills are a demonstration of how preparedness can bring peace of mind and reduce fear when the real event happens.

In addition to these school drills, Japan's government has implemented extensive infrastructure projects designed to withstand earthquakes. Buildings are constructed with the latest seismic technology, including shock absorbers and flexible frames that allow structures to sway rather than crumble during an earthquake. The mindset is that while earthquakes cannot be avoided, the damage they cause can be minimized through thoughtful design and strategic planning. This proactive acceptance—that earthquakes are a natural and recurring part of life—has led to one of the safest and most resilient urban environments in the world.

2. The Role of "Shikata ga nai" in Earthquake Preparedness

The Japanese phrase "shikata ga nai," which loosely translates to "it can't be helped," is a cornerstone of the culture of acceptance. This doesn't mean that challenges are shrugged off with indifference; rather, it reflects the idea that some things are beyond our control and must be dealt with pragmatically. In the case of earthquakes, "shikata ga nai" embodies the understanding that earthquakes are inevitable and must be faced head-on, not avoided or feared.

This cultural mindset fosters an approach where rather than expending energy on resistance or denial, people focus on what can be done in the face of the inevitable. In Japan, once an earthquake occurs, it is not uncommon for individuals and entire communities to calmly assess the damage and immediately begin the process of recovery. The psychological and emotional response is one of acceptance: recognizing that disaster has struck, but that it is possible to rebuild, regroup, and recover. This doesn't mean the shock or the pain of loss isn't felt; rather, it indicates a deep cultural commitment to moving forward constructively.

3. Adaptability in Response to Crisis

Acceptance in Japan doesn't mean passivity; instead, it fuels adaptability. One of the most compelling examples of how acceptance fosters adaptability is the quick and efficient response to natural disasters, particularly after the Great East Japan Earthquake in 2011. The aftermath of the disaster demonstrated the remarkable resilience and adaptability of the Japanese people.

Within hours of the earthquake, emergency response teams were mobilized. Shelters were set up, roads were cleared, and power was restored in record time. The Japanese people didn't succumb to the shock of the disaster—they adapted swiftly, implementing contingency plans that had been developed long before the earthquake struck. These efforts were not accidental; they were the result of a culture deeply ingrained with the belief that in life's most challenging moments, the ability to adapt and respond effectively is paramount.

This adaptability is also evident in Japan's disaster recovery efforts. After an earthquake, it is common to see entire neighborhoods rebuild within a few years, with a renewed sense of solidarity. This adaptability, fueled by a culture of acceptance, is not limited to physical reconstruction; it extends to the emotional and psychological resilience of the community. Recovery efforts are not rushed but are based on a long-term vision, ensuring that each step of the rebuilding process is handled thoughtfully and effectively. In this way, Japan's culture of acceptance allows for a more sustainable form of recovery that recognizes the need for both immediate response and long-term planning.

4. Acceptance as a Collective Strength

In Japanese culture, acceptance is not just an individual trait—it is a collective strength. This idea of group resilience is crucial in understanding how Japanese society deals with crises. In the aftermath of an earthquake, it is not uncommon for communities to band together to help those in need. Volunteers often step in to support recovery efforts, and there is a profound sense of communal responsibility that is ingrained in the culture.

This collective approach to crisis management is particularly evident in the way Japanese communities respond to post-disaster recovery. People don't wait for the government to fix everything; they take matters into their own hands, sharing resources, offering emotional support, and physically rebuilding homes and infrastructure. The acceptance of crisis is framed as a communal challenge that requires cooperation, teamwork, and resilience from everyone involved.

This collective strength, derived from cultural acceptance, is a key factor in Japan's ability to respond to natural disasters with efficiency and resilience. It demonstrates that when individuals acknowledge the inevitability of challenges and work together to find solutions, communities can adapt in ways that are both swift and sustainable.

5. Lessons for the Modern World

Japan's approach to acceptance in the face of natural disasters offers valuable lessons for the modern world, particularly in an era marked by uncertainty and rapid change. The global community faces its own challenges, from climate change to political instability, and while we may not be able to control or prevent many of these crises, we can learn from Japan's example of resilience. Acceptance doesn't mean giving up; it means understanding that the world is unpredictable, but that we have the capacity to adapt to whatever comes our way.

Incorporating the principles of acceptance into our own lives means recognizing what is within our control and focusing on that. It's about cultivating adaptability—the ability to bend without breaking, to adjust when necessary, and to approach challenges not with resistance, but with a willingness to evolve. Just as Japan has learned to adapt to earthquakes, we too can learn to adapt to the challenges of the modern world.

By embracing acceptance, we free ourselves from the paralyzing fear of uncertainty. We stop resisting what cannot be controlled and, instead, begin to focus on how we can respond more effectively, both individually and collectively. Just as the Japanese have demonstrated time and again, the power of acceptance lies not in passive surrender, but in the active engagement with the world as it is, with a mindset that seeks solutions and growth in the face of adversity.

In a world increasingly defined by rapid changes and unexpected events, we can all take a page from Japan's book and cultivate the resilience to thrive amid uncertainty. Through acceptance, we build not only our ability to survive but our capacity to thrive, no matter what life throws our way.

Tools: Guided Journaling to Process Loss, Failure, or Change

Journaling is one of the most effective tools for processing deep emotional experiences, such as loss, failure, or significant life changes. When faced with adversity, it's easy to become overwhelmed by emotions that seem too complex or too heavy to manage. Guided journaling provides a way to break down those emotions, explore them in depth, and ultimately come to a place of acceptance or understanding. It's a practice that allows us to reflect, express our feelings, and gain clarity during challenging moments.

The power of journaling lies in its ability to help us externalize our internal world. When we put our thoughts on paper, they become more tangible. What once felt overwhelming and chaotic can be organized and explored in a way that brings new perspectives. Guided journaling, in particular, uses specific prompts to lead you through your emotional process, helping you reflect with intention and gain insight.

In the context of loss, failure, or change, journaling can be an especially useful tool for transforming painful experiences into opportunities for growth. It allows you to move through grief, navigate the fear of failure, and find peace amidst change, using writing as a means of processing and healing.

1. Journaling as a Tool for Acceptance

In the Japanese cultural framework, acceptance is an integral part of overcoming adversity. The concept of "shikata ga nai" (it cannot be helped) reflects the idea of accepting the uncontrollable in order to move forward with clarity. Guided journaling can help you practice acceptance by encouraging you to confront your feelings of helplessness, frustration, and grief head-on, rather than avoiding or suppressing them. Through this process, you can come to a place of peace where you acknowledge the truth of your situation while also seeking to understand how to move forward.

Exercise: "What Is Beyond My Control?"

Start by asking yourself: *What parts of my current situation are beyond my control?* Write down your thoughts. If you find yourself struggling with acceptance, try writing about the emotional resistance you feel towards this loss or change. What are the specific emotions you're experiencing (anger, sadness, regret, confusion)?

Then, ask yourself: *What can I control moving forward?* This exercise helps shift the focus away from what's outside your control and refocuses your energy on the aspects of your situation that are actionable. The process of journaling can create a sense of relief as you start to see how you might be able to regain some sense of agency, even in the face of uncontrollable events.

2. Using Journaling to Process Loss and Failure

Loss and failure are universal experiences. Whether we're grieving the end of a relationship, the death of a loved one, or the failure of a personal goal, these experiences can leave us feeling isolated, lost, or uncertain. Journaling helps us navigate these emotions by allowing us to work through them in a structured way. It provides a private space to be honest with ourselves about how we're feeling, what we're afraid of, and what we might need to heal.

Exercise: "The Grief Map"

Create a "Grief Map" where you write down the different stages or emotions you're currently experiencing. These might include shock, anger, sadness, guilt, or relief. For each emotion, write a brief description of what it feels like in your body. Does your anger manifest in a clenched jaw? Does your sadness weigh on your chest? Try to notice any physical sensations that arise as you explore each emotion. This can help you understand the full depth of your grief or failure.

Once you've mapped out your emotions, reflect on each one. Ask yourself, *What does this emotion tell me about what I need right now? What might be the next step I can take to move forward?* This journaling process allows you to reflect not just on the pain, but on the potential for healing, which is often hidden underneath.

3. Reflecting on Change: Embracing the New Normal

Change is often a catalyst for growth, but it can also feel deeply unsettling. Whether it's a major life transition, a career change, or a shift in personal identity, change disrupts our sense of stability. Guided journaling helps us confront the anxiety that comes with change by offering a structured way to reflect on how we feel about the transition, what we've learned from the experience, and what we might be able to do next.

Exercise: "The New Normal"

Start by acknowledging how change is impacting your life. Write about what's different, what you're grieving, and what's uncertain. This exercise helps you gain clarity on how the change is affecting you emotionally. Next, reflect on the aspects of your life that are still stable or positive despite the changes. Even in the midst of disruption, there are often elements of life that remain constant.

Write about what aspects of your life you've learned to appreciate in a new way because of this change. What strengths have emerged that you didn't know you had? What have you learned about yourself or others? Focusing on the growth that comes from navigating change can help you find new meaning and direction during challenging transitions.

4. Journaling to Cultivate Resilience

Resilience is the ability to bounce back from challenges, to remain grounded even in the face of adversity. It is closely linked to the ability to adapt and adjust to life's difficulties. Journaling can be a powerful tool for building resilience by encouraging you to reflect on your past challenges, the lessons you've learned, and how those lessons can help you navigate future obstacles.

Exercise: "Resilience Rewind"

Think back to a difficult moment in your life—whether it was a personal failure, loss, or a time when things felt especially hard. Write about the situation, your feelings at the time, and how you responded. Were there moments where you surprised yourself with your strength? Reflect on the resources (both internal and external) that helped you through that period. Did you rely on friends, family, or faith? Did you use specific coping strategies, like mindfulness or exercise?

Then, ask yourself: *What would I do differently if I faced a similar challenge again?* Write about how you've grown from that experience and what lessons you can take forward into your current life. This exercise helps to reframe your past challenges as opportunities for growth, which enhances your overall resilience.

5. Integrating Journaling into Your Daily Routine

Journaling isn't just a tool for processing intense emotions—it can be a daily practice that enhances your overall well-being. Making journaling a part of your daily routine allows you to process emotions in real-time, so they don't accumulate and become overwhelming. Even if you're not going through a major life event, journaling provides an opportunity to reflect on the small, daily challenges that shape your emotional landscape.

Exercise: "The Daily Check-In"

Start by setting aside time every evening (or whenever works best for you) to reflect on your day. Ask yourself: *What went well today? What challenges did I face? How did I feel throughout the day?* Write about the emotions that surfaced and how you responded to them. Be as honest and non-judgmental as possible.

Over time, this practice will help you become more attuned to your emotions, and you may notice patterns that you can address proactively. By integrating journaling into your routine, you'll develop a habit of reflection that helps you process the ups and downs of life more effectively, without letting the weight of emotions build up over time.

Guided journaling offers a powerful tool for processing loss, failure, and change. By providing a structured way to reflect on and understand your emotions, it helps you move through difficult experiences with greater clarity and resilience. Whether you're dealing with the grief of loss, the sting of failure, or the fear of change, journaling offers a safe space to explore, accept, and ultimately heal. Through consistent practice, you'll build emotional resilience that empowers you to face life's challenges with strength and acceptance, turning obstacles into opportunities for growth.

Exercises: Practice Reframing Setbacks with a "Growth Lens"

Setbacks are an inevitable part of life, but how we view and respond to them can drastically impact our personal growth and resilience. One of the most powerful tools for transforming setbacks into opportunities for growth is the practice of reframing—taking a setback and looking at it through a different lens. By reframing a situation, we can shift our focus from frustration and failure to understanding and development. This is where adopting a "growth lens" becomes essential.

A growth lens is based on the concept of "growth mindset," a term coined by psychologist Carol Dweck. This mindset is the belief that our abilities and intelligence can be developed through dedication, hard work, and learning from challenges. When we approach setbacks with a growth lens, we begin to see them not as insurmountable obstacles but as stepping stones on the path to improvement. This shift in perspective is not about denying the pain or difficulty of a setback, but rather about transforming how we engage with it.

The following exercises will guide you in practicing the reframing of setbacks. They are designed to help you see challenges through a growth lens and to foster resilience, adaptability, and self-compassion. Let's begin.

1. The "Learning Opportunity" Exercise

One of the simplest ways to reframe a setback is to see it as a learning opportunity. This exercise encourages you to ask the question: *What can I learn from this?* When you encounter a setback, your first reaction might be to feel disappointed, frustrated, or even defeated. Instead of staying in those emotions, shift your attention to the learning potential of the situation.

Steps:

- Identify a recent setback you've experienced. It could be a project that didn't go as planned, a personal disappointment, or something in your work or relationships.

- Write down the details of the setback without judgment. Allow yourself to feel the emotions, but focus on describing the facts.

- Ask yourself: *What went wrong, and why?*

- Then, shift your perspective and ask: *What is there to learn from this? How can I grow from this experience?*

- Write down any lessons you can extract from the situation. Even if the setback was painful or discouraging, there's likely something valuable to gain from it—whether it's a new skill, a realization about yourself, or better strategies for next time.

Reflection: How did this shift in thinking impact your feelings about the setback? Did reframing the situation help you feel more empowered and open to finding solutions?

2. The "Strengths Reframe" Exercise

Another way to reframe setbacks is by focusing on the strengths that you exercised during the challenge. When we face difficulties, we often focus on what went wrong or what we could have done better. However, this exercise encourages you to reflect on the qualities or strengths you demonstrated during the setback. Recognizing these can help you see that even in failure, you are developing resilience, problem-solving skills, and other valuable traits.

Steps:

- Reflect on a recent setback. Think about the actions you took, the decisions you made, and how you responded during the setback.

- Identify at least three strengths you exhibited during this time. These could be emotional (like patience, resilience, or self-control), cognitive (like critical thinking or problem-solving), or behavioral (like perseverance or communication).

- Write about how these strengths helped you navigate the situation, and how they contributed to your personal growth, even if the outcome wasn't what you wanted.

- Ask yourself: *What strengths did I discover or develop as a result of this experience?*

Reflection: Did this exercise help you see the value in the process, rather than just focusing on the result? Recognizing your strengths can help you see that setbacks are not just failures but also opportunities to practice and refine your abilities.

3. The "Reframe the Narrative" Exercise

Our self-talk can have a powerful impact on how we view setbacks. Negative self-talk can reinforce the idea that we are incapable, unlucky, or destined to fail. The key to reframing setbacks is to change the narrative we tell ourselves about them. By doing so, we can transform a moment of failure into a moment of growth and perseverance.

Steps:

- Think of a recent setback that caused you frustration, anger, or sadness. Pay attention to the thoughts that surfaced at the time. These thoughts might include phrases like, *I'm not good enough,* or *I'll never be successful.* Write them down.

- Challenge these thoughts by asking yourself: *Is this really true? Is there any evidence to the contrary?* Often, the thoughts we have about setbacks are exaggerated or self-critical, not based on objective reality.

- Now, reframe the narrative by writing a new, more positive version of the story. Focus on how you handled the setback, what you learned, and how you can apply this lesson in the future. For example, instead of thinking *I failed*, try reframing it as *I encountered a challenge, but I have the ability to learn from it and grow stronger.*

- Repeat this reframing process for other setbacks, making it a habit to rewrite your internal narrative whenever things don't go as planned.

Reflection: How does reframing the narrative impact your self-esteem? Does focusing on learning, effort, and resilience help you feel more confident and optimistic?

4. The "What's Next?" Exercise

When a setback happens, it's easy to get stuck in the past—thinking about what could have been, what should have happened, or how things went wrong. The *What's Next?* exercise encourages you to look ahead and consider how you can use the setback as a stepping stone toward future success. Rather than dwelling on the failure, this exercise shifts your focus toward action and possibility.

Steps:

- Identify a setback that left you feeling stuck or uncertain about the future.

- Ask yourself: *What's next for me?* What can I do now to take the next step forward, regardless of how small it might seem? Sometimes, even the smallest forward movement is enough to regain momentum and begin moving out of the stagnation that comes with failure.

- Write down at least three actionable steps you can take to move past this setback. These steps don't have to be monumental—they can be as simple as seeking advice, learning more about a particular topic, or making a plan to try again.

- Break these steps down into manageable tasks that feel achievable. The goal is to build momentum and reduce the feeling of overwhelm.

Reflection: How does shifting your attention to the future, rather than lingering on the past, help you regain a sense of control and hope? Are you now able to view the setback as part of your journey, rather than something that defines you?

5. The "Gratitude Reframe" Exercise

Gratitude is one of the most powerful reframing tools because it shifts our focus from what's wrong to what's right in our lives. This exercise encourages you to find the good—even in the most challenging situations. Practicing gratitude helps break the cycle of negativity that can accompany setbacks and opens us up to the possibility of growth.

Steps:

- Reflect on the setback you've experienced and write down three things about it that you are grateful for. This might be hard at first, especially if you're feeling discouraged, but challenge yourself to find something positive.

- Ask yourself: *What has this setback taught me? What strengths or insights have I gained as a result of this situation?*

- Make a list of other things in your life that you are grateful for during this time. It could be supportive relationships, a job you enjoy, or personal accomplishments. Gratitude has a way of putting setbacks into perspective, reminding us that not all is lost.

Reflection: How does practicing gratitude help you shift your mindset? Does focusing on what you have, rather than what you lack, make the setback feel more manageable?

By consistently practicing these reframing exercises, you'll begin to see setbacks not as failures but as opportunities for growth. The more you train your mind to see challenges through a growth lens, the more resilient and adaptable you'll become. Every setback, no matter how difficult, is an opportunity to learn, build strength, and grow. And with each practice of reframing, you will shape your ability to navigate life's uncertainties with confidence and clarity, ultimately fostering a mindset that thrives in the face of adversity.

CHAPTER SIX
STRENGTH IN LETTING GO

After embracing acceptance through *shikata ga nai*, we encounter a deeper truth: acceptance opens the door to letting go. While acceptance helps us make peace with what is, letting go empowers us to move forward unburdened. This progression from acceptance to release is beautifully demonstrated in Japanese culture, where the art of letting go isn't seen as defeat, but as a path to freedom.

During my time in Japan, I was struck by a recurring theme that appeared not just in the design of the country, but in the way people lived their daily lives: minimalism. It wasn't just about the tidy spaces or the carefully curated décor. It was a philosophy, a way of being that permeated everything from the art of tea ceremonies to the way people approached relationships, possessions, and even emotions. It was as if everything was intentionally pared down to its essential elements, creating an environment where each thing had its purpose and meaning.

Building on our practice of acceptance, one of the most profound experiences I had was during a visit to a small, traditional home in Kyoto. The space was simple yet elegant. The furniture was sparse—just a few tatami mats on the floor, a small wooden table, and a single lantern casting soft light across the room. The walls were plain, with only a few carefully chosen objects on display: a small vase with a single flower, a calligraphy scroll, and a piece of pottery.

What stood out to me was the absence of clutter. There were no knick-knacks or excess items, nothing extraneous. It wasn't just a physical emptiness—it was a kind of mental space as well. The simplicity seemed to invite calmness, focus, and presence. It was as if every item in that room was there with intention, and everything that wasn't there had been consciously released. It became clear to me that minimalism, in this sense, wasn't about deprivation—it was about clarity, purpose, and the ability to let go.

The concept of detachment was central to this experience. Japanese minimalism, as I observed, wasn't just about reducing possessions—it was about cultivating a sense of freedom through letting go. It wasn't about emptying oneself out; it was about making room for what truly mattered. In fact, I came to realize that the art of detachment was not about renouncing the world or avoiding attachments, but about mastering the ability to let go of the things that no longer served us—whether that was physical possessions, outdated beliefs, or emotional burdens.

A particularly poignant lesson came from a conversation I had with an older Japanese gentleman who was a master of Ikebana, the Japanese art of flower arranging. He shared with me how each flower arrangement was about balance—finding beauty not just in the flowers themselves, but in the empty spaces between them. In the same way, he explained, life's richness comes from knowing what to hold onto and what to release. "To arrange flowers," he said, "is to understand when to let go."

This lesson in detachment didn't just apply to objects, but to experiences, expectations, and even people. In Japanese culture, the concept of "mottainai" encourages people to not waste anything— whether that be time, resources, or emotions. But it also includes the wisdom of knowing when something has outlived its purpose and when it is time to release it. As we learned through shikata ga nai, it is about giving things their due respect and then allowing them to pass, creating space for new experiences and growth.

I began to understand that letting go is not a passive act of abandonment—it is an active process of clearing out the old to make room for the new. Just like a garden needs to be pruned to allow for healthy growth, we too need to let go of the clutter in our lives— whether physical or emotional—in order to grow.

In contrast, I noticed that many of us, particularly in the West, often cling to things—whether they are physical items, emotional attachments, or even outdated beliefs. It's as if we fear that without them, we will lose ourselves. But I realized that in holding onto everything, we are weighed down. The more we cling, the less room we have to grow, to change, or to evolve.

Reflecting on this, I thought back to a personal experience. A few years ago, I had been holding onto a job that no longer served me. I was too attached to the idea of stability and the security it offered, even though I was deeply unhappy. I didn't want to let go of what I had worked so hard for, but it was clear that the job was draining me, leaving me with little energy for the things that mattered most. Finally, I made the difficult decision to leave, and while the process was painful and filled with uncertainty, it was also liberating. This release, born from true acceptance, it was only by letting go of that old, draining chapter of my life that I was able to move forward and discover new opportunities that aligned with my true purpose.

In Japan, the idea of letting go is not seen as weakness or failure, but as a form of strength. It requires self-awareness, emotional intelligence, and the wisdom to discern when to hold on and when to release. In the West, we tend to view attachment as something we must strive for—be it to possessions, success, or relationships. But in Japan, the focus is on balance and understanding when enough is enough.

By embracing the wisdom of letting go, I began to understand the profound impact it can have on our emotional and psychological well-being. We hold on to many things in life—whether they are material possessions, past experiences, or even unresolved emotions—because we fear that without them, we'll lose our sense of identity or purpose. However, detachment is not about loss; it is about creating space for new things, new ideas, and new possibilities to take root.

Japanese minimalism taught me that detachment does not mean indifference. It means being present with what is essential and releasing the rest. It means knowing that true strength comes not from holding on to everything, but from the wisdom to let go when the time is right. And, perhaps most importantly, it taught me that there is great power in simplicity, clarity, and the freedom to release what no longer serves us.

Subsequently, we will check the deeper implications of this philosophy and how we can apply it to various aspects of our lives—whether it be in our personal growth, relationships, or career. Like the minimalist spaces in Japan that allowed for simplicity and clarity, we too can cultivate a life where we intentionally release what doesn't serve us, making space for what truly matters. Letting go, it turns out, is not a loss but a path to strength and transformation. This philosophy of letting go is key to understanding the paradox of strength: sometimes, we must release control to gain true mastery over our lives.

The Japanese Wisdom of Letting Go

In Japan, the idea of letting go is embedded deeply in cultural practices, from the art of tea ceremonies to Zen Buddhism and the philosophy of wabi-sabi. These teachings don't just encourage letting go of material possessions; they advocate for a deeper release—of attachments, expectations, and rigid control.

Take, for instance, the practice of Zen gardening. The process involves cultivating a garden that is not only simple and minimal but also ever-changing. The garden is designed with the knowledge that over time, the plants will grow, shift, and evolve. There's no attempt to control this change; instead, there's an acceptance of impermanence. The gardener's role isn't to command the landscape but to work with it, adjusting as it shifts and letting go of the need for permanence or rigidity.

In Zen, this concept extends beyond physical landscapes and into the inner landscape of the mind. The practice of mindfulness, which is central to Zen, involves letting go of our attachment to thoughts, emotions, and judgments. Rather than trying to control or suppress them, we simply observe them without attachment. This act of letting go—of not clinging to our thoughts and feelings—actually leads to a greater sense of control over our emotional responses and reactions. It's through non-resistance, not force, that we gain mastery over ourselves.

A striking example of this is found in the Japanese concept of *mushin*, often translated as "the mind of no mind." In martial arts, particularly in the practice of kendo (the art of Japanese swordsmanship), *mushin* refers to a state of mental clarity and openness, where the practitioner is not overthinking or trying to control every movement. Instead, the practitioner is fully present, responding to the situation with intuition rather than forceful will. It's a paradox: in letting go of the need to control the outcome, the practitioner gains the ability to move freely and react swiftly. The act of letting go in this case enhances control.

This idea extends beyond martial arts and into other aspects of life. When we let go of the need to micromanage our relationships, for instance, we often create deeper, more authentic connections. When we release the fear of failure, we open ourselves up to learning and growth. The more we surrender the need for control, the more control we actually gain over our happiness and peace of mind.

The Paradox in Practice: Embracing Flexibility

One of the greatest ironies of life is that when we surrender our need for rigid control, we become more adaptable and flexible, and in turn, more able to navigate the inevitable changes and uncertainties of life. In this sense, letting go becomes a form of control—not control over outcomes, but control over our ability to adapt to the unpredictable nature of life.

In the modern world, this flexibility is more important than ever. We live in a time marked by rapid change—technological advancements, social shifts, and environmental challenges—all of which demand a flexible mindset. When we try to control these external factors, we only end up frustrated and overwhelmed. But when we accept the fluid nature of these circumstances, we find the strength to move with them rather than against them.

Take, for example, the experience of navigating a career change. When we are overly attached to a specific path or job title, we may resist the idea of switching careers or trying something new. The fear of uncertainty and loss of control can paralyze us. But when we let go of the rigid idea that we must stay on a single path, we open ourselves up to new possibilities and opportunities. This doesn't mean we give up on our goals or ambitions. Instead, it means we trust that there are multiple routes to success, and sometimes the most fulfilling path is the one that emerges when we let go of our preconceived notions.

The Strength of Releasing Control

This paradox—letting go to gain control—also applies to our emotional lives. Many people hold onto past hurts, grudges, and unresolved emotions because they believe that by holding onto them, they retain control over their feelings and experiences. But in reality, this emotional attachment often keeps us stuck in the past, preventing us from moving forward.

In the same way that a gardener must let go of old leaves to allow for new growth, we too must release our emotional attachments in order to grow. This doesn't mean forgetting or suppressing our emotions; rather, it means acknowledging them, processing them, and then letting them go. By doing so, we regain control over our emotional state, freeing ourselves from the weight of past pain and disappointment.

This process can be incredibly liberating. For example, when I let go of the anger and frustration I had been holding onto after a difficult breakup, I found that my emotional health improved dramatically. Instead of trying to control my feelings or cling to the pain, I allowed myself to feel what I needed to feel and then chose to release it. In doing so, I regained my sense of agency and control over my emotional well-being.

The Paradoxical Strength of Letting Go

The more we understand this paradox of strength—the idea that letting go is not an act of weakness, but a pathway to true strength—the more we realize that our lives are not defined by what we hold on to, but by what we are willing to release. This includes not only our physical possessions and emotional attachments but also our need for control over every aspect of our existence.

By letting go, we open ourselves up to a greater sense of freedom and possibility. We gain control over our lives not by tightening our grip, but by loosening it—allowing the flow of life to guide us, while we remain centered and resilient. This is the strength of flexibility, adaptability, and the wisdom to know when to hold on and when to release.

Letting go is not about passivity; it's about being in control of our response to life's challenges. It's about accepting that some things are beyond our control, and trusting that by releasing them, we make room for something greater. This is the paradox of strength: by letting go, we gain the control we seek—not over everything, but over ourselves.

Neural correlates of acceptance and commitment therapy

The study *Neural Correlates of Acceptance and Commitment Therapy* sheds light on a fascinating link between the practice of acceptance and observable changes in brain activity. Specifically, it reveals that acceptance-based strategies, central to Acceptance and Commitment Therapy (ACT), reduce activation in the amygdala, the brain's emotional center responsible for processing fear, stress, and other heightened emotional states. This scientific insight helped me understand why acceptance, though seemingly counterintuitive, has such a powerful impact on our well-being.

In the thick of my recovery, I often felt the emotional surge that comes with frustration and helplessness. Physical pain from my spinal injuries was one thing, but the emotional toll—the "what ifs," the fear of never regaining full mobility—could spiral out of control. There were nights when those emotions consumed me, leaving me in a state of heightened anxiety. Reflecting back, these moments were prime examples of the amygdala's overactivity, a biological response to perceived threats.

However, as I began embracing acceptance, guided by both the Japanese concept of *shikata ga nai* and my conversations with nurses and visitors, something shifted. The study explains this process: when individuals practice acceptance—allowing their emotions to exist without judgment or avoidance—it decreases amygdala activity. Instead of the brain perceiving a constant "threat" in negative emotions, acceptance reframes them as natural, reducing their emotional intensity. The result? A calmer, more balanced emotional state.

I remember vividly one particular interaction with a nurse who noticed I was unusually tense during a physical therapy session. She gently reminded me, "Your frustration is natural. Let it come, then let it go." At first, I found this advice puzzling. Wasn't frustration something to fight against, to overcome? But over time, I realized the wisdom in her words. By allowing myself to feel frustration without clinging to it or trying to suppress it, the emotion lost its grip on me. This wasn't resignation—it was liberation.

The imaging results from the study make this process tangible. Reduced amygdala activation means that the brain perceives less "danger" in the emotional experience. Acceptance, in essence, rewires the brain's relationship with stress. Instead of treating emotional discomfort as an enemy to be avoided, the brain begins to treat it as a transient experience, no more threatening than a passing cloud. This physiological shift creates room for clarity, focus, and thoughtful action—qualities that are impossible to access when the amygdala is in overdrive.

It also helped me understand why avoidance, though tempting, often backfires. When we suppress or avoid difficult emotions, the brain perceives those emotions as even more threatening. The amygdala's response intensifies, creating a feedback loop of anxiety and stress. The study clarifies that acceptance short-circuits this loop, allowing the prefrontal cortex—the brain's rational, decision-making center—to regain control. In a sense, acceptance isn't passive; it's an active reclaiming of agency over our mental and emotional states.

This insight is beautifully echoed in Japanese culture. I saw it in the calm demeanor of the hospital staff, who approached even chaotic situations with a steady sense of composure. They weren't emotionally detached; rather, they had a deeply ingrained ability to stay present without being overwhelmed. It wasn't just a cultural trait—it was a skill, and as the study shows, one rooted in a neurological process that we can all cultivate.

Understanding the science behind acceptance deepened its meaning for me. It's not just a philosophical idea or a cultural practice—it's a biological mechanism that changes how we experience the world. The study gave me a framework for what I had been experiencing intuitively during recovery. When I let go of the fight against my emotions and simply allowed them to exist, I wasn't giving in—I was allowing my brain to recalibrate, to find its way back to balance.

This, I realized, is why acceptance works. It's not a passive surrender but an active process that quiets the storm within, giving us the clarity and resilience to face whatever comes next.

Practical Steps: Simplifying One Area of Your Life

PICTURE: A FLOW CHART FOR THE STEPS

In the quest for control and success, it's easy to accumulate more than we need—whether it's possessions, commitments, or habits. But the paradox is clear: by simplifying one area of our lives, we can gain a deeper sense of control and clarity. This doesn't mean eliminating everything, but rather intentionally letting go of what doesn't serve us. In Japanese culture, this principle of simplicity is deeply ingrained, from the minimalist approach to design in a Zen garden to the practice of *wabi-sabi*—finding beauty in simplicity and imperfection.

Let's explore how simplifying one area of your life—whether it's your possessions, commitments, or habits—can free you from the burden of unnecessary complexity and allow you to focus on what truly matters.

Step 1: Declutter Your Physical Space

Our environment has a profound impact on our mental and emotional state. Clutter, whether it's piles of books, unused gadgets, or clothes that no longer serve us, can contribute to feelings of stress and overwhelm. By decluttering your physical space, you're not just making room for new things; you're creating space for new thoughts, new opportunities, and a clearer state of mind.

In Japan, the practice of minimalism is not just about reducing physical items but also about enhancing the quality of life by surrounding oneself with only what is necessary and beautiful. The concept of *shibui*, a Japanese aesthetic, celebrates simplicity, subtlety, and the understated beauty of objects that are functional yet elegant.

How to Start

- **Assess Your Space**: Look around your living or working space and identify areas that are overcrowded or disorganized. Are there items you rarely use or wear? Is there clutter you've been holding onto out of habit rather than necessity?

- **Sort and Let Go**: Take the time to go through each room or area. Ask yourself: *Do I really need this? Does it serve a* *purpose or bring me joy?* If it doesn't, it's time to let it go. Be honest about the items you've been holding onto because of sentimentality or guilt. Remember, letting go doesn't mean you're losing something valuable—it means you're making room for more meaningful things.

- **Implement the "One-In-One-Out" Rule**: Once you've decluttered, make a commitment to bring in only what adds true value to your life. For example, for every new item you acquire, commit to letting go of something else. This helps prevent future accumulation and keeps your space intentionally minimal.

By simplifying your physical space, you not only make your environment more peaceful, but you also create mental clarity and a sense of calm. You might find that this simplicity allows you to focus more deeply on the tasks at hand, whether it's work, relationships, or personal growth.

Step 2: Evaluate and Streamline Your Commitments

In today's fast-paced world, it's easy to overcommit ourselves. Whether it's professional obligations, social events, or family responsibilities, we often feel the need to say "yes" to everything. This can lead to burnout, overwhelm, and a lack of time for the things that truly matter. Just like a blade that needs to be sharpened, our energy and attention need to be focused and honed in order to be effective.

In Japan, there is a strong cultural emphasis on the value of *ma*—the space between things, or the importance of balance and pacing. In a culture that often prioritizes work, people understand that true productivity and peace come from finding balance and not overcommitting. This concept can be incredibly useful when evaluating our own commitments.

How to Start

- **Identify Your Current Commitments**: Take an honest look at all the things you've committed to—work, family obligations, social activities, hobbies. Are there any commitments that are draining your energy or that you no longer feel passionate about?

- **Prioritize**: Determine which commitments are aligned with your values and long-term goals. What truly brings you joy, fulfillment, or growth? What can you let go of without guilt?

- **Set Boundaries**: Learn to say "no" or "not right now." It's okay to decline invitations or turn down opportunities that aren't a good fit for your life. Saying no doesn't mean you're being selfish; it means you're prioritizing what truly matters.

- **Practice Time Blocking**: Schedule time for yourself each day to recharge, reflect, or simply relax. Make it non-negotiable. By allocating time for yourself, you can more effectively manage the commitments that do matter.

By streamlining your commitments, you free up time and mental space to focus on the things that truly enhance your life. This isn't about being busy for the sake of it—it's about intentionality. By simplifying your schedule, you allow more room for creativity, personal growth, and meaningful relationships.

Step 3: Simplify Your Habits

Habits shape our daily lives, but not all habits are created equal. Many of us operate on autopilot, engaging in routines and activities that we don't consciously choose. These habits can be draining, distracting, or even harmful, preventing us from living with intention. Simplifying your habits means identifying which ones are serving you and which ones are keeping you stuck in patterns that no longer align with your goals.

The Japanese concept of *kaizen*—the idea of continuous improvement through small, incremental changes—can be applied to our habits. Rather than trying to overhaul everything all at once, kaizen encourages us to focus on small, manageable changes that lead to long-term transformation.

How to Start

- **Track Your Habits**: Start by keeping a simple journal or log of your daily habits. What do you do first thing in the morning? What are your most frequent activities throughout the day? Are there habits that you do automatically, but that don't serve your well-being?

- **Identify the Habits That Matter**: Focus on the habits that contribute to your physical, emotional, and mental health. These might include eating healthy, exercising, reading, or spending quality time with loved ones.

- **Eliminate Unnecessary Habits**: What habits can you reduce or eliminate? Maybe it's scrolling mindlessly on social media, eating junk food late at night, or procrastinating on important tasks. Let go of these distractions and create space for healthier habits.

- **Introduce One Small Positive Habit**: If you're trying to build a new habit, start small. Instead of aiming to exercise for an hour every day, start with 10 minutes of movement each morning. Gradually build upon this habit over time.

- **Use Habit Stacking**: This technique, popularized by James Clear in *Atomic Habits*, involves linking a new habit to an existing one. For example, after you brush your teeth (an established habit), you might meditate for 2 minutes (the new habit you're trying to form).

By simplifying your habits, you gain more mental energy and focus, allowing you to spend your time on the things that matter most. Over time, these small changes add up, helping you live a more intentional and fulfilling life.

Step 4: Practice Mindfulness and Present-Moment Awareness

The final step in simplifying an area of your life is to cultivate mindfulness and present-moment awareness. Our tendency to rush through life or dwell on the past or future can distract us from what's truly important. In Japanese culture, there's a deep appreciation for the present moment, particularly in practices like tea ceremonies, where every step is deliberate and mindful.

Mindfulness helps us cut through the noise and focus on what's in front of us, fostering a deeper sense of clarity and control. By focusing on the present, we simplify our mental landscape, enabling us to fully engage with whatever we are doing.

How to Start

- **Commit to a Daily Mindfulness Practice**: Whether it's meditation, deep breathing, or mindful walking, set aside time each day to practice mindfulness. This will help you become more present and less overwhelmed by the demands of life.

- **Practice Single-Tasking**: Instead of juggling multiple tasks at once, focus on one thing at a time. Whether it's writing an email, cooking dinner, or having a conversation, give it your full attention.

- **Observe Without Judgment**: When you experience stressful or challenging moments, take a step back and observe your thoughts and feelings without judgment. Notice where you're attaching yourself to a particular outcome or trying to control the situation.

Mindfulness allows you to simplify your experience by focusing on what's happening right now. It helps you release the need to control everything and instead embrace the present moment with clarity and peace.

Generally, simplicity is not about eliminating everything from your life, but about choosing what truly matters. By simplifying one area of your life—whether it's possessions, commitments, or habits—you can create more space for what is meaningful. In doing so, you not only declutter your environment but also clear your mind and soul, allowing you to live with greater intention and peace. This practice of simplicity is not just a one-time event; it's a continual process of letting go and refining, helping you cultivate the control and resilience you need to thrive in a chaotic world.

By following these practical steps, you will start to experience the transformative power of simplicity, creating space for more authentic connections, a clearer mind, and a deeper sense of control over your life.

The Fire Doesn't Destroy—It Transforms

The phrase "the fire doesn't destroy—it transforms" encapsulates one of the most powerful lessons in life and growth. Just as fire purifies and reshapes metal into something stronger and more refined, the challenges and hardships we face can transform us into better versions of ourselves—if we approach them with the right mindset. The process of transformation through adversity, much like the forging of a katana, is about enduring the heat, pressure, and challenges to become something sharper, stronger, and more resilient.

In many ways, fire serves as a metaphor for life's trials and tribulations. We often view difficulties and painful experiences as destructive forces that threaten our well-being, but if we shift our perspective, we can begin to see them as the crucibles through which we are reshaped. The fire might feel unbearable in the moment, but it is in the flames that our most significant transformations take place.

Embracing the Heat

When we face adversity, our instinct is often to flee from it. We want to avoid the discomfort, the uncertainty, the pain. We are wired to seek comfort and security, and anything that threatens that sense of stability can feel overwhelming. However, in nature, fire serves as both a destructive and a regenerative force. It can raze a forest to the ground, but it also clears space for new growth. Similarly, the struggles we face can strip us of our old, limiting beliefs, habits, and patterns, creating the space for new opportunities and a new way of being.

It's important to recognize that transformation isn't easy. Just like a katana undergoes extreme heat to become strong, we too must endure heat—whether it's the fire of failure, rejection, loss, or grief. But each challenge we face is an opportunity for growth. The heat, though uncomfortable, is not meant to break us. Rather, it is a necessary part of our evolution.

For example, consider the experience of someone who loses their job or goes through a breakup. At first, it feels like everything is falling apart. The fire is intense, and it feels like destruction is imminent. But as time passes and healing begins, the individual may discover new strengths, new opportunities, and a deeper understanding of who they are and what they truly want in life. The fire has not destroyed them— it has transformed them.

Fire as a Catalyst for Change

The fire of hardship can be a catalyst for positive change if we approach it with the right mindset. Transformation often requires us to let go of old patterns, beliefs, and attachments that no longer serve us. Just as the forging of a katana requires the smith to carefully control the temperature and pressure to shape the metal, we too must allow the heat of life's challenges to mold us into something better.

Take, for instance, the Japanese practice of *wabi-sabi*, which celebrates the beauty of imperfection and the process of decay and renewal. In this mindset, flaws are not seen as weaknesses but as elements that contribute to the uniqueness and depth of an object or experience. Similarly, the fire of hardship does not diminish our worth. Rather, it highlights our resilience, adaptability, and capacity to learn and grow.

In the face of hardship, the key is to stop viewing ourselves as victims of circumstance and instead embrace the notion that we are active participants in our transformation. Like the katana being shaped in the forge, we too are being honed and sharpened through our struggles. The fire isn't destroying us—it is refining us, making us stronger and more capable of facing future challenges with grace and courage.

The Role of Resilience

Resilience is the ability to withstand and recover from adversity. It's not about avoiding hardship but about learning how to navigate through it without losing our sense of self or purpose. Just as the katana is repeatedly folded, heated, and hammered to enhance its strength, we too must endure hardship to build our inner resilience.

But resilience isn't something we are simply born with—it is a skill that can be cultivated over time. It is built through our experiences, our willingness to face challenges head-on, and our ability to learn from failure. Resilience allows us to stay grounded when things get tough and to rise again when we are knocked down.

To develop resilience, we must first learn to embrace the discomfort of transformation. Just as the fire makes the katana blade more durable, our own challenges help us develop mental toughness and emotional strength. In this way, every setback is an opportunity to grow stronger, and every moment of adversity is a chance to refine our character.

Transformation Through Adversity

Consider the process of *kaizen*, the Japanese principle of continuous improvement. This philosophy emphasizes the importance of small, incremental changes over time. It's not about big, sweeping actions or radical shifts; it's about consistently making small adjustments that lead to a greater transformation. Just as a blade is repeatedly folded and heated to increase its strength and sharpness, we too are shaped by the small, everyday challenges we face.

In our own lives, transformation can occur in both small and large ways. Some challenges may feel overwhelming, while others may seem more manageable. But whether the fire is small or large, it has the potential to transform us if we approach it with the right mindset. The key is not to resist the heat but to endure it, knowing that it is part of the process of becoming who we are meant to be.

This process of transformation is often messy, unpredictable, and uncomfortable. But it is through this very discomfort that we grow. Just as the katana undergoes numerous stages of refinement, we too must go through stages of growth, learning, and change. The fire that we face in our lives is not meant to destroy us—it is meant to mold us into the strongest, sharpest versions of ourselves.

Fire and the Alchemy of Personal Growth

The alchemists of old believed that fire could turn base metals into gold. This idea of transformation—turning something common into something precious—can be applied to our own lives. The struggles we face, though they may feel painful, are the very things that can transform us into something more resilient, wiser, and more capable of achieving our deepest aspirations.

By embracing the fire of change, we undergo a process of personal alchemy. We take the raw material of our lives—our experiences, emotions, failures, and successes—and through the fire, we refine it into something stronger, more purposeful, and more meaningful. It is in this way that hardship becomes not just something to endure, but something to embrace as a tool for growth.

When we stop fearing the fire and start using it as a catalyst for personal transformation, we begin to see challenges not as obstacles, but as opportunities for growth. We become the blacksmiths of our own lives, shaping and sharpening ourselves with each trial and each victory.

The fire that we encounter in life is not an enemy—it is a powerful ally. It transforms us, refines us, and prepares us for the next chapter of our journey. Just as a katana is made stronger through fire, folding, and tempering, we too are shaped by the challenges and adversities we face.

So, when life presents its fiery trials, remember this: the fire doesn't destroy—it transforms. Embrace the heat, endure the process, and allow yourself to be reshaped. Through this transformation, you will become more resilient, more capable, and more aligned with the person you are meant to be. The fire is not the end—it is the beginning of your journey toward strength, wisdom, and authenticity.

As we let go of what no longer serves us, we create space for deeper self-reflection. This emptiness becomes fertile ground for the inner work that lies ahead. The journey from acceptance to letting go prepares us for the profound self-examination that will guide our transformation.

PART III:
REFLECTION – NAIKAN

CHAPTER SEVEN
THE MIRROR WITHIN

It was a chilly autumn morning when I found myself walking along a stone path toward a quiet, ancient temple nestled in the hills of Kyoto. The air was crisp, and the gentle rustling of the leaves created a peaceful melody. I had been traveling through Japan for a few weeks, soaking in the beauty of the country's rich culture and history. But this particular visit was different. This time, I was about to experience something deeply personal, something that would challenge me to examine my life in ways I had never considered before.

Naikan, which translates to 'inside looking' or 'looking within,' is a structured approach designed to help individuals gain a deeper understanding of themselves and their relationships with others. It is a practice that encourages introspection and self-discovery, allowing individuals to examine their lives with greater clarity and awareness.

The temple, as I would soon learn, was a place not just for spiritual devotion, but also for deep reflection—a practice known as *Naikan*.

Naikan, which translates to "inside looking" or "looking within," is a traditional Japanese method of self-reflection. It is a structured approach designed to help individuals assess their relationships with others and, ultimately, themselves. As I stood outside the temple's wooden doors, I had no idea that in the hours to come, I would experience a process that would force me to confront the depths of my own thoughts and emotions.

The temple was peaceful and serene, bathed in the golden light of early morning. The sound of a distant bell echoed through the grounds, signaling the beginning of the practice. Inside, the atmosphere was minimalist, with bare walls, tatami mats on the floor, and soft, muted lighting. I was welcomed by a gentle, middle-aged Japanese man named Hiroshi, who introduced himself as my guide for the Naikan session.

Hiroshi explained that the practice of Naikan was rooted in the teachings of the Buddhist monk Ishin Yoshimoto, who developed it in the 1940s. The method involved reflecting on three key questions, which were designed to illuminate the dynamics of one's relationships and personal life:

1. **What have I received from this person?**

2. **What have I given to this person?**

3. **What troubles and difficulties have I caused this person?**

Approaching these questions without judgment is crucial. Naikan is not about self-criticism or dwelling on one's shortcomings. Instead, it's about cultivating a compassionate and accepting mindset as you turn your attention inward. Think of Naikan as a gentle guide, helping you illuminate the path toward greater self-awareness and understanding.

These simple, yet profound questions were the cornerstone of Naikan, and Hiroshi explained that we would spend several hours in reflection, beginning with one person—our mother. The idea was that by examining our relationship with the person who brought us into the world, we could uncover deeper truths about ourselves and our connections with others. As I sat down on the tatami mat in the quiet space, I was struck by how the room itself encouraged contemplation—a space devoid of distraction, designed to facilitate deep thought.

We started with the first question: *What have I received from this person?* As I sat quietly, I began to think about my mother. In the stillness of the room, I was able to strip away the noise of daily life and reflect on everything she had given me over the years—her love, her sacrifices, the lessons she imparted to me, both spoken and unspoken. I thought about the nights she stayed up late helping me with my homework, the hugs she gave me when I was afraid, and the endless support she offered during difficult times. The list seemed endless, yet in the busyness of life, I had rarely stopped to acknowledge it fully.

The next question was more challenging: *What have I given to this person?* I was taken aback by how quickly I struggled with this one. What had I truly given her, aside from the occasional "thank you" or act of kindness? I realized that, like many people, I often took the relationship for granted. I had focused so much on what I had received, but I hadn't given enough thought to how I could reciprocate. In that quiet room, I recognized how much more I could have done to show my appreciation, love, and support.

Finally, Hiroshi asked the third and most difficult question: *What troubles and difficulties have I caused this person?* This was the question that brought me to tears. I thought of the times I had disappointed her, the moments when I had been too absorbed in my own life to notice her needs, the selfish moments when I took her love for granted. I thought about the arguments we'd had, the times I had failed to communicate, and how I had sometimes taken her for granted. The truth was that I had caused her pain—not intentionally, but through my own immaturity and lack of awareness.

As I sat in silence, reflecting on these three questions, I began to feel the weight of my own humanity. I realized how often I had been unaware of the ways in which I impacted those around me. We often see the world through our own lens, our own narrative, but we rarely take the time to step outside of that and see things from the perspective of others. Naikan had forced me to do exactly that. It had challenged me to take an honest, unflinching look at the impact I had on the people in my life.

What struck me most about this practice was not just the answers to the questions, but the profound sense of clarity and understanding that emerged from them. It was as if the temple itself had absorbed all the noise and distractions of my life, leaving only the raw, unvarnished truth. For the first time in a long while, I felt deeply connected to the person I was reflecting on—not just as a mother, but as a fellow human being, with her own struggles, joys, and complexities.

After the reflection, Hiroshi led me through a brief meditation, guiding me to acknowledge my feelings of gratitude, guilt, and love. It was a powerful experience, one that opened my heart in ways I hadn't expected. As I left the temple that day, I felt a renewed sense of clarity and connection to myself and to those I love. The Naikan practice had shown me the importance of looking inward and embracing the complexity of human relationships.

In the days that followed, I continued to reflect on the questions posed during the practice. I found myself revisiting the experience during quiet moments, applying the questions to other relationships in my life—friends, colleagues, and even strangers. The more I used Naikan as a lens for understanding my connections, the more I realized how essential it is to truly understand our impact on the people around us. The simplicity of the questions didn't make the answers easy to find, but they made me realize how much I had to learn about myself, my relationships, and the world around me.

In many ways, Naikan is a mirror. It forces us to look at ourselves honestly and without judgment. And while that process can be uncomfortable, it is ultimately freeing. When we understand the depths of our relationships and the true nature of our interactions with others, we begin to grow. This experience in the temple, though brief, taught me that the process of looking within is not just about finding fault or remorse. It is about understanding, learning, and ultimately transforming ourselves into better versions of who we are meant to be.

The temple, the practice, and the questions they offered all pointed to the same truth: true growth comes from honest reflection. But be prepared, as this honest reflection may sometimes lead to uncomfortable realizations. It might reveal hidden aspects of yourself—your 'shadows'—that you may have been avoiding or denying. This is not a setback; it is an invitation to deeper growth. By acknowledging these shadows, you can begin the transformative journey of confronting them and integrating them into your path toward wholeness. And through this kind of reflection, we can begin to create deeper, more meaningful connections with others—and, more importantly, with ourselves.

What is Naikan? A Structured Self-Reflection Tool Based on Three Questions

Naikan is a Japanese self-reflection practice that offers a profound yet simple way to deepen one's understanding of relationships and personal behavior. Originating in the mid-20th century, Naikan, which translates roughly to "looking inside" or "inside looking," has become a widely respected tool for self-examination. Its structured approach encourages individuals to reflect on their lives, the people in it, and how they've interacted with them—ultimately leading to greater self-awareness, gratitude, and personal growth.

At its core, Naikan is based on three key questions, which may seem deceptively simple at first but invite a deep exploration of one's actions, attitudes, and emotions. These questions are designed to help individuals uncover the hidden dynamics of their relationships, particularly with those closest to them, and assess their own roles in those relationships. While the practice is rooted in Buddhist philosophy, particularly in the teachings of the monk Ishin Yoshimoto, it is not tied to any specific religious practice and can be embraced by people from all walks of life.

The three central questions that form the heart of Naikan are:

1. **What have I received from this person?**

2. **What have I given to this person?**

3. **What troubles and difficulties have I caused this person?**

These questions are designed to uncover multiple layers of insight, helping individuals move beyond surface-level understandings of relationships and delve into more nuanced and often uncomfortable areas of self-awareness.

The Three Key Questions of Naikan

1. What Have I Received from This Person?

The first question focuses on gratitude and acknowledgment. In our busy, day-to-day lives, it is easy to take others for granted—especially those who are closest to us, like family members, friends, or even colleagues. We might go through life assuming that others are always there to give and support us, but we rarely stop to actively reflect on the ways in which we have benefited from their presence. This question invites you to pause and think deeply about the gifts—both tangible and intangible—that you have received from the person you are reflecting on.

This question is not just about the obvious things: the material support, the help with specific tasks, or the kindness shown during difficult times. It is also about the emotional and psychological support someone may have offered, often without us even realizing it. This could be the patience they've shown when we were struggling, the understanding they offered when we were down, or even the sacrifices they made to improve our lives. In reflecting on these gifts, we begin to develop a deeper appreciation for the people in our lives, and we begin to acknowledge the interconnectedness of human relationships.

The impact of this question is subtle but profound. When you start to recognize all the ways a person has helped you, you realize how much they have shaped who you are. This awareness fosters gratitude, helping you cultivate a deeper sense of appreciation and humility toward others.

2. What Have I Given to This Person?

The second question flips the perspective and asks us to consider what we have contributed to the other person's life. This question invites us to evaluate how we show up in relationships. We are often so focused on what we are receiving that we overlook the importance of our own actions and contributions. Naikan challenges us to look inward and ask whether we've truly reciprocated in meaningful ways.

What we give to others goes beyond material gifts or actions; it encompasses emotional support, time, attention, and energy. This question pushes us to assess whether we have been a good friend, partner, family member, or colleague. It forces us to take responsibility for our behavior and recognize if we've been neglectful or inattentive. In doing so, it helps us take accountability for our role in nurturing or weakening relationships.

This can be a difficult question to answer honestly, especially if we find that we have been less giving or more self-absorbed than we would like to admit. It encourages self-reflection on whether our actions have matched our intentions and whether we've been consistent in our contributions. In relationships, the act of giving is not always reciprocal in the way we expect, but Naikan helps us assess if we are fulfilling our side of the equation with care, generosity, and attention.

3. What Troubles and Difficulties Have I Caused This Person?

The third question is perhaps the most challenging, as it asks us to confront the ways we may have caused pain, disappointment, or difficulty for the other person. It's easy to blame others for the challenges in our relationships, but Naikan encourages us to look at our own actions, words, and behavior and how they may have contributed to the issues at hand.

This question doesn't just ask about the obvious instances of conflict or harm—it goes deeper into our attitudes, our lack of awareness, and the unintended consequences of our actions. How have we been selfish, thoughtless, or insensitive? How have we neglected or hurt others without meaning to? These reflections aren't about guilt or shame, but about taking responsibility for the ways we have impacted others.

Often, when we think about our relationships, we see them through a lens of what others have done to us, or what they haven't done. But Naikan asks us to confront the fact that we, too, have a role to play in the dynamics of every relationship. It encourages us to examine our behavior honestly, without excuses, and recognize the areas where we have fallen short. This doesn't mean we blame ourselves for everything that goes wrong, but rather, we become more mindful of our own actions and their effects on others.

How Naikan Works: The Process

Naikan isn't just about reflecting on these three questions in isolation. The process is often carried out over an extended period of time, typically in a retreat-like environment, where participants engage in periods of silence, journaling, and deep introspection. During this time, individuals may reflect on the relationships they want to examine, whether it's their parents, a spouse, or even a colleague. They are encouraged to sit with their thoughts and feelings without distractions, allowing the process to unfold naturally.

Naikan's method may also involve revisiting past events or conversations, carefully considering each question and its implications. The idea is not to focus on achieving perfect answers, but rather to engage deeply with the process, allowing insights to emerge organically. The practice requires patience, as the answers to these questions may not always be clear right away. It takes time to unpack the complexity of our feelings, especially when it comes to our relationships with others.

The benefits of Naikan are both immediate and long-lasting. By practicing self-reflection through these three simple questions, we develop a deeper awareness of ourselves and others. We begin to recognize our own patterns of behavior, both positive and negative, and how they affect the people in our lives. We develop greater empathy and understanding, which enhances our capacity for compassion and forgiveness.

Naikan also encourages emotional healing, as it helps individuals process unresolved feelings or conflicts from the past. It allows people to make amends, seek forgiveness, and move forward in their relationships with a clearer sense of purpose and direction. By taking time to reflect on our interactions with others, we begin to cultivate a mindset of self-improvement and continuous growth.

Perhaps most importantly, Naikan helps us reconnect with the fundamental truths of our lives—the interconnectedness of all people, the significance of our relationships, and the importance of gratitude. Through Naikan, we learn that personal growth is not a solitary endeavor, but something that is deeply intertwined with the lives of others.

Therefore, Naikan is not simply a method of reflection; it is a transformative practice that helps us uncover the hidden layers of our relationships and our own behavior. By asking three simple but powerful questions, Naikan allows us to explore the depths of our connections, cultivate empathy, and ultimately become better versions of ourselves. It teaches us that the path to true personal growth isn't through self-centeredness or superficial stability, but through an honest, mindful examination of the ways we impact the world and the people around us.

The Science of Introspection: How Reflection Rewires the Brain

Introspection—the practice of examining one's own thoughts, emotions, and behaviors—has been a core element of human self-awareness for centuries. Ancient philosophies, such as Buddhism and Stoicism, often emphasized the importance of self-reflection for personal growth and well-being. In modern psychology, introspection has evolved from a spiritual practice into a well-established tool for mental health, emotional regulation, and cognitive development. But what does science have to say about the practice of looking inward? How does the act of reflecting on our experiences and emotions actually change the brain? Let's explore the fascinating science behind introspection and how it rewires the brain to improve our mental and emotional health.

The Brain's Neuroplasticity: The Power of Change

The brain is not a static organ. Rather, it is highly adaptable and capable of rewiring itself throughout life. This phenomenon, known as neuroplasticity, refers to the brain's ability to reorganize itself by forming new neural connections in response to learning, experiences, and conscious effort. Introspection plays a significant role in promoting neuroplasticity by encouraging active mental engagement, which helps strengthen neural pathways associated with self-awareness, emotional regulation, and cognitive flexibility.

When we engage in reflective practices, we activate different areas of the brain that are involved in higher-order functions such as problem-solving, decision-making, and self-regulation. For instance, the prefrontal cortex, which is responsible for executive functions, becomes more active during periods of introspection. This part of the brain helps us plan, think critically, and regulate our impulses. By consciously reflecting on our actions, decisions, and feelings, we train the prefrontal cortex to become more efficient at managing our thoughts and emotions, ultimately leading to greater self-control and resilience.

Moreover, studies show that the process of introspection helps to strengthen the connections between the prefrontal cortex and the limbic system, which governs our emotions. By reflecting on emotional experiences, we can process these emotions in a more balanced and controlled manner, reducing the risk of emotional reactivity and promoting emotional intelligence.

Introspection and the Default Mode Network (DMN)

When we turn our attention inward, reflecting on our thoughts, feelings, and memories, the brain activates a network of regions collectively known as the Default Mode Network (DMN). The DMN includes areas such as the medial prefrontal cortex, the posterior cingulate cortex, and the angular gyrus, which are involved in self-referential thinking, memory retrieval, and social cognition. Essentially, the DMN is the brain's "background network," activated when we are not focused on the external world but instead are reflecting on ourselves and our experiences.

The DMN is crucial for mental processes such as self-awareness, future planning, and understanding others' perspectives. This network allows us to create a coherent narrative of our lives and make sense of our past and present experiences. During introspection, the DMN is particularly active as we reflect on our thoughts and feelings, often providing insights that help us make sense of complex situations or emotional experiences.

However, the DMN can also become problematic when it becomes overactive, leading to rumination—a repetitive, often negative cycle of self-reflection that can contribute to mental health issues such as anxiety and depression. Therefore, while introspection has significant benefits, it is important to balance reflective practices with mindfulness techniques that allow us to detach from negative thought patterns and remain present in the moment.

Reflection and Emotional Regulation

One of the most powerful ways that introspection rewires the brain is by enhancing our emotional regulation abilities. Emotional regulation refers to the ability to monitor, evaluate, and modify our emotional reactions in response to different situations. Effective emotional regulation is critical for mental well-being, as it allows us to handle stress, manage conflict, and respond to challenging situations in a measured way.

Research suggests that engaging in introspective practices, such as journaling or meditative reflection, strengthens the brain's emotional regulation systems. For example, reflective practices activate the prefrontal cortex, which helps us process emotions more effectively and reduce the influence of the amygdala—the brain region associated with emotional reactions like fear and anger. Over time, regular introspection can lead to increased emotional resilience, as the brain becomes better equipped to manage intense feelings and recover from emotional distress.

Moreover, introspection allows us to identify patterns in our emotional responses. By reflecting on situations where we have reacted impulsively or excessively, we can identify triggers and habitual thought patterns that contribute to these emotional responses. This awareness allows us to make more conscious choices in how we react in the future, thereby fostering greater emotional intelligence and empathy for others.

Introspection and Cognitive Flexibility

Cognitive flexibility is the ability to switch between different perspectives, adapt to changing circumstances, and consider alternative solutions to problems. It is a vital skill for problem-solving and creativity, and it is essential for personal growth. Introspection enhances cognitive flexibility by encouraging us to examine our assumptions, beliefs, and mental models, allowing us to become more open-minded and adaptable.

When we reflect on our experiences, we are forced to evaluate our thoughts and behaviors from different angles, which helps us develop a more nuanced understanding of ourselves and the world around us. For instance, reflecting on a conflict with a colleague might prompt us to consider their point of view, challenge our assumptions, and think about alternative ways we could have handled the situation. By practicing introspection regularly, we develop the cognitive flexibility needed to approach challenges with a broader perspective and a more open mindset.

Additionally, introspection can foster creativity by encouraging divergent thinking—the ability to generate multiple solutions to a problem. When we reflect on our experiences, we are not just trying to make sense of the past, but also exploring possibilities for the future. This process of mental exploration promotes creativity, as we begin to think about different potential outcomes and solutions that we might not have considered before.

The Role of Mindfulness in Introspection

Mindfulness, the practice of being present and fully engaged with the current moment, plays a key role in enhancing the benefits of introspection. While introspection involves reflecting on past experiences, mindfulness helps us observe these experiences without judgment, allowing us to gain insights without becoming overwhelmed by emotions or negative thought patterns.

Studies have shown that mindfulness meditation can lead to changes in brain areas related to emotional regulation, attention, and self-awareness. For example, mindfulness has been linked to increased gray matter density in the prefrontal cortex, the hippocampus, and other areas of the brain associated with memory, emotional regulation, and self-reflection. These changes suggest that mindfulness practices not only improve our ability to reflect on ourselves but also enhance our capacity to respond to life's challenges with greater clarity and calmness.

Moreover, mindfulness helps us engage in introspection without falling into the trap of rumination. By practicing mindfulness, we can observe our thoughts and feelings with curiosity and openness, rather than getting caught in negative thought loops. This combination of mindfulness and introspection creates a powerful feedback loop that promotes mental clarity, emotional balance, and cognitive growth.

The science of introspection reveals how this age-old practice can rewire the brain, enhancing our emotional regulation, cognitive flexibility, and self-awareness. Through introspection, we activate key brain networks, strengthen our emotional resilience, and cultivate greater mental clarity. As we reflect on our thoughts, behaviors, and experiences, we not only gain valuable insights but also promote neuroplasticity—the brain's ability to adapt and change. By practicing introspection regularly, we can develop a mindset that is more adaptable, creative, and emotionally intelligent, helping us navigate the challenges of life with greater ease and clarity.

Exercises: Guided Naikan Practice Focusing on Gratitude and Accountability

The practice of Naikan, a Japanese form of self-reflection, offers a profound method of examining our relationships, actions, and emotional experiences. It is structured around three key questions that promote deep introspection, helping individuals process their past actions and relationships in a meaningful way. By applying this practice, we can cultivate a stronger sense of gratitude and personal accountability, which can lead to lasting growth and transformation.

In this section, we will guide you through an exercise based on the Naikan principles, focused specifically on gratitude and accountability. This exercise will allow you to reflect on your life, your relationships, and the ways in which you have contributed to or been affected by those around you.

Understanding Naikan and Its Core Questions

Naikan, a method developed by Yoshimoto Ishin, translates roughly to "looking inside." The practice is rooted in three main questions, which are designed to create a balanced and honest reflection of one's interactions and personal impact. These three questions serve as the foundation for deepening your sense of self-awareness, gratitude, and accountability:

1. **What have I received from [this person]?**

2. **What have I given to [this person]?**

3. **What troubles and difficulties have I caused [this person]?**

These three simple yet powerful questions allow you to evaluate not just your actions but also the emotions and intentions behind them. Through repeated application of these questions, you begin to view your relationships through a lens of appreciation and responsibility, which naturally encourages gratitude and accountability.

Now, let's explore how to incorporate these three Naikan questions into an exercise that focuses on cultivating gratitude and personal responsibility. This exercise can be done alone, in a journal, or even in a guided meditation session.

Step 1: Choose a Relationship

To begin this Naikan practice, identify a relationship in your life that you'd like to reflect on. This could be a close family member, a friend, a colleague, or even someone who has significantly impacted your life in some way. If you're new to Naikan, it's often helpful to start with a relationship that feels neutral—neither too painful nor too close. The goal is to foster a balanced perspective, so choose someone you feel safe reflecting on at this point in your journey.

If you're open to it, you can also consider a relationship that may require healing. Introspection into relationships that are strained or complicated can bring powerful insight and growth, but it's important to approach these with gentleness and compassion toward yourself.

Step 2: Answer the Three Naikan Questions

Now that you've chosen your focus person, take a deep breath and begin by reflecting on each of the three Naikan questions. These questions are meant to guide you in a compassionate yet honest examination of your interactions, contributions, and any unintended harm. Take your time with each question, writing your thoughts down or reflecting silently.

1. What have I received from [this person]?

Start with an attitude of gratitude. What has this person given you—whether material, emotional, or even just their presence in your life? Think deeply about both large and small contributions they have made. Perhaps they've supported you in difficult times, offered their wisdom, or simply been a steady presence. Try to approach this question with an open heart, recognizing the value they've brought to your life, both directly and indirectly.

Example:

- "My mother has always supported me emotionally, even when I've made mistakes."

- "My friend offered me advice that changed my perspective on my career."

2. What have I given to [this person]?

Next, reflect on the ways in which you have given to this person. This doesn't have to be grand gestures—sometimes the small, everyday acts are the most meaningful. What have you offered them in terms of support, care, or companionship? This question invites you to consider how your actions have impacted the other person. It encourages self-recognition of how you show up in the relationship, not only through actions but also through your energy and presence.

Example:

- "I have shared my thoughts and feelings openly with them, even when it was hard."

- "I helped them during a stressful time, making sure they felt supported and heard."

3. What troubles or difficulties have I caused [this person]?

This is the most challenging of the three questions, but also one of the most important. Reflect on any moments where your actions may have unintentionally or intentionally caused this person pain, frustration, or inconvenience. It is crucial here to avoid self-blame or guilt; instead, approach this question with a spirit of accountability and ownership. Understand that, as human beings, we sometimes act in ways that hurt others, even when it's not our intention. The key is to recognize these actions and take responsibility.

Example:

- "I was distracted when they needed my attention, and I didn't realize how much that affected them."

- "I sometimes become defensive when they offer feedback, which likely makes them feel unheard."

Step 3: Reflect on the Patterns

After you've answered the three questions for your chosen person, take a moment to reflect on the patterns that have emerged in your answers. Are there any themes of imbalance—where you might have received more than you've given, or vice versa? Are there recurring instances where you've unintentionally caused harm or difficulty?

This is an opportunity to practice humility and self-awareness. Rather than focusing on the guilt or discomfort of acknowledging mistakes, embrace this reflection as an opportunity to grow. Consider the following points as you reflect:

- Are there ways in which you could improve your actions to bring more balance into the relationship?

- What can you do to express more gratitude toward this person in your life moving forward?

- How can you show up more fully in this relationship, with greater awareness of your impact?

Step 4: Create an Action Plan for Gratitude and Accountability

Once you've completed your reflection, it's time to turn your insights into action. Think about how you can shift your mindset in this relationship moving forward. Your answers to the three Naikan questions may highlight areas where you can express more gratitude, offer more support, or be more mindful of the impact of your actions.

Consider these action steps:

1. **Gratitude:**

- Write a letter or message to this person, expressing your appreciation for what they've given you.

- Reflect on ways you can show gratitude regularly (e.g., checking in with them, offering a gesture of kindness, acknowledging their support).

2. **Accountability**

163

- Identify specific actions you can take to remedy any harm you may have caused. This might include apologizing for past mistakes, being more mindful of their needs, or setting better boundaries.

- Make a commitment to show up more authentically in the relationship, understanding the impact of your actions and words.

3. **Growth**

- Commit to a practice of ongoing reflection on your relationships. Revisit the Naikan questions periodically to monitor how you're progressing in your gratitude and accountability.

- Use what you've learned from this reflection to deepen your connection with the person and enhance your own personal growth.

The Naikan practice is a transformative tool that encourages gratitude and accountability, two key elements in fostering healthy and meaningful relationships. By answering the three simple but powerful questions, you can deepen your understanding of how your actions affect those around you and how you can contribute more fully to the lives of others.

Incorporating these insights into your daily life will not only strengthen your relationships but will also foster a deeper sense of self-awareness, emotional growth, and personal responsibility. By using Naikan as a practice, you open the door to continuous self-improvement and the cultivation of a katana mindset—a mindset rooted in reflection, gratitude, and the willingness to evolve.

The Role of Self-Reflection in Personal Growth

The study *The Role of Self-Reflection in Personal Growth*, published in the *Journal of Personality and Social Psychology*, reveals that regular self-reflection can increase emotional intelligence by 23%. This finding is both compelling and deeply resonant with my experiences during recovery in Japan, particularly as I began exploring the practice of *Naikan*—a structured form of introspection that originated in Japanese culture.

At the core of the study is the idea that self-reflection acts as a mirror for our inner world. It helps us better understand not only our own emotions but also how they influence our interactions with others. Emotional intelligence, as described in the study, isn't just about managing one's emotions—it's about recognizing patterns, fostering empathy, and responding thoughtfully rather than reactively. When I began practicing *Naikan*, I saw how these qualities emerged through deliberate, structured introspection.

During my hospital stay, a fellow patient shared the concept of *Naikan*, which translates to "inner looking." He explained its simplicity yet profound depth. The practice involves reflecting on three questions:

1. What have I received from others?

2. What have I given to others?

3. What troubles or difficulties have I caused others?

At first, these questions struck me as unassuming. Yet, as I began incorporating them into my days, they opened doors to emotional clarity I hadn't accessed before. For example, when I thought about the first question—what I had received from others—I was reminded of the unwavering care of the nurses, who not only managed my physical healing but also offered encouragement when I felt despondent. This wasn't just gratitude; it was a realization of the deep interconnectedness between my recovery and the efforts of those around me.

The study sheds light on why this kind of reflection is transformative. Regular introspection rewires neural pathways, enhancing our ability to process emotions with greater clarity. It also activates regions in the brain associated with empathy, such as the anterior cingulate cortex and the prefrontal cortex, strengthening our capacity to connect with others on a deeper level. When we repeatedly engage in reflective practices, these neural changes compound, leading to a significant increase in emotional intelligence over time.

This growth was evident in my reflections on the third question: what difficulties I had caused others. Initially, this question felt uncomfortable. Who wants to dwell on their mistakes or shortcomings? But as the study notes, authentic self-reflection requires courage—the willingness to confront not only our strengths but also our flaws. I began to see how my impatience, especially in the early days of my recovery, may have placed unnecessary strain on those caring for me. Recognizing this wasn't about self-criticism; it was about accountability. It spurred me to express gratitude more frequently and to approach others with greater understanding.

The practice also deepened my empathy. Reflecting on what I had given to others highlighted moments where I could have been more attentive, more present. This wasn't about self-judgment—it was about cultivating an awareness that allowed me to act differently moving forward. As the study emphasizes, regular self-reflection fosters a feedback loop: increased awareness leads to better emotional regulation, which in turn enhances our relationships.

What struck me most about *Naikan* was its simplicity. Unlike the Western emphasis on self-improvement as a path to personal achievement, *Naikan* encourages humility. It asks us to see ourselves not as isolated individuals but as part of a web of relationships. This perspective shifts the focus from "What can I gain?" to "What have I received, and how can I contribute?"

The findings from the study align beautifully with this approach. By increasing emotional intelligence, self-reflection doesn't just benefit the individual—it strengthens the bonds that connect us to others. This realization was transformative for me. It wasn't just about becoming more emotionally aware—it was about becoming more human.

Through *Naikan*, and supported by the insights from this study, I began to understand that personal growth isn't a solitary endeavor. It's a process that unfolds in the context of our relationships, shaped by the interplay of receiving, giving, and recognizing our impact on others. And in that recognition, we find not only emotional intelligence but also a deeper sense of purpose and belonging.

Deep Self-Reflection: The Naikan Stage

The **Naikan** stage invites you to turn inward, fostering a practice of structured reflection that deepens your understanding of yourself and your relationships. Derived from the Japanese term meaning "looking inside," Naikan isn't about self-criticism or dwelling on faults; instead, it's a guided journey of self-discovery that brings clarity, gratitude, and emotional balance.

Stage Recognition

Recognizing when you're in the Naikan stage is essential for embracing its transformative potential. This stage often follows a period of acceptance (Shikata ga nai), as you begin to seek understanding of your emotions, behaviors, and patterns.

- **Key Indicators:**

    - A strong desire to understand why you react the way you do in certain situations.

    - Feeling disconnected from your true self or unsure about your life's direction.

    - A pull to examine past experiences and their influence on your present.

- **Behavioral Patterns:**

    - Spending more time reflecting on your choices and relationships.

    - Questioning long-held beliefs or assumptions about yourself.

    - Seeking meaning in past successes and failures.

- **Relationship Dynamics:**

    - A shift in how you perceive others, with growing curiosity about their perspectives.

    - Realizations about your role in relationship conflicts or patterns.

Self-Assessment Exercise:

- Ask yourself:

    - What have I received from others lately?

    - What have I given to others?

    - What difficulties have I caused others?
      These three Naikan questions help uncover hidden

patterns in your interactions and foster a sense of accountability and gratitude.

Stage Completion Markers

As you work through the Naikan stage, you'll notice profound shifts in your understanding of yourself and your relationships:

- **Mindset Shifts:**

    - Moving from blame or self-pity to accountability and gratitude.

    - Greater clarity about your values, priorities, and emotional triggers.

- **Behavioral Changes:**

    - A more thoughtful approach to relationships, driven by empathy and understanding.

    - Reduced impulsivity, as you become more deliberate in your actions.

- **Emotional Milestones:**

    - Finding peace with past mistakes or regrets.

    - A sense of closure and renewed connection to your inner self.

- **Relationship Developments:**

    - Strengthened bonds, as you take responsibility for your role in past conflicts.

    - The ability to see others' contributions to your life with fresh gratitude.

Next Stage Preparation

Naikan naturally transitions into **Kaizen**, the stage of continuous improvement, as your insights fuel a desire for purposeful action. Signs you're ready include:

- **Internal Signals:**
    - A clear understanding of where you want to grow and what needs improvement.
    - A renewed sense of empowerment and curiosity about personal transformation.

- **Transition Challenges:**
    - Overanalyzing the past and becoming stuck in reflection instead of moving forward.
    - Difficulty letting go of newly uncovered emotions, such as guilt or regret.

- **Preparation Exercises:**
    - **Actionable Insight:** Choose one revelation from your Naikan reflection and create a plan to address it, such as mending a strained relationship or changing a harmful habit.
    - **Gratitude Journal:** Regularly write about people or events you're thankful for, integrating positivity into your reflections.

Regression Warnings

Reflection, though powerful, can sometimes lead to regression if not handled with balance. Be mindful of these signs:

- **Early Warning Signs:**
    - Overdwelling on past mistakes or painful memories.

- Slipping into self-criticism instead of constructive reflection.

- **Common Triggers:**

  - External pressure to suppress your emotions or move on prematurely.

  - Confrontations that force you to revisit unresolved conflicts.

- **Stages to Avoid Regressing To:**

  - Falling back into denial or avoidance (Shikata ga nai).

  - Retreating to surface stability (Genki) instead of embracing deeper truths.

- **Recovery Practices:**

  - Revisit the Naikan questions to ground yourself in gratitude and accountability.

  - Practice mindfulness to stay present rather than fixated on the past.

Stage Integration

The Naikan stage isn't a one-time process—it's a skill to carry forward, enriching your journey through the subsequent stages.

- **Building on Reflection:**

  - Use your insights as a guide for decision-making in daily life.

  - Incorporate reflection practices into regular routines, such as weekly journaling.

- **Sustaining Progress:**

- Balance reflection with action, ensuring you don't get stuck in introspection.

- Seek feedback from trusted friends or mentors to gain external perspectives on your growth.

- **Integration Exercise:**

    - Write a letter to someone who has deeply impacted your life. Share your gratitude and reflect on how their presence has shaped your journey.

The Naikan stage is a powerful gateway to self-awareness and growth. By looking inward with honesty and compassion, you gain the clarity needed to move forward with purpose and intentionality. This stage prepares you not only to improve yourself but also to enrich your connections with others, paving the way for continuous progress in the Kaizen stage.

CHAPTER EIGHT

CONFRONTING YOUR SHADOWS

Confronting Your Shadows: A Personal Regret

In the process of self-reflection, as we turn our attention inward, we may stumble upon uncomfortable truths about ourselves - the 'shadows' that lurk in the corners of our being. These shadows may be the regrets we've buried, the fears we've denied, or the unfulfilled potential we've ignored. While it's tempting to keep these shadows hidden, confronting them is an essential part of the transformative journey.

The weight of regret is an invisible burden, quietly accumulating over time. It doesn't announce itself in the moment but grows with reflection, becoming a shadow that follows us everywhere. For me, one such shadow took root during an ordinary day—a day that became etched in my memory as a poignant reminder of how much we take for granted until it's too late.

It was a summer afternoon, and I was busy—caught up in work, messages, errands, and the seemingly endless to-do list of daily life. My phone buzzed. It was my friend, Haruto. He rarely called, so I assumed it was something trivial, perhaps a question or a favor. I glanced at the screen, saw his name, and let it ring.

"I'll call him back later," I thought. But I didn't.

The days turned into weeks, and Haruto's call became a forgotten item on my mental checklist. It wasn't until another friend reached out to inform me that Haruto had passed away in a sudden accident that I understood the gravity of that unanswered call. The words hit like a thunderclap. My first thought wasn't disbelief or sorrow—it was regret.

Regret that I hadn't answered. Regret that I didn't know why he had called. Regret that my busy, preoccupied self had placed everything else above a simple act of connection.

This shadow lingered, deepening as I replayed that moment over and over in my head. What had Haruto wanted to say? Was it important? Would it have made a difference to him, to me, to the fleeting thread of connection we had left? These questions had no answers, only echoes.

The Nature of Shadows

Regrets like this one are the shadows of our lives. They may not always be visible, but they are there—lurking, growing in the corners of our memory. They stem from the moments we didn't show up, the words we left unspoken, the actions we failed to take. Some are small and fleeting, while others leave a lasting mark, shaping the way we view ourselves and the world.

In many ways, shadows are unavoidable. To live is to make choices, and to make choices is to sometimes make the wrong ones. Yet, it is not the presence of these shadows that defines us, but how we confront them.

Confronting a shadow means stepping into discomfort and facing the parts of ourselves we'd rather leave hidden. It means taking responsibility, acknowledging our flaws, and seeking ways to grow from those moments of failure or inaction.

Cultural perspectives on shame and accountability can significantly influence how we confront our shadows. In Japan, the emphasis on collective harmony and responsibility creates a different approach compared to the West's focus on individualism. Understanding these cultural nuances can offer valuable insights into how shame and regret are processed and addressed.

The Call You Can't Return

The unanswered call from Haruto taught me more than just the importance of prioritizing people over tasks. It forced me to confront a deeper truth: the fear of facing my own inadequacy. At its core, regret is not just about what we didn't do—it's about what it says about us. My regret was a mirror, reflecting my tendency to get lost in the whirlwind of my own priorities, to forget the fragility of time and connection.

Haruto's memory became a quiet teacher in my life. Though I could never return that call or change what had happened, I could change how I approached my relationships moving forward. I started answering calls more often, even when they came at inconvenient times. I became more intentional about reaching out to friends and family, about expressing gratitude and love in the present instead of waiting for some undefined "later."

There is immense power in facing our regrets head-on. It's tempting to push them aside, to bury them beneath excuses or distractions. But regret, when acknowledged and examined, becomes a tool for growth. It teaches us where we've fallen short and where we can do better. It gives us a roadmap for the kind of person we aspire to be.

I began to ask myself difficult questions:

- Why didn't I answer Haruto's call?

- Was it truly because I was busy, or was it a deeper reluctance to engage in a moment of vulnerability or connection?

- How many other "Haruto moments" might I have missed in my life, simply because I was too caught up in my own world?

These questions were uncomfortable, but they were necessary. They forced me to confront not just the regret itself, but the underlying patterns and behaviors that had led to it.

A Lesson in Shadows

In Japanese culture, there is a concept called **kintsugi**—the art of repairing broken pottery with gold. The philosophy behind kintsugi is that flaws and imperfections are not something to hide but something to embrace and even highlight. Our shadows, much like the cracks in kintsugi pottery, are part of who we are. They shape us, teach us, and ultimately make us more resilient if we're willing to learn from them.

Regret, when viewed through the lens of kintsugi, becomes a golden thread. It reminds us of our humanity, our fallibility, and our capacity for growth. Haruto's call became my golden thread. Though I could not repair the past, I could use that experience to guide my future—to create deeper connections, to be more present, and to embrace the fleeting, precious moments of life.

Moving Forward

Confronting your shadows doesn't mean erasing them. It means acknowledging their presence and allowing them to inform your actions moving forward. For me, the shadow of that unanswered call remains—it is a part of my story. But it no longer weighs me down. Instead, it serves as a reminder to live more intentionally, to prioritize people over tasks, and to embrace vulnerability, even when it feels inconvenient or uncomfortable.

We all carry shadows, and we all have moments we wish we could undo. But within those shadows lies an opportunity for transformation. By facing them with courage and honesty, we can turn our regrets into lessons, our failures into growth, and our shadows into light.

The process of confronting shadows is not always easy. It may lead to moments of deep introspection and even the realization of hitting rock bottom. But within this vulnerability lies the potential for profound personal growth. By facing our shadows head-on, we not only heal old wounds but also create space for greater authenticity, resilience, and self-acceptance.

Cultural Contrasts: Japanese vs. Western Approaches to Shame and Accountability

Shame and accountability are universal human experiences, but the ways in which cultures interpret, express, and respond to them vary dramatically. Japan and the West offer two distinct frameworks for understanding these concepts, each shaped by history, values, and societal expectations. While both cultures emphasize personal responsibility, the paths they take toward accountability and the role of shame within those journeys reveal fundamental differences in worldview and priorities.

The Role of Shame in Japan: A Collective Mirror

In Japan, shame is deeply intertwined with the concept of **"giri"** (obligation) and **"ninjo"** (personal feelings). These cultural forces create a delicate balance between societal expectations and individual emotions, with shame acting as a social mechanism to maintain harmony.

Shame in Japan is collective by nature. When someone fails or commits a mistake, the ripple effects extend beyond the individual to their family, workplace, or community. This interconnectedness is rooted in the cultural emphasis on **"wa"** (harmony). The individual is seen not as a solitary entity but as part of a larger whole, and their actions—positive or negative—reflect on the entire group.

177

This collective lens means that accountability often takes the form of **atonement** or visible gestures of remorse. Public apologies, resignations, and even acts of self-sacrifice are common responses to mistakes or transgressions. These acts are not just about repairing the individual's reputation but also about restoring balance and trust within the community.

Examples from Japanese Culture:

1. **Public Apologies:** When scandals occur in Japan—whether in politics, business, or entertainment—it is customary for the person at fault to hold a press conference where they bow deeply and express sincere regret. This gesture, known as **ojigi**, is more than symbolic; it is an acknowledgment of responsibility and a request for forgiveness.

2. **Kaishaku (Taking Responsibility):** Historically, in the era of the samurai, shame was so powerful that failure often led to **seppuku** (ritual suicide) as an ultimate form of accountability. While this extreme practice no longer exists, the legacy remains in the modern expectation of profound accountability.

3. **Group Over Self:** In schools and workplaces, collective responsibility often means that a group will apologize for the actions of one member. If a student misbehaves, their classmates might also express remorse to the teacher, reinforcing the idea that the individual's shame is shared by the group.

Western Views on Shame: A Personal Burden

In contrast, Western cultures, particularly those in the United States and Europe, view shame primarily as an individual experience. The emphasis is on personal accountability and self-redemption, driven by values like independence, self-expression, and personal freedom.

Shame in the West is often internalized, focusing on how the individual feels about their actions rather than their impact on the broader community. While public accountability is still valued, it tends to center on personal growth and change rather than collective harmony.

Key Differences in Western Accountability:

1. **Focus on Forgiveness and Redemption:** In Western cultures, accountability often includes an expectation of forgiveness. An individual might apologize and then take steps to demonstrate personal growth, with the ultimate goal of moving forward. Examples abound in public life, where figures who face scandal often seek redemption through acts of charity, rehabilitation, or personal development.

2. **Shame vs. Guilt:** Western psychology makes a distinction between **shame** (feeling like a bad person) and **guilt** (feeling bad about specific actions). The latter is often seen as more constructive, as it encourages individuals to address their behavior without internalizing the belief that they are inherently flawed.

3. **Individual Over Group:** Accountability in the West is usually confined to the individual. A person's mistake is not typically seen as a reflection of their family or community. This perspective stems from the cultural emphasis on individual autonomy and the belief that people should not bear responsibility for others' actions.

Points of Convergence and Divergence

While Japanese and Western approaches to shame and accountability differ significantly, there are areas of overlap. Both cultures value accountability and recognize the importance of addressing mistakes. However, their motivations and methods diverge:

Aspect	Japanese Approach	Western Approach
Focus	Collective impact, restoring harmony	Individual growth, seeking redemption
Expression of Shame	Public, visible gestures (e.g., apologies)	Private reflection, verbal apologies
Accountability	Group responsibility, visible atonement	Personal responsibility, long-term change
Role of Shame	Social mechanism, reinforces community norms	Personal emotion, catalyst for self-improvement

Strengths and Challenges of Each Approach

1. **Japanese Strengths:**

   o The collective emphasis fosters a strong sense of community and mutual accountability.

   o Public acts of remorse demonstrate sincerity and commitment to making amends.

   o Shame as a social mechanism encourages people to act in ways that preserve harmony.

Challenges:

   o The intense pressure to avoid shame can discourage openness and vulnerability.

180

- Public accountability may feel performative if not accompanied by genuine change.

2. **Western Strengths:**

- The focus on personal growth allows individuals to learn from their mistakes without fear of excessive judgment.

- Differentiating shame and guilt helps individuals address behaviors rather than internalizing failure.

- Autonomy in accountability supports diverse paths to redemption.

Challenges:

- The individual focus can sometimes neglect the broader impact on communities or relationships.

- A lack of visible gestures of remorse may be perceived as insincere or inadequate.

There is wisdom to be found in both approaches. From Japan, we can learn the value of acknowledging the collective impact of our actions and the importance of visible accountability. From the West, we can embrace the idea that mistakes are opportunities for personal growth and that self-forgiveness is a crucial part of moving forward.

By blending these perspectives, we can approach shame and accountability with greater balance—acknowledging our role within a community while also taking responsibility for our individual growth. Whether through a public apology, a private reflection, or a commitment to meaningful change, the ultimate goal is the same: to turn moments of failure into opportunities for transformation.

Tools: Shadow Journaling—Acknowledging and Embracing Your Flaws

Shadow journaling is a powerful practice that invites us to confront, acknowledge, and embrace the parts of ourselves we often try to hide—our "shadow selves." This term, popularized by psychologist Carl Jung, refers to the hidden, often suppressed aspects of our personality, including our flaws, insecurities, fears, and even unrealized potential. While these shadows might seem negative at first glance, they carry valuable lessons and opportunities for growth.

Shadow journaling helps us engage with these aspects in a structured and compassionate way, creating space for self-acceptance and transformation. Below, we'll explore what shadow journaling entails, why it's important, and how to begin this journey toward self-awareness and healing.

What is Shadow Journaling?

Shadow journaling is the practice of writing specifically about the thoughts, emotions, and behaviors that you might typically avoid or deny. It's about bringing the unseen into the light—not to judge or fix it, but to understand it. Through this process, you acknowledge your flaws, explore their origins, and discover how they influence your life.

Rather than running from discomfort, shadow journaling encourages you to lean into it, revealing insights that can help you grow. It is not about wallowing in negativity but about creating a safe, reflective space to uncover hidden truths and integrate them into your conscious self.

Why Acknowledge Your Shadows?

1. **Self-Acceptance:** By facing your flaws, you learn to accept yourself as a whole person. True self-love requires

182

acknowledging the parts of yourself that are difficult to look at.

2. **Improved Relationships:** Unresolved shadows often project outward, leading to misunderstandings and conflicts. Recognizing and addressing your shadow traits can lead to healthier, more empathetic interactions.

3. **Personal Growth:** Your shadows hold the key to untapped potential. For instance, the insecurity that drives perfectionism might also fuel a desire for excellence, which can be harnessed positively.

4. **Reduced Emotional Triggers:** When you confront and process your inner wounds, external situations are less likely to provoke strong, unhelpful emotional reactions.

5. **Aligned Authenticity:** Integrating your shadow allows you to live more authentically, no longer weighed down by the need to hide parts of yourself.

How to Begin Shadow Journaling

Step 1: Create a Safe Space

- Find a quiet, private environment where you feel secure to reflect deeply.

- Use a notebook dedicated solely to shadow journaling, or create a digital file where you can freely write.

Step 2: Set an Intention

Start each session by clarifying your purpose. For example:

- "I want to understand why I feel resentment in certain situations."

- "I want to explore my fear of failure."

Write your intention at the top of the page to guide your reflections.

Step 3: Use Prompts to Explore Your Shadows

Shadow journaling can feel intimidating without direction, so prompts can help you dive into specific areas. Some effective prompts include:

- **What are my biggest insecurities, and how do they affect my decisions?**

- **What am I most afraid of others discovering about me? Why?**

- **When have I felt jealousy or resentment, and what does that reveal about my unmet needs?**

- **What is a recurring conflict I experience in relationships, and how might I contribute to it?**

- **What emotions am I uncomfortable expressing, and why?**

Step 4: Practice Radical Honesty

Write without filtering or judging your thoughts. Shadow journaling works best when you are brutally honest with yourself. Let go of the fear of what you might discover, knowing that awareness is the first step to growth.

Step 5: Reflect and Reframe

After journaling, take a moment to read what you've written. Ask yourself:

- What patterns or themes do I notice?

- How has this aspect of my shadow served or hindered me?

- How can I embrace this shadow in a way that aligns with my growth?

Practical Exercises for Shadow Journaling

1. "What I Hide from Others" Exercise

Divide a page into two columns:

- **Left column:** List the traits, habits, or emotions you hide from others.

- **Right column:** For each item, explore why you hide it. Does it stem from fear, shame, or societal pressure? What might happen if you embraced or shared this part of yourself?

2. "Mirror Moments" Reflection

Recall a recent situation where someone triggered a strong emotional reaction in you—anger, jealousy, frustration, or insecurity. Write about:

- What specifically upset you?

- Could this reaction reflect something within yourself that you haven't accepted?

For example, if you felt irritated by someone's arrogance, ask whether you struggle with self-confidence or fear appearing arrogant yourself.

3. "Dear Shadow" Letter

Write a letter to a part of yourself you've been avoiding or suppressing. For example:

- "Dear Perfectionist,"

- "Dear Insecure Self,"

Acknowledge its presence, express gratitude for how it has tried to protect you, and discuss how you'd like to work together moving forward.

4. "Rewriting the Narrative" Exercise

Identify a past mistake or failure that you frequently replay in your mind. Write about:

- What you learned from the experience.

- How this event shaped your character or values.

- What you would tell your younger self about this moment now.

Tips for Effective Shadow Journaling

1. **Be Patient:** Confronting your shadows can be uncomfortable. Progress might be slow, and that's okay.

2. **Practice Compassion:** Treat yourself with the same kindness you would offer a close friend.

3. **Incorporate Mindfulness:** Before journaling, try a few minutes of deep breathing or meditation to calm your mind and center your focus.

4. **Seek Support if Needed:** If shadow work unearths deep or painful emotions, consider discussing your findings with a trusted friend, mentor, or therapist.

Shadow journaling is not about "fixing" yourself; it's about understanding and embracing all facets of your humanity. Your flaws, insecurities, and hidden emotions are not burdens to eliminate—they are parts of your story that deserve compassion and integration.

As you explore your shadows, remember that the process itself is an act of courage. By shining a light into your inner depths, you pave the way for transformation, authenticity, and growth. Each shadow you acknowledge brings you closer to becoming a fully realized version of yourself.

Action Steps: Create a "Forgiveness Letter" for Yourself or Others

Forgiveness is a transformative act. It's not about excusing harmful behavior or minimizing pain—it's about releasing the heavy burden of resentment, guilt, or regret that holds us back. Writing a "forgiveness letter" is one of the most powerful tools for achieving this release. Whether directed toward yourself or someone else, this process helps clarify emotions, acknowledge pain, and foster healing.

Forgiveness doesn't mean forgetting or condoning; it means choosing peace over prolonged suffering. Let's explore how to craft a forgiveness letter that can guide you toward emotional freedom and growth.

Why Write a Forgiveness Letter?

Forgiveness letters are therapeutic for several reasons:

1. **Clarity:** Writing helps organize complex emotions, allowing you to process what happened and how it affected you.

2. **Empowerment:** By taking control of your narrative, you shift from feeling powerless to feeling proactive in your healing.

3. **Emotional Release:** Putting your thoughts into words can provide a sense of closure, even if the person you're addressing never sees the letter.

4. **Self-Compassion:** If the letter is for yourself, it encourages you to let go of self-blame and treat yourself with kindness.

Steps to Write a Forgiveness Letter

1. Set the Stage

Find a quiet, comfortable place where you won't be interrupted. Gather your materials—a notebook or digital device—and center yourself with a few deep breaths.

2. Decide on the Recipient

- **If writing to yourself:** Reflect on past actions, mistakes, or decisions that you've been holding against yourself.

- **If writing to someone else:** Consider someone who has hurt you or someone toward whom you feel lingering resentment.

3. Reflect on the Hurt

Before writing, spend some time reflecting on the following:

- What exactly happened?

- How did it make you feel?

- How has holding onto this pain affected your life?

This reflection ensures that your letter is rooted in honesty and understanding.

4. Structure the Letter

Your forgiveness letter can be structured into three main parts:

I. Acknowledge the Hurt

Start by clearly stating what happened and how it made you feel. Use "I" statements to express your perspective without assigning blame.

For example:

- *"I felt betrayed when you didn't support me during a difficult time."*

- *"I regret the way I handled that situation and how it hurt the people around me."*

This step is about validating your emotions, not dismissing them.

II. Express Understanding

If possible, try to understand the reasons behind the actions (yours or the other person's). This doesn't mean justifying the behavior but recognizing the humanity in imperfection. For example:

- *"I understand that you were going through your own struggles and may not have realized how your actions affected me."*

- *"I recognize that I made that choice out of fear and insecurity, and I didn't know any better at the time."*

III. Grant Forgiveness

Conclude by expressing your decision to forgive. Be specific about what you're releasing and why. For example:

- *"I forgive you for the pain you caused me because I no longer want to carry this anger."*

- *"I forgive myself for making mistakes, knowing that I'm learning and growing every day."*

Sample Forgiveness Letters

Example 1: Forgiving Someone Else

Dear [Name],

I want to take a moment to express something that has weighed heavily on my heart. When [specific event] happened, I felt [describe emotions, e.g., hurt, betrayed, confused]. It left me questioning [describe impact, e.g., your self-worth, the relationship, etc.].

As I reflect on this, I've come to understand that we were both navigating our own challenges. I realize that [acknowledge their perspective, if possible]. This understanding doesn't erase the pain, but it helps me see the situation with more compassion.

Today, I choose to let go of the resentment I've been holding onto. I forgive you for [specific hurt], and I release myself from the grip of this pain. While I may never forget what happened, I want to move forward with a lighter heart.

Sincerely,
[Your Name]

Example 2: Forgiving Yourself

Dear Me,

I've been carrying the weight of [specific mistake or regret], and it's time to address it. When I [describe event or decision], I felt [describe emotions, e.g., ashamed, disappointed, guilty]. I've spent too much time replaying this moment, wondering how I could have acted differently.

But as I write this, I realize that I was doing the best I could with what I knew at the time. I acted out of [acknowledge your motivations, e.g., fear, confusion], and while the outcome wasn't ideal, it taught me valuable lessons about [describe insights gained].

Today, I choose to forgive myself. I release the guilt and self-judgment that have held me back. I am not defined by my mistakes; I am defined by how I grow from them. Moving forward, I will treat myself with the kindness and understanding I deserve.

With love,
[Your Name]

Practical Tips for Writing

1. **Write Freely:** Don't worry about grammar, spelling, or structure. Focus on expressing yourself honestly.

2. **Take Breaks:** If the process becomes overwhelming, pause and return when you're ready.

3. **Be Patient:** Forgiveness is a journey, not a one-time act. Writing the letter is a step in the right direction, but healing takes time.

4. **Decide Whether to Send It:** Most forgiveness letters are for your own healing, not necessarily to be shared. However, if you feel that sharing it with the recipient will bring closure, ensure that the timing and context are appropriate.

Post-Letter Reflection

After writing your forgiveness letter, take a moment to reflect:

- How do you feel now compared to before you started writing?

- What insights did you gain from this process?

- How can you carry this sense of release and understanding into your daily life?

Consider creating a ritual to mark the completion of your forgiveness letter. For instance, you might fold it and store it in a meaningful place, shred it to symbolize release, or burn it as a gesture of letting go.

Forgiveness isn't about forgetting the hurt; it's about choosing freedom over pain. Writing a forgiveness letter is an act of courage and self-compassion, allowing you to reclaim your energy and focus on growth. Whether forgiving yourself or others, this practice can be a profound step toward healing and peace.

Remember, forgiveness is not a sign of weakness—it's a testament to your strength and resilience. Through this process, you're not only transforming your relationship with the past but also forging a brighter, more empowered future.

Mindfulness practice leads to increases in regional brain gray matter density

The study *Mindfulness Practice Leads to Increases in Regional Brain Gray Matter Density* by Hölzel et al. uncovers something fascinating: meditation doesn't just alter how we think—it physically reshapes our brains. Specifically, mindfulness practices have been shown to increase gray matter density in areas of the brain associated with learning, emotional regulation, and self-awareness. This discovery resonates deeply with my experiences practicing *Naikan* and other reflective traditions during my recovery in Japan.

I remember one quiet morning in the hospital when I tried a basic meditation technique introduced by a visiting counselor. She suggested simply focusing on my breath, observing thoughts without judgment, and gently returning to the present moment when my mind wandered. It sounded straightforward, but as I sat there, it became clear how chaotic my thoughts had been—endless loops of frustration, regret, and fear about the future. This initial attempt was both humbling and eye-opening. Over time, I began to notice subtle changes. My focus improved, I was less reactive to minor frustrations, and I felt a growing sense of calm, even in difficult moments.

What struck me later, after learning about this study, was the idea that these changes weren't just psychological—they were biological. Hölzel and her team used MRI scans to show that regular mindfulness practice increases gray matter density in the hippocampus (involved in learning and memory) and the prefrontal cortex (key for self-awareness and decision-making). This aligns with the shifts I felt in my ability to process emotions and reflect more deeply. It wasn't that the challenges I faced had disappeared—it was that I had a new capacity to engage with them thoughtfully rather than react impulsively.

This understanding dovetails with the principles of *Naikan*. When practicing *Naikan*, I often reflected on the three foundational questions: *What have I received? What have I given? What troubles have I caused others?* These aren't easy questions—they require honesty, vulnerability, and the willingness to confront both the good and the bad. Yet, I found that the act of sitting with these reflections had a grounding effect, similar to my experiences with mindfulness. There's a deliberate stillness that allows the mind to process not just what's happening in the present, but how past actions, relationships, and events weave into the larger story of one's life.

Hölzel's study highlights why these practices feel so transformative. The structural changes in the brain, particularly in the anterior cingulate cortex and the amygdala, explain the improved ability to manage emotions and approach life with a sense of clarity. For example, the anterior cingulate cortex, which plays a role in decision-making and emotional regulation, becomes more robust with mindfulness practice. This might be why I found myself less consumed by frustration during my recovery and more able to appreciate small moments of connection or progress.

Interestingly, the study also discusses the reduction of amygdala activation—a part of the brain often associated with fear and stress responses. This made me reflect on how *Naikan* and mindfulness both shift focus outward, from self-centered worries to a broader understanding of one's role in a network of relationships. By cultivating gratitude and accountability through *Naikan*, I was also retraining my brain to respond to challenges with less fear and more composure.

One key insight from the study is that these changes don't happen overnight. Much like the forging of a katana, where repeated hammering and tempering gradually shape raw steel into a balanced blade, the benefits of mindfulness and reflective practices accumulate through consistent effort. In my own journey, this was a reminder to embrace patience—not just with the practice itself, but with the process of personal growth.

Perhaps what I appreciated most about *Naikan* and mindfulness, supported by Hölzel's findings, is how they encourage a shift from passive reaction to active engagement with life. They teach us that transformation isn't about escaping challenges but about reshaping how we meet them—by building mental resilience, fostering curiosity, and cultivating deeper awareness. In doing so, they illuminate the path to genuine learning and growth, both within and beyond the brain's structure.

CHAPTER NINE

THE GIFT OF ROCK BOTTOM

The journey of confronting our shadows, of facing those uncomfortable truths about ourselves, can sometimes lead us to a place we never anticipated: rock bottom. It's that point where the ground seems to crumble beneath our feet, and we're left feeling lost and vulnerable. But what if this very experience, as daunting as it seems, held the potential for profound transformation?

Rock bottom is a place no one ever plans to visit. It's the moment when the ground crumbles beneath you, leaving nothing but a void of uncertainty. Yet, within that emptiness, a strange and profound clarity can emerge—a clarity I witnessed firsthand during my time in a Japanese hospital.

It was late in the afternoon when I first met Mrs. Sato, a woman in her sixties undergoing treatment for advanced cancer. She was frail, her frame almost swallowed by the oversized hospital robe. Yet, when I stepped into her room, her presence felt larger than life. Her eyes held an unshakable calm that seemed to radiate across the sterile walls of the ward.

Mrs. Sato wasn't alone in her battle. Her daughter visited daily, and the nurses—efficient yet compassionate—attended to her with a quiet reverence. Despite the grim prognosis, Mrs. Sato's demeanor was far from defeated. She greeted every visitor with a warm smile, her voice soft yet steady.

I couldn't help but wonder: How does one face such adversity with so much grace?

The Fall and the Foundation

As I got to know Mrs. Sato, she shared snippets of her life story. She'd been through what she described as her "real" rock bottom decades before her illness—a period of financial ruin after her husband's business collapsed. She spoke of the nights she cried herself to sleep, unsure of how to feed her young daughter or keep a roof over their heads.

"What changed?" I asked her one afternoon, genuinely curious about the resilience she seemed to embody.

She smiled faintly, looking out the window toward the garden below. "I stopped fighting the fall," she said. "When you hit the bottom, there's no further to go. All you can do is look up and decide how to rise."

Mrs. Sato explained how that period of despair became the foundation for a life rebuilt with intention. She took small steps: selling handmade crafts, leaning on friends, and accepting help when it was offered. It wasn't easy, and the scars of that time lingered, but those scars, she said, were a testament to her survival.

In Japan, there's a cultural acceptance of hardship that contrasts starkly with the Western tendency to avoid or mask pain. Concepts like *mono no aware*—an appreciation for the impermanence of life—and *wabi-sabi*—finding beauty in imperfection—infuse Japanese culture with a sense of resilience. This mindset doesn't glorify suffering but rather acknowledges it as an inevitable part of the human experience.

Mrs. Sato embodied these principles. Her illness had brought her to a second rock bottom, but instead of resisting it, she allowed herself to adapt and find meaning in the moments that remained. She taught me that rock bottom isn't just a place of despair; it's also a place of potential.

Rock bottom, while often associated with despair and defeat, can be a catalyst for profound change. It can be a turning point where we shed old patterns, beliefs, and attachments that no longer serve us, creating space for new growth and a more authentic way of being.

A Shared Moment of Strength

One afternoon, I walked into Mrs. Sato's room to find her daughter sitting by her side, holding her hand. They were laughing about something, their heads tilted close together. It was a scene of intimacy and love that felt almost sacred.

"What are you laughing about?" I asked, smiling at the warmth between them.

Mrs. Sato looked at me and said, "I told her that if I'd known this hospital had such good pudding, I'd have come here sooner."

We all laughed, and in that moment, I realized something profound. Rock bottom isn't always about the external circumstances—it's about the inner decision to keep going, even when life seems unbearably hard. Mrs. Sato had found joy in the smallest things, not despite her situation but because she had chosen to embrace it fully.

As I reflect on Mrs. Sato's story, I see her as a living testament to the gift of rock bottom. It's a paradoxical gift, wrapped in pain and struggle, but one that offers the opportunity to rebuild, redefine, and rise.

Rock bottom forces you to confront what truly matters. It strips away the superficial and demands honesty, courage, and vulnerability. It's not a place anyone wants to be, but for those who find themselves there, it can become the starting point for a life of deeper meaning and authenticity.

Navigating rock bottom requires resilience—the ability to bounce back from adversity. It also calls for acceptance—acknowledging the reality of the situation without judgment. And perhaps most importantly, it's about finding strength in vulnerability—allowing ourselves to lean on others and ask for help when needed. By embracing these qualities, we can transform the experience of hitting rock bottom into a powerful opportunity for growth and self-discovery.

Mrs. Sato's journey reminded me that resilience isn't about avoiding the fall—it's about finding the strength to rise after the impact. In her quiet acceptance and determination, I saw the true essence of human spirit, and I carried that lesson with me long after I left the hospital.

Why Hitting Bottom is a Starting Point

There's a saying in Japanese: *Nana korobi ya oki*—"Fall seven times, rise eight." It speaks to the resilience embedded in the human spirit, the ability to rise after each fall. But what happens when the fall is so deep it feels impossible to get up? What happens when you hit rock bottom?

Surprisingly, for many, rock bottom becomes the foundation for profound transformation. In the depths of despair, we confront truths we might otherwise ignore. We shed the weight of pretenses and discover the raw strength needed to rebuild. As paradoxical as it sounds, rock bottom is not an end—it is a beginning.

The Clarity of Hitting Bottom

Rock bottom strips away the noise of life. It clears the distractions, revealing the essence of what truly matters. When you've lost a job, a relationship, or even your sense of identity, the superficial concerns—status, appearances, fleeting comforts—fall away. What remains is raw and often painful, but it is also real.

Consider the story of John, a man who had built his entire identity around his high-paying corporate job. He drove the latest car, lived in an upscale apartment, and outwardly seemed to have it all. But when a sudden economic downturn left him unemployed, his carefully constructed world collapsed.

At first, John was consumed by shame and anger. He blamed himself, the economy, and even his colleagues. But as the months wore on, he began to reflect deeply on his life. He realized he had spent years chasing external validation while neglecting his relationships and passions. With no job to distract him, he reconnected with his love for painting—a hobby he had abandoned in his twenties.

What began as a way to pass time eventually turned into a thriving career as an artist. Today, John describes losing his job as the best thing that ever happened to him. "It forced me to face myself," he said. "And I discovered a version of me I actually like."

Transformation Through Hardship

Hardship has a way of forcing growth in ways comfort never can. In Japan, there's a cultural appreciation for the beauty that can emerge from adversity. The art of *kintsugi*—repairing broken pottery with gold—reflects this philosophy. The cracks, rather than being hidden, are highlighted, turning the object's history of breakage into something unique and beautiful.

One such story comes from Naomi, a single mother in rural Japan who lost everything in a devastating earthquake. Her home was reduced to rubble, and she and her two children lived in a temporary shelter for months. It was during this time that Naomi discovered a strength she didn't know she possessed.

Determined to rebuild her life, she began volunteering at the shelter, helping others who had lost even more than she had. Over time, this led to a job coordinating disaster relief efforts, and eventually, she started a nonprofit focused on community resilience. Naomi's experience of hitting bottom became the foundation for a life dedicated to making a difference.

"Before the earthquake, I thought my life was set," she said. "I didn't realize how much I could grow until I had no choice but to start over."

The Turning Point

The pivotal moment at rock bottom is often a choice: to stay down or to rise. It's a decision to face the pain head-on and transform it into something meaningful. This turning point doesn't happen overnight. It requires time, reflection, and the willingness to embrace discomfort.

One of the most powerful examples of this comes from Viktor Frankl, a psychiatrist and Holocaust survivor. In his memoir *Man's Search for Meaning*, Frankl recounts how, even in the unthinkable suffering of a concentration camp, he found meaning by focusing on his purpose—helping others and holding onto the vision of reuniting with his wife.

Frankl's experience highlights a universal truth: Even in the darkest moments, we have the power to choose how we respond. Rock bottom, while excruciating, offers the clarity to make that choice.

Finding Strength in Vulnerability

Hitting bottom also teaches us the value of vulnerability. In our lowest moments, we often rely on the support of others. Asking for help, admitting struggles, and accepting kindness require courage. Yet, these acts of vulnerability can forge deeper connections and remind us that we're not alone.

Take the story of Sara, a woman who spiraled into debt after her small business failed. For months, she hid her struggles from her friends and family, ashamed of her perceived failure. But when she finally opened up, she was met with unexpected support. Her friends helped her find a financial counselor, and her parents offered her a temporary place to stay while she rebuilt her life.

Sara's rock bottom became a lesson in humility and connection. "I thought admitting failure would make people respect me less," she said. "But it actually brought me closer to the people who cared about me."

When you've been at rock bottom, you gain a perspective that others may never understand. You learn to appreciate the small victories—a kind word, a moment of peace, a step forward. You also develop a resilience that comes from knowing you've survived the worst.

This perspective is what makes stories of transformation so inspiring. They remind us that adversity, while painful, is not permanent. It is a chapter, not the entire story.

Practical Steps: Creating a "Rock-Bottom Toolkit"

When life's challenges bring you to your lowest point, having tools to navigate the darkness can make all the difference. A "rock-bottom toolkit" is a collection of coping mechanisms, strategies, and support systems that help you endure, heal, and ultimately rise stronger. Building this toolkit is about preparation, self-awareness, and the willingness to lean on resources when needed.

1. Identify Your Emotional Anchors

During times of crisis, emotions can feel overwhelming. Having specific practices or reminders that ground you can help regain stability.

- **Journaling:** Writing down your thoughts and feelings can bring clarity and reduce emotional intensity. Use prompts like, "What am I feeling right now?" or "What do I need to release?"

- **Breathing Exercises:** Deep breathing signals to your brain that it's safe to calm down. Try box breathing—inhale for four counts, hold for four counts, exhale for four counts, and hold again.

- **Affirmations or Mantras:** Choose grounding phrases such as, "This is temporary," or "I have the strength to get through this."

2. Build a Support Network

One of the hardest parts of hitting rock bottom is feeling isolated. A strong support network reminds you that you're not alone.

- **Friends and Family:** Identify a few trusted people you can turn to for emotional support. Be honest with them about your struggles and needs.

- **Professional Help:** Therapy or counseling can be invaluable for processing emotions and finding new perspectives.

- **Community Groups:** Whether it's a support group, faith-based organization, or hobby club, being part of a community fosters connection and belonging.

Action Step: Write down three people you can call when you feel overwhelmed and commit to reaching out to at least one during tough times.

3. Develop Healthy Coping Mechanisms

Unhealthy coping, like numbing with alcohol or avoidance, may provide short-term relief but worsens long-term pain. Your toolkit should include healthier alternatives.

- **Physical Activity:** Exercise releases endorphins, which can boost your mood. Even a 10-minute walk can make a difference.

- **Creative Outlets:** Painting, playing music, or even cooking can provide an emotional release.

- **Meditation:** Mindfulness practices help you stay present and reduce anxiety about the future or regret about the past.

4. Create a Self-Care Plan

Taking care of your basic needs may feel impossible when you're at rock bottom, but small acts of self-care can restore a sense of control.

- **Prioritize Sleep:** Sleep is crucial for mental resilience. Create a bedtime routine with calming activities like reading or listening to soothing music.

- **Nourish Your Body:** Focus on simple, balanced meals. If cooking feels daunting, keep healthy snacks like nuts or fruits on hand.

- **Hydrate:** Drinking water seems basic, but dehydration can worsen fatigue and irritability.

Action Step: Write down three self-care rituals you can commit to, even on your hardest days.

5. Find Meaning in Small Victories

At rock bottom, even the smallest win matters. Recognizing and celebrating these victories builds momentum for larger changes.

- **Set Micro-Goals:** Instead of focusing on major achievements, aim for manageable tasks like making your bed, calling a friend, or going outside for five minutes.

- **Keep a Gratitude Journal:** Write down one thing you're grateful for each day, no matter how small. This practice rewires your brain to notice the positive.

Example: When you're at your lowest, doing the laundry may feel monumental. Celebrate it. Acknowledge, "I showed up for myself today."

6. Establish Your Non-Negotiables

Your non-negotiables are the practices and boundaries you refuse to compromise, even in tough times. These are the anchors that keep you steady.

- **Daily Check-Ins:** Spend five minutes each day asking, "What do I need right now?"

- **Protected Time:** Reserve a specific time for yourself, whether it's a quiet morning walk or a nightly wind-down ritual.

- **Boundary Setting:** Learn to say no to commitments or people that drain you, even if it feels uncomfortable.

7. Embrace the Power of Perspective

Shifting your mindset during hardship is a cornerstone of resilience.

- **Reframe the Narrative:** Instead of seeing rock bottom as failure, view it as a turning point. Ask, "What can I learn from this?"

- **Visualization:** Picture yourself overcoming the challenge and moving toward a brighter future.

- **Inspirational Stories:** Read books or watch documentaries about others who've overcome adversity to remind yourself of what's possible.

8. Prepare for Future Challenges

Your rock-bottom toolkit isn't just for immediate recovery; it's a lifelong resource. The lessons you learn now will strengthen you for whatever comes next.

- **Document Your Journey:** Keep a journal of what worked for you during this time. It can become a guide for future hardships.

- **Regular Maintenance:** Revisit and update your toolkit as your life evolves.

- **Teach Others:** Sharing your strategies with friends or loved ones reinforces your own resilience.

Your Personalized Toolkit

As you work through these steps, take the time to personalize your rock-bottom toolkit. What works for one person might not work for another. The key is to build something that resonates with you and feels accessible, even in your darkest moments.

Example Toolkit:

1. Emotional Anchor: Breathing exercises and journaling.

2. Support Network: Three friends and a therapist.

3. Healthy Coping: Morning yoga and sketching.

4. Self-Care Plan: Eight hours of sleep, hydration, and simple meals.

5. Small Wins: List three accomplishments at the end of each day.

6. Non-Negotiables: One hour of "me time" daily.

PART IV:
IMPROVEMENT – KAIZEN

CHAPTER TEN

THE POWER OF SMALL CHANGES

Kaizen, a Japanese term meaning 'continuous improvement,' is a philosophy that emphasizes the power of small, consistent changes. It's about making gradual, incremental progress rather than seeking massive, overnight transformations. The beauty of Kaizen lies in its sustainability and accessibility—it's a mindset that anyone can adopt to improve any area of their life.

In the heart of a bustling factory on the outskirts of Osaka, there was a man named Mr. Tanaka, whose life revolved around the art of improvement. To the untrained eye, Mr. Tanaka's job seemed monotonous: he assembled small components for electronics, repeating the same motions every day. Yet, to him, each motion was a puzzle to solve, a step to refine.

Mr. Tanaka wasn't just assembling parts; he was perfecting a system. His obsession wasn't born from pressure or competition—it stemmed from pride in his craft. Each day, he asked himself the same question: *How can I do this better?*

The Kaizen Moment

One morning, while working at his station, Mr. Tanaka noticed something small: the time it took to reach for a particular tool added up over the day. To most, this would seem insignificant—a mere two seconds per task. But Mr. Tanaka understood the power of accumulation. If he could shave off those two seconds, he would save over 30 minutes across his shift.

Determined, he rearranged his workstation, placing frequently used tools within arm's reach. The change seemed minor, almost laughable, but the results were immediate. Not only did he finish his tasks faster, but he also felt a renewed sense of flow in his work.

When his supervisor noticed the improvement, Mr. Tanaka was asked to share his method. Soon, his small adjustment inspired other workers to assess their stations. A culture of continuous improvement spread across the factory, transforming its efficiency without a single major overhaul.

The key to Kaizen is to start small. Don't try to change everything at once. Instead, focus on making one small improvement at a time. This could be something as simple as drinking an extra glass of water each day, setting aside five minutes for mindfulness, or decluttering one corner of your desk. These small changes may seem insignificant at first, but they create a ripple effect, building momentum and leading to significant improvements over time.

The Ripple Effect

Mr. Tanaka's story illustrates the core of *kaizen*, a Japanese philosophy of continuous, incremental improvement. It's not about dramatic changes or sweeping innovations; it's about the small, consistent adjustments that compound over time.

Years later, Mr. Tanaka reflected on his career. He wasn't famous or wealthy, but his commitment to improvement had left a lasting impact. The factory he worked in became a model of efficiency, and his practices were adopted far beyond its walls. More importantly, Mr. Tanaka carried the principles of *kaizen* into his personal life, transforming his relationships, health, and happiness one small step at a time.

The story of Mr. Tanaka teaches us that the path to transformation doesn't require monumental efforts. Instead, it calls for consistent, intentional actions. Whether in a factory, a home, or a life, the smallest changes can lead to the biggest outcomes when pursued with patience and persistence.

As we delve into the power of small changes in this chapter, think of Mr. Tanaka and his relentless pursuit of efficiency. But the power of small changes isn't a passive phenomenon—it requires discipline. While starting small is important, it's equally important to maintain consistency and commitment to those small actions. This is where discipline comes in—the bridge between intention and action. In the next chapter, we'll explore how discipline can sustain the momentum created by Kaizen and lead to lasting transformation. His story is a reminder that no matter where you start, progress is always within reach—one small step at a time.

What is Kaizen? The Science and Art of Incremental Improvement

Kaizen, a Japanese term that translates to "continuous improvement," is more than a methodology—it's a mindset. Rooted in the words *kai* (change) and *zen* (good), Kaizen emphasizes small, consistent actions that compound over time to create meaningful transformation. Unlike dramatic overhauls, which can be intimidating and unsustainable, Kaizen encourages us to focus on manageable steps, creating a steady rhythm of progress.

The Origins of Kaizen

The concept of Kaizen emerged in post-World War II Japan as a response to the country's economic recovery challenges. During this period, Japanese businesses adopted principles from American productivity systems, such as the Plan-Do-Check-Act (PDCA) cycle, while integrating their cultural values of precision and mindfulness.

Toyota became one of the earliest and most prominent adopters of Kaizen, embedding it into their manufacturing processes. Workers on assembly lines were encouraged to identify inefficiencies and propose solutions, regardless of their position in the hierarchy. This approach not only improved productivity but also cultivated a sense of ownership and pride among employees.

Kaizen soon extended beyond factories, finding its place in healthcare, education, and personal development. Its core philosophy—that small, intentional improvements lead to significant change—resonated across disciplines.

The Science Behind Kaizen

At its core, Kaizen aligns with principles of behavioral science and neuropsychology. Here's how it works:

1. **Small Wins Build Momentum**

   When we set a goal that feels overwhelming, our brains often respond with resistance, activating the amygdala, the part of the brain responsible for fear and stress. Kaizen bypasses this response by breaking goals into tiny, achievable steps. Each small success triggers a dopamine release, reinforcing the behavior and encouraging us to take the next step.

For example, instead of committing to an hour-long workout, Kaizen suggests starting with five minutes of stretching. This minor action feels manageable and serves as a gateway to larger commitments over time.

2. **Neuroplasticity Through Repetition**

   The brain's ability to rewire itself, known as neuroplasticity, thrives on consistent practice. Kaizen leverages this by encouraging daily repetition of small actions. Over time, these actions form new neural pathways, turning once-daunting tasks into automatic habits.

3. The Power of Compound Interest

Kaizen operates on the principle of compound growth. Just as small financial investments grow exponentially over time, small improvements accumulate, leading to significant transformation. James Clear, author of *Atomic Habits*, explains this beautifully: improving by 1% every day results in a 37-fold improvement over a year.

Kaizen in Practice

Kaizen isn't limited to factories or organizations—it's a philosophy that can transform all areas of life.

- **In Health:** Instead of aiming to lose 20 pounds immediately, start by drinking an extra glass of water each day or taking a 10-minute walk.

- **In Relationships:** Small acts of kindness, such as leaving a note of appreciation or spending five uninterrupted minutes with a loved one, can strengthen bonds over time.

- **In Work:** Focus on organizing one drawer of your desk rather than tackling the entire office in one go.

The beauty of Kaizen lies in its adaptability. Whether applied to personal goals or complex systems, the principles remain the same: start small, stay consistent, and trust the process.

The Art of Kaizen: Mindfulness Meets Progress

What sets Kaizen apart from other productivity methods is its emphasis on mindfulness. Unlike approaches that prioritize speed or output, Kaizen encourages us to be present in the process of improvement.

For instance, when reorganizing a workspace, Kaizen invites us to reflect on why each item belongs where it does. This attention to detail fosters a deeper connection to the task, transforming mundane activities into opportunities for growth and reflection.

Kaizen also teaches patience. In a world that glorifies quick fixes, it reminds us that true transformation takes time. The art of Kaizen lies in embracing the journey, knowing that each small step is part of a larger, meaningful process.

Kaizen as a Way of Life

At its heart, Kaizen is more than a tool for improvement—it's a philosophy for living. It challenges the notion that change has to be disruptive or overwhelming. Instead, it shows us that progress is always within reach, no matter how small the starting point.

By adopting the principles of Kaizen, we learn to celebrate small victories, cultivate resilience, and approach life with curiosity and purpose. In doing so, we transform not only our habits but also our mindset, unlocking the potential for continuous growth.

Exercises: Create a 1% Improvement Plan for One Area of Life

The philosophy of 1% improvement, deeply rooted in the Kaizen mindset, emphasizes making small, consistent changes that compound over time. Unlike drastic overhauls, this approach is manageable and sustainable, allowing you to build momentum and confidence in your ability to grow. This exercise will guide you in creating a 1% improvement plan for one area of your life—be it health, relationships, work, or personal growth.

Step 1: Choose One Area of Focus

To begin, select a single area of life where you want to see growth. By narrowing your focus, you channel your energy into a specific goal rather than spreading yourself too thin. Consider the following categories:

1. **Health:** Physical fitness, nutrition, sleep.

2. **Relationships:** Family, friendships, romantic connections.

3. **Career:** Productivity, skills, networking.

4. **Personal Growth:** Hobbies, education, mindfulness.

Exercise:
Write down the area you've chosen and why it matters to you.

- **Example:** "I want to focus on physical fitness because it will give me more energy and improve my mental well-being."

Step 2: Define Your Current Baseline

Understanding where you are now is crucial for tracking progress. Take a moment to reflect honestly on your current habits and routines in the chosen area.

Exercise:
Answer the following questions:

- What does my typical day look like in this area?

- What is working well?

- What are the challenges or barriers I face?

Example (Physical Fitness):

- **Current routine:** "I rarely exercise, and I sit for long periods during the day."

- **What's working:** "I walk to the grocery store a couple of times a week."

- **Challenges:** "I feel too tired after work to commit to a full workout."

Step 3: Visualize a 1% Improvement

Now, imagine what a 1% improvement would look like. It should feel small enough to be achievable but meaningful enough to make a difference over time.

Exercise:
Brainstorm micro-changes you could make. Choose one that feels manageable.

- **Examples for Physical Fitness**
  1. Take the stairs instead of the elevator once a day.
  2. Add one extra glass of water to your daily routine.
  3. Stretch for five minutes before bed.

Write down your chosen micro-change.

- **Example:** "I will do 10 minutes of light stretching after work."

Step 4: Break It Down into Tiny Steps

Even a small goal can feel overwhelming without a clear path. Breaking it down into tiny, actionable steps makes it easier to follow through.

Exercise:
Create a checklist for your chosen micro-change.

- **Example (Stretching):**
  1. Choose a quiet space in my home.

2. Set a timer for 10 minutes.

3. Follow a simple stretching routine (e.g., neck rolls, forward folds).

By dividing the task into smaller actions, you reduce decision fatigue and increase the likelihood of success.

Step 5: Establish a Routine with Habit Stacking

To make your micro-change stick, attach it to an existing habit or routine. This is known as habit stacking, a powerful technique for embedding new behaviors.

Exercise:
Identify a habit you already perform daily and pair it with your micro-change.

- **Example:** "After I take off my shoes at the end of the day, I will spend 10 minutes stretching."

Write down your habit stack:

- **After I _____, I will _____.**

Step 6: Track and Reflect on Progress

Consistency is key to improvement. Tracking your progress not only reinforces the habit but also motivates you to keep going.

Exercise:
Choose a method to track your habit:

- Use a simple calendar to mark off each day you complete the habit.

- Use a habit-tracking app like Habitica or Streaks.

- Keep a journal to note how you feel after completing the task.

At the end of each week, reflect on your progress:

- What went well?

- What could be improved?

Step 7: Gradually Increase the Challenge

Once the initial micro-change feels easy and natural, you're ready to build on it. The beauty of 1% improvement is that each small win sets the stage for bigger changes.

Exercise:
Write down ways to increase the challenge slightly:

- If your goal is stretching for 10 minutes, extend it to 15 minutes after two weeks.

- If your goal is walking one extra block, aim for two blocks the following week.

Example: "I'll add one additional stretch to my routine every week."

Sample 1% Improvement Plans

Here are some examples of how this exercise could look for different areas:

Health: Better Nutrition

- **Micro-change:** Add one vegetable to your daily meals.

- **Steps:**

    1. Research simple vegetable recipes.

    2. Buy fresh or frozen veggies during weekly grocery shopping.

    3. Incorporate them into one meal daily.

- **Habit stack:** "After I plate my dinner, I will add a serving of vegetables."

Relationships: Strengthening Connections

- **Micro-change:** Send one thoughtful text or message to a friend each day.

- **Steps:**

    1. Make a list of friends you want to reconnect with.

    2. Choose one person each morning.

    3. Send a short but meaningful message.

- **Habit stack:** "After I drink my morning coffee, I will text a friend."

Work: Improving Productivity

- **Micro-change:** Plan your top three priorities for the day.

- **Steps:**

    1. Keep a small notebook or use a digital planner.

    2. Write down three tasks each morning.

    3. Review them at the end of the day.

- **Habit stack:** "After I check my email in the morning, I will list my top three priorities."

The 1% improvement approach is a reminder that meaningful change doesn't require dramatic leaps—it thrives on small, steady steps. By crafting and implementing your improvement plan, you're not just altering habits; you're building a mindset of growth and resilience.

What's one small change you can start today? Write it down, take action, and watch how these incremental shifts transform your life. The journey of a thousand miles truly begins with a single step—or, in this case, a single percent.

Small steps to significant change

The Harvard Business Review article *Small Steps to Significant Change* highlights a remarkable insight: making consistent, tiny improvements of just 1% daily can compound to a staggering 37x improvement over a year. This finding resonates deeply with the Japanese principle of *Kaizen*, which focuses on continuous, incremental progress rather than sweeping, dramatic change.

When I first came across this idea during my recovery, it felt counterintuitive. Like many people, I had grown up believing that real transformation required major effort and visible results. But as I began to observe *Kaizen* in action—through Japanese systems, culture, and even personal habits—it became clear that the magic lay in its simplicity and consistency.

One vivid example of this principle was watching how a nurse adjusted the hospital's daily routine. Instead of overhauling procedures all at once, she introduced tiny tweaks: repositioning tools for easier access, streamlining patient charts to reduce errors, and even suggesting small ergonomic changes to prevent staff fatigue. These adjustments, seemingly insignificant on their own, created noticeable improvements in efficiency and morale over time. What struck me was how natural and sustainable these changes were—there was no burnout or resistance because each step felt manageable.

Reflecting on my own life, I realized how often I had sabotaged myself by setting massive, unrealistic goals. After the accident, even the smallest tasks—like sitting upright or taking a few steps—felt monumental. But inspired by this principle, I started focusing on what I could improve by 1%. One day, it was extending my physiotherapy exercises by a single repetition. The next, it was holding a stretch a few seconds longer. Over weeks, these small efforts compounded into measurable progress.

The idea is deeply rooted in science, as highlighted in the HBR article. Small, consistent changes not only lead to long-term transformation but also bypass the brain's resistance to big shifts. When a goal feels too ambitious, our brain perceives it as a threat, triggering stress and avoidance. However, incremental changes keep us within our comfort zone, building confidence and momentum as we go. Each success, however small, reinforces the belief that change is possible—a critical factor in sustaining effort over time.

In the article, they also emphasize the concept of "positive compounding." Just as 1% improvements build over time, so too can 1% declines. It was a sobering reminder of how easy it is to slide backward when we neglect small habits. Missing one day of practice or indulging in one unhealthy choice may seem inconsequential, but over time, these actions accumulate just as powerfully. This duality makes *Kaizen* not just a method of improvement but a mindset of vigilance and self-awareness.

What I found most profound about *Kaizen* was its accessibility. You don't need special tools, enormous willpower, or perfect circumstances to begin. All it takes is asking: *What is one small thing I can improve today?* This approach transformed my recovery from overwhelming to achievable, one tiny step at a time. And as the article suggests, it's a strategy that works not only for personal growth but for organizations, relationships, and life as a whole.

Continuous Improvement: The Kaizen Stage

The **Kaizen** stage represents a commitment to continuous, incremental improvement in every aspect of life. Derived from the Japanese words "kai" (change) and "zen" (good), Kaizen is not about dramatic overhauls but the small, consistent steps that lead to significant, sustainable transformation. This stage embodies the essence of progress, encouraging you to refine your habits, skills, and mindset day by day.

Stage Recognition

Recognizing when you're in the Kaizen stage is vital to making the most of its opportunities. This stage often follows Naikan, as the clarity gained from self-reflection drives a desire for purposeful, meaningful change.

- **Key Indicators:**

    - Feeling motivated to make improvements but unsure where to start.

    - A growing awareness of small, inefficient habits or patterns.

    - A desire for consistent growth rather than quick fixes.

- **Behavioral Patterns:**

    - Taking incremental actions to improve your skills, relationships, or daily routines.

    - Monitoring progress through journaling, checklists, or habit trackers.

    - Focusing on process-oriented goals rather than outcome-driven ones.

- **Relationship Dynamics:**

  - Strengthened connections through small, thoughtful acts of support or kindness.

  - A shift toward collaboration and mutual growth with those around you.

Self-Assessment Exercise:

- Ask yourself:

  - What area of my life feels stagnant or inefficient?

  - What small changes could I make to improve it?

  - How can I break larger goals into manageable steps?

Stage Completion Markers

Completing the Kaizen stage involves mastering the art of incremental progress and recognizing the profound impact of small changes:

- **Mindset Shifts:**

  - Believing that growth is a journey rather than a destination.

  - Embracing failure as a natural part of the improvement process.

- **Behavioral Changes:**

  - Establishing consistent routines that align with your goals.

  - Celebrating small wins while maintaining focus on long-term progress.

- **Emotional Milestones:**
  - Developing patience and resilience during setbacks.
  - Feeling more confident in your ability to create meaningful change.
- **Relationship Developments:**
  - Inspiring others through your dedication to steady improvement.
  - Building deeper trust and reliability in relationships.

Next Stage Preparation

Kaizen naturally transitions into **Omoiyari**, the stage of compassion, as your personal growth enables you to contribute positively to others. Signs you're ready to move forward include:

- **Internal Signals:**
  - A sense of fulfillment from your progress and a desire to share it with others.
  - Growing awareness of how your actions impact those around you.
- **Transition Challenges:**
  - Balancing self-improvement with external responsibilities.
  - Avoiding perfectionism or becoming overly critical of yourself.
- **Preparation Exercises:**

- **Reflect on Impact:** Consider how your growth benefits others and identify ways to extend that impact.

- **Collaborative Goals:** Partner with a friend or mentor on a small improvement project, fostering mutual growth.

Regression Warnings

While Kaizen emphasizes steady progress, it's easy to fall back into old habits or become overwhelmed by setbacks. Be mindful of these signs:

- **Early Warning Signs:**
  - Losing motivation due to impatience with results.
  - Overcommitting to too many changes at once.

- **Common Triggers:**
  - Stressful life events that disrupt routines.
  - Negative feedback or perceived failure in your efforts.

- **Stages to Avoid Regressing To:**
  - Retreating to passivity or avoidance (Shikata ga nai).
  - Falling into complacency and surface-level stability (Genki).

- **Recovery Practices:**
  - Revisit your original goals and break them into smaller steps.
  - Seek encouragement from supportive friends or mentors.

Stage Integration

The lessons of Kaizen extend beyond this stage, becoming a lifelong approach to growth and adaptability.

- **Building on Progress:**
  - Continuously apply the principle of small improvements to new challenges and opportunities.
  - Share your strategies and insights with others, fostering a culture of growth.

- **Sustaining Momentum:**
  - Regularly review and update your goals to stay aligned with your evolving priorities.
  - Use setbacks as learning experiences rather than reasons to give up.

- **Integration Exercise:**
  - Identify one habit you've successfully improved and reflect on its impact. Consider how you can apply the same method to another area of your life.

Kaizen teaches that even the smallest changes can yield profound results when practiced consistently. As you embrace this stage, you'll find that the journey itself becomes the reward—a continual process of growth, learning, and self-discovery. With each step forward, you not only transform yourself but also create ripples of positive change in the world around you.

CHAPTER ELEVEN
DISCIPLINE OVER MOTIVATION

In our pursuit of continuous improvement, of refining our habits and actions through Kaizen, we often encounter a crucial bridge that carries us from intention to lasting change: discipline. Discipline is the steady force that sustains the momentum created by small changes, ensuring that those incremental improvements blossom into significant transformations.

I remember the first time I watched a traditional Japanese martial arts practice. It wasn't a grand tournament or an exhibition—just a quiet dojo in Kyoto where students trained under their sensei's watchful eye. The air smelled faintly of polished wood and sweat, and the only sounds were the soft shuffle of bare feet on the tatami mats and the occasional sharp crack of a bokken—wooden practice sword—meeting its mark.

At the center of it all stood a martial artist, perhaps in his late forties. He wasn't the tallest or the most imposing figure in the room, but there was something magnetic about him. His movements were precise and controlled, each strike deliberate, each stance unwavering. Unlike some of the younger students, who occasionally stole glances at the clock or wiped their brows in exhaustion, this man moved as though time and fatigue didn't exist.

As the session ended and the students bowed to their sensei, I struck up a conversation with him. Curious about what drove him to practice with such unwavering dedication, I asked, "How do you stay so motivated?"

He smiled, almost amused by my question. "Motivation?" he said, shaking his head. "Motivation is fleeting. Some days, you feel it; some days, you don't. Discipline is what keeps you going. It's not about feeling like it. It's about showing up, no matter what."

His words stayed with me, challenging my own assumptions about what it takes to achieve mastery or accomplish meaningful goals. Like many people, I'd often relied on bursts of inspiration to kickstart new habits or tackle difficult tasks. But here was someone who embodied the idea that the key to success wasn't in waiting for motivation to strike—it was in building a foundation of discipline that made action inevitable.

Discipline acts as the bridge between the initial spark of motivation and the consistent action required for true growth. While motivation might ignite the fire within us, it's discipline that provides the steady fuel, ensuring that the flames don't die down when faced with challenges or distractions. It's the unwavering commitment to showing up, even when we don't feel like it, that sets the stage for lasting change.

The Quiet Power of Discipline

Discipline isn't flashy. It doesn't come with the adrenaline rush of a motivational speech or the dopamine hit of a New Year's resolution. Instead, it's like the steady beat of a drum, setting the rhythm for consistent action, day after day.

Watching that martial artist train reminded me that discipline is a choice—a series of small, daily decisions to prioritize long-term goals over short-term comforts. While motivation might push you to start something, discipline is what ensures you finish.

The Japanese concept of **shugyo**, often translated as "austere training," embodies this idea. In martial arts, shugyo isn't about mastering techniques quickly; it's about enduring the process, embracing the grind, and finding meaning in the repetition. Whether it's practicing the same kata (sequence of movements) hundreds of times or sitting in zazen (seated meditation) for hours, shugyo teaches that growth comes from perseverance, not passion.

The lesson of discipline isn't confined to the dojo. It applies to every aspect of life, from work to relationships to personal development. Think about the tasks you find hardest to stick with—exercising regularly, eating healthily, or staying focused at work. Often, the problem isn't that you don't care about these things; it's that you're waiting to feel motivated to act on them.

But here's the truth: motivation is unreliable. It's tied to emotion, and emotions are fickle. One bad day, one moment of doubt, and your motivation can vanish. Discipline, on the other hand, is like a muscle. The more you use it, the stronger it becomes.

Consider how the martial artist I met approached his training. He didn't rely on excitement or enthusiasm to fuel his practice. Instead, he had routines, rituals, and habits that made training a non-negotiable part of his day. When you build structures like these into your own life, discipline becomes less about willpower and more about creating an environment where the right actions are automatic.

The Danger of Over-Reliance on Motivation

One of the biggest myths in personal development is that you need to feel inspired to take action. While motivation can spark change, it often leads to a cycle of start-and-stop behavior. You feel motivated, make a big push, burn out, and then wait for motivation to return. This approach is not only inefficient but also demoralizing.

In contrast, discipline is steady and predictable. It acknowledges that some days will be harder than others, but it also ensures that progress continues, no matter how small. Over time, the consistent effort fueled by discipline often outpaces the erratic bursts of motivation.

Building Discipline: Lessons from Martial Arts

The martial artist's practice offered several insights into cultivating discipline:

1. **Commit to Showing Up:** The first step in building discipline is consistency. Whether it's going to the gym, writing for 30 minutes, or meditating, the act of showing up—even imperfectly—builds momentum.

2. **Embrace Repetition:** Mastery comes from doing the same thing over and over again. Repetition might feel tedious, but it strengthens neural pathways, making the action second nature.

3. **Focus on Process, Not Outcomes:** Discipline thrives when you prioritize the journey over the destination. Instead of fixating on the results you want, focus on the daily actions that will get you there.

4. **Build Rituals and Routines:** Like the warm-ups and cooldowns in martial arts training, rituals signal to your brain that it's time to engage in a specific activity.

5. **Practice Self-Compassion:** Discipline doesn't mean being harsh on yourself. Just as a martial artist learns from mistakes, you can use setbacks as opportunities to grow rather than reasons to quit.

When I left the dojo that evening, I felt a newfound respect for the quiet, enduring power of discipline. Watching the martial artist train reminded me that transformation isn't about dramatic breakthroughs—it's about the quiet, unglamorous work of showing up every day.

In your own journey, ask yourself: Are you relying on fleeting bursts of motivation, or are you building the discipline to keep moving forward? The choice to act, even when it's hard, is what sets the truly resilient apart.

And it's through these small, disciplined actions that momentum is born—a force that propels us forward on the path toward mastery and long-term growth. Just as a katana is sharpened through the disciplined repetition of honing, we too refine our skills, habits, and character through the consistent practice of discipline. This is how we transform intentions into reality and create a life of purpose and fulfillment.

As the martial artist told me before I left, "The blade is forged in fire, but it's sharpened through discipline. Without it, even the strongest steel is useless." This unwavering dedication showcased the power of discipline – a force far more enduring than fleeting motivation.

Why Discipline Outlasts Motivation

Motivation and discipline are often seen as two sides of the same cBoin, but they serve fundamentally different roles in personal growth and achievement. While motivation is the spark that ignites action, discipline is the steady flame that keeps it burning. Understanding why discipline outlasts motivation is key to building a life where progress isn't left to chance but becomes a predictable outcome of your daily habits.

Motivation is emotional by nature. It can come from external sources like an inspiring speech, a moving story, or the excitement of starting something new. Internal motivation might arise from a desire to improve, achieve a goal, or overcome a challenge.

The problem? Motivation is unreliable.

Think about how many times you've started a project or a fitness routine fueled by the energy of motivation. In the beginning, you're eager and optimistic. But as the novelty wears off and obstacles arise, that initial excitement fades. Motivation fluctuates because it depends on factors like mood, environment, and external rewards—all of which can change daily.

For example, you might feel motivated to wake up early and exercise after watching a video about the benefits of fitness. But what happens when your alarm goes off, and it's cold outside, or you didn't sleep well? In that moment, motivation often vanishes, leaving you with a choice: act or stay in bed.

This is where discipline steps in.

Discipline: The Steady Flame

Discipline is not an emotion; it's a decision. It's the ability to act regardless of how you feel in the moment. While motivation relies on inspiration, discipline thrives on commitment and structure.

Discipline doesn't ask, "Do I feel like it?" It simply says, "This is what I do."

Consider an athlete training for a marathon. They don't rely on motivation to complete every run, especially on days when they're tired or the weather is bad. Instead, they follow a training plan, trusting the process even when it's difficult. Over time, this consistency builds strength, endurance, and confidence—results that motivation alone could never achieve.

Why Discipline Wins

1. **Discipline Creates Consistency**

   Motivation comes and goes, but discipline builds a routine. When you rely on discipline, your actions become habits. Habits don't require willpower—they're automatic, like brushing your teeth or locking the door when you leave home. This consistency is what leads to long-term success.

2. **Discipline Builds Resilience**

   Motivation is often tied to positive emotions, but life isn't always positive. Discipline equips you to push through hard days, setbacks, and failures. It teaches you to embrace discomfort and stay focused on your goals, even when circumstances aren't ideal.

3. **Discipline Fosters Self-Trust**

   Every time you follow through on a commitment, you reinforce your belief in yourself. This self-trust becomes a powerful motivator, creating a positive feedback loop. You don't need to rely on external inspiration because you know you can depend on your own discipline.

4. **Discipline Prioritizes Long-Term Goals**

   Motivation is often short-term—it's easy to feel motivated to achieve a small win or avoid an immediate problem. Discipline, on the other hand, aligns your actions with your long-term values and goals. It keeps you moving forward, even when progress is slow or invisible.

Science of Discipline

Research in psychology highlights why discipline is more sustainable than motivation.

- **The Habit Loop**: In his book *The Power of Habit*, Charles Duhigg explains how habits form through a loop of cue, routine, and reward. Discipline helps establish this loop, ensuring that positive behaviors are repeated until they become second nature.

- **Delayed Gratification**: Studies like the famous Marshmallow Test show that people who can delay gratification—choosing long-term rewards over immediate pleasures—tend to achieve more success in life. Discipline strengthens this ability by training the brain to focus on the bigger picture.

- **Neuroplasticity**: Discipline rewires the brain by creating new neural pathways. Repeated actions strengthen these pathways, making disciplined behavior easier over time. Motivation might start this process, but discipline sustains it.

Practical Examples

1. **Fitness**: Many people start exercising because they feel motivated to get fit. However, those who succeed in maintaining a fitness routine often rely on discipline—committing to workouts even when they're tired or busy. Over time, this discipline turns into a habit, and the question of "Should I exercise today?" disappears.

2. **Work**: Writers, artists, and entrepreneurs often talk about the importance of showing up every day, regardless of inspiration. As novelist William Faulkner famously said, "I only write when inspiration strikes. Fortunately, it strikes at nine every morning."

3. **Personal Growth**: Imagine someone trying to build mindfulness through meditation. In the beginning, they might feel motivated by the promise of reduced stress. But as they sit down to meditate day after day, it's discipline—not motivation—that keeps them going, especially when results aren't immediate.

Building Discipline

So how do you cultivate discipline in your own life?

1. **Start Small**: Discipline doesn't mean overhauling your life overnight. Begin with small, manageable actions, like drinking a glass of water every morning or setting a timer for 10 minutes of focused work.

2. **Create Routines**: Build structures that make disciplined behavior automatic. For example, if you want to exercise more, lay out your workout clothes the night before or schedule workouts at the same time every day.

3. **Focus on Process**: Shift your attention from outcomes to actions. Instead of obsessing over losing 10 pounds, focus on eating a healthy meal today.

4. **Track Progress**: Use tools like habit trackers or journals to celebrate small wins. Seeing your consistency in action reinforces discipline and motivates you to keep going.

5. **Be Patient**: Building discipline takes time. Don't expect perfection—just aim to be better today than you were yesterday.

Motivation might inspire you to start, but discipline ensures you finish. It's the bridge between where you are and where you want to be. By cultivating discipline, you create a foundation of consistent action that outlasts the highs and lows of emotion.

As the Japanese martial artist reminded me, "Motivation can be fickle, but discipline is your true ally. It's not about how you feel—it's about what you've committed to becoming."

Practical Tips: Habit Stacking, Accountability Systems, and Removing Barriers

Discipline is built on consistency, and consistency thrives when supported by practical systems. By incorporating habit stacking, accountability systems, and removing barriers, you create an environment where disciplined action becomes not only achievable but also sustainable. Let's explore how each of these strategies can help you cultivate the kind of discipline that endures.

Habit Stacking: Building New Habits onto Existing Routines

Habit stacking is a method introduced by James Clear in *Atomic Habits*. It involves attaching a new habit to an existing one, leveraging the structure of what you already do daily. This approach simplifies creating new routines because it integrates change into what's familiar.

How Habit Stacking Works

The basic formula for habit stacking is:

After [current habit], I will [new habit].

This creates a mental link between the two behaviors, making the new habit easier to remember and perform.

Examples of Habit Stacking

- **Health**: After I brush my teeth, I will do 10 squats.

- **Productivity**: After I pour my morning coffee, I will write down three priorities for the day.

- **Mindfulness**: After I sit down at my desk, I will take three deep breaths.

Why It Works

Habit stacking capitalizes on the brain's ability to create associations. By tying the new habit to something you already do without thinking, you bypass the need for motivation or reminders. Over time, the stacked habit becomes as automatic as the original one.

Accountability Systems: Staying on Track with Support

Discipline can feel isolating if you think you're entirely on your own. Accountability systems introduce external checks that keep you motivated and consistent, even when your internal drive wanes.

Types of Accountability Systems

1. **Accountability Partners**: Pair up with someone who shares similar goals or who can act as a mentor. Check in regularly to share progress, setbacks, and plans.

   o Example: Commit to exercising three times a week with a friend who can join you or at least check in to ensure you follow through.

2. **Public Commitments**: Announce your goals to a group or on social media. The fear of disappointing others can be a powerful motivator.

   o Example: Share your intention to complete a 30-day fitness challenge online.

3. **Professional Support**: Work with a coach, therapist, or mentor who can provide guidance, encouragement, and constructive feedback.

4. **Accountability Tools**: Use apps and trackers designed to keep you on course.

   o Example: Apps like Habitica gamify habits by rewarding consistent behavior with points and challenges.

The Role of Positive Pressure

Accountability systems introduce a layer of positive pressure, encouraging you to follow through because someone else is invested in your success. Knowing that you're not working toward your goals in isolation can make a significant difference.

Removing Barriers: Simplify the Path to Action

Sometimes, the biggest obstacle to discipline is friction—anything that makes it harder to take action. Removing barriers clears the way, making the disciplined choice the easiest one.

Common Barriers to Discipline

1. **Decision Fatigue**: Too many choices can lead to inaction.

2. **Procrastination**: Putting off tasks because they feel overwhelming or unpleasant.

3. **Environment**: Physical or mental clutter that distracts from your goals.

How to Remove Barriers

1. **Streamline Decisions**

- o Eliminate unnecessary choices by creating routines. For example, plan meals for the week or choose a specific time to work on a project daily.

- o Example: Lay out your workout clothes the night before, so you don't have to decide what to wear in the morning.

2. **Break Down Tasks**

- o Large tasks can feel intimidating. Divide them into smaller, manageable steps.

- o Example: Instead of "write a book," start with "write 200 words today."

3. **Optimize Your Environment**

- o Design your space to encourage positive habits and discourage distractions.

- o Example: Keep healthy snacks visible and easy to reach, while storing junk food out of sight.

4. **Automate When Possible**

- o Use technology to take care of repetitive tasks, freeing your mental energy for more important actions.

- o Example: Set up automatic bill payments to avoid late fees and unnecessary stress.

5. **Prepare for Obstacles**

- o Anticipate challenges and plan solutions in advance.

- o Example: If you're prone to skipping workouts when it's raining, create a backup plan for an indoor routine.

Combining These Strategies

For maximum effectiveness, combine habit stacking, accountability systems, and barrier removal. Here's how this might look in practice:

- **Goal**: Improve fitness by walking 10,000 steps daily.

  - **Habit Stacking**: After I finish breakfast, I will put on my walking shoes.

  - **Accountability System**: Share my step count with a friend every evening.

  - **Removing Barriers**: Keep my walking shoes near the door and set reminders on my phone.

Building discipline doesn't have to rely on willpower alone. By stacking habits, leveraging accountability systems, and removing barriers, you create an environment where success becomes the default. Each small action reinforces your commitment to your goals, turning discipline into a natural part of your daily life.

As the Japanese proverb says, "Even dust, when piled up, becomes a mountain." Small, consistent efforts, supported by practical strategies, lead to profound transformation over time.

Action Steps: Design a "Discipline Calendar"

Discipline thrives on clarity, consistency, and accountability. A "discipline calendar" is a tool that brings all three together, helping you visualize your progress and stay committed to your goals. Unlike a to-do list, which focuses on daily tasks, a discipline calendar tracks behaviors that contribute to long-term growth. It's not about perfection but about consistency and reflection.

Here's how to design a discipline calendar and make it a practical tool for your transformation journey.

Step 1: Define Your Focus Areas

Before creating your discipline calendar, identify the habits or behaviors you want to build. These should align with your larger goals and values. To avoid overwhelm, start with two or three areas of focus.

Examples of Focus Areas:

1. **Health**: Exercise, hydration, or consistent sleep.

2. **Work**: Daily deep work sessions or learning a new skill.

3. **Personal Development**: Journaling, meditation, or reading.

4. **Relationships**: Regular check-ins with loved ones or expressing gratitude.

Tip: Choose habits that are specific and measurable. Instead of "be healthier," opt for "walk 30 minutes daily."

Step 2: Choose Your Format

Your discipline calendar can be digital, physical, or a mix of both. The key is accessibility—pick a format you'll interact with daily.

Popular Formats:

1. **Paper Planner or Journal**: Ideal for people who enjoy analog tools. Use a blank calendar template or create one in a notebook.

2. **Wall Calendar**: A large calendar on display keeps your goals visible and top of mind.

3. **Digital Tools**: Apps like Google Calendar, Notion, or habit-tracking apps like Habitica or Streaks can automate reminders and progress tracking.

Step 3: Break It Into Daily, Weekly, and Monthly Goals

Your discipline calendar should balance daily actions with longer-term milestones. Breaking it down helps you stay consistent without losing sight of the bigger picture.

Daily Goals:

- These are your non-negotiable habits.

- Example: Drink 8 glasses of water, write 500 words, or spend 10 minutes meditating.

Weekly Goals:

- Focus on habits that need less frequent attention.

- Example: Call a family member, declutter a room, or complete a training module.

Monthly Goals:

- Use these as checkpoints to measure progress and adjust as needed.

- Example: Evaluate fitness improvements or track progress in a learning project.

Step 4: Create a Tracking System

Your calendar should include a simple way to log whether you completed a habit or goal. This could be as straightforward as checking a box or coloring a square for each successful day.

Ideas for Tracking:

1. **Habit Tracker Grid**: Create a grid with days of the month along one axis and habits along the other. Mark each completed habit with a check, star, or colored dot.

2. **Color-Coded Calendar**: Assign a color to each habit and fill in the days you complete them. For example, blue for exercise, green for mindfulness, and yellow for learning.

3. **Streak Counters**: Track how many consecutive days you've maintained a habit. Apps often have this feature built-in.

Step 5: Add Motivational Elements

Make your discipline calendar a source of encouragement. Incorporate visuals or notes that inspire you to keep going.

Ideas for Motivation:

1. **Affirmations**: Write motivational quotes or personal affirmations on your calendar.

   o Example: "Small steps every day lead to big changes."

2. **Rewards**: Attach small rewards to milestones.

   o Example: Treat yourself to a favorite meal after completing a 30-day streak.

3. **Progress Notes**: Add a section to jot down how you feel after completing a habit.

Step 6: Reflect and Adjust

A discipline calendar isn't set in stone—it's a dynamic tool. Regular reflection ensures it evolves with your needs and goals.

Weekly Reflection:

- Review your calendar at the end of each week.

- Ask yourself:

    o Which habits were easy to maintain?

    o Where did I struggle?

    o What adjustments can I make for next week?

Monthly Reflection:

- Evaluate your overall progress and celebrate wins.

- Adjust habits or goals based on what's working and what's not.

Example: A Week in a Discipline Calendar

Focus Areas: Health, Productivity, Relationships

Day	Exercise	Deep Work	Gratitude Practice
Monday	✓	✓	✓
Tuesday	✓	✗	✓
Wednesday	✓	✓	✗
Thursday	✗	✓	✓
Friday	✓	✓	✓
Saturday	✗	✓	✓
Sunday	✓	✗	✓

At the end of the week, review the patterns. Perhaps you struggled with exercise mid-week or skipped deep work on weekends. Use this data to tweak your approach for the next week.

A discipline calendar isn't just a tool—it's a commitment to yourself. By designing a system that tracks your progress, motivates you, and adapts to your needs, you create a sustainable path to long-term growth.

Remember, discipline is a practice, not a destination. Celebrate your progress, learn from your setbacks, and keep moving forward. Over time, the consistent effort you document in your calendar will forge the resilience and strength needed to face life's challenges with confidence.

CHAPTER TWELVE
MOMENTUM THROUGH MASTERY

T hrough the consistent practice of discipline, as we commit to those small, intentional actions that pave the path of Kaizen, we begin to generate a powerful force: momentum. Momentum is the steady accumulation of positive energy that propels us forward, making our journey toward mastery feel not only achievable but also exhilarating. It's the fruit of our disciplined efforts, the tangible reward for showing up day after day, even when progress seemed slow or invisible.

In the serene corners of a Japanese garden, a bonsai tree sits quietly, its gnarled branches reaching out in miniature perfection. It's easy to marvel at its delicate beauty, but what's less obvious is the story of patience and mastery that shaped it. Every curve of its trunk, every twist of its branches, was guided by years—sometimes decades—of dedicated care. The tree wasn't rushed, nor was its growth left to chance. Instead, it grew slowly, intentionally, under the watchful eye of its caretaker.

I remember the first time I truly understood what it meant to cultivate momentum. It wasn't in a career-defining project or a sudden burst of inspiration—it was in the presence of a bonsai.

A Chance Encounter

On a quiet morning during a trip to Kyoto, I found myself in a garden that seemed suspended in time. The air carried the faint aroma of pine, and the sounds of the bustling city faded into the background. Amid the carefully raked gravel paths and lush greenery, I spotted an elderly gardener hunched over a bonsai tree. He worked with delicate precision, trimming a single branch with scissors so fine they looked like a surgeon's tool.

Curiosity drew me closer, and soon I was immersed in his story.

"This tree," he explained in soft, deliberate Japanese, "is over forty years old. Every year, I adjust its wires, trim its leaves, and shape its growth. But I don't rush. The tree moves at its own pace, and so must I."

At first, I couldn't wrap my head around it. Forty years? How could someone dedicate so much time to such a tiny tree? But the more he spoke, the more I understood. The bonsai wasn't just a tree—it was a symbol of disciplined growth, of achieving mastery by embracing slow, steady momentum.

Lessons from the Bonsai

The bonsai tree embodies principles that are easily overlooked in today's fast-paced world. Its growth isn't dramatic or flashy; it's gradual, almost imperceptible. And yet, over time, it transforms into something extraordinary.

1. Patience Creates Progress

The gardener doesn't expect instant results. Each small adjustment contributes to the tree's long-term beauty and health. Similarly, momentum in our lives doesn't come from dramatic leaps but from consistent, purposeful actions.

2. Intentionality Over Speed

Every decision—the angle of a wire, the removal of a branch—is made with care. This level of intentionality ensures that the tree grows in harmony with its environment. In our own lives, being deliberate about our choices fosters sustainable progress.

3. Mastery Through Repetition

The gardener's skill isn't innate; it's cultivated through years of practice. In the same way, mastery in any area of life comes from showing up, day after day, even when progress feels invisible.

Momentum, like the growth of a bonsai, is a testament to the power of continuous improvement and disciplined action. It's the culmination of countless small steps, each building upon the last, creating a force that propels us forward. Just as the bonsai is shaped through patient, persistent care, we too are molded by our consistent efforts, our unwavering commitment to showing up, even when the results aren't immediately visible.

My Personal "Bonsai Moment"

Years after that encounter, I found myself reflecting on the bonsai's lessons during a challenging period in my life. I was stuck in a cycle of overcommitment, chasing too many goals at once. Progress felt frustratingly slow, and I began questioning whether my efforts were worth it.

One evening, as I revisited photos from my trip to Kyoto, I stumbled upon a picture of that bonsai tree. Its quiet elegance reminded me of the gardener's words: "The tree moves at its own pace, and so must I."

It was a turning point. I realized that in my rush to achieve, I was neglecting the importance of steady, intentional growth. Inspired by the bonsai, I began focusing on small, consistent efforts instead of chasing instant results. Slowly but surely, I started regaining momentum—not through grand gestures, but through daily actions that aligned with my values.

The Bonsai and the Katana

The principles of bonsai cultivation align beautifully with the metaphor of the katana. Just as the bonsai is shaped through patient, meticulous care, the katana is forged through cycles of heating, folding, and tempering. Both processes require time, discipline, and an unwavering commitment to mastery.

Momentum, like the growth of a bonsai tree or the forging of a katana, isn't about speed. It's about persistence. It's about showing up consistently, even when progress feels slow. Over time, those small efforts compound into something remarkable.

Finding Your Bonsai

We all have our "bonsai"—an area of life where we want to grow but often feel frustrated by the slow pace. It might be a skill you're trying to master, a relationship you're nurturing, or a career path you're forging. Whatever it is, the bonsai teaches us that growth doesn't happen overnight. It happens in the quiet moments, through the small, steady actions we take every day.

As you reflect on your own journey, ask yourself:

- Where am I rushing, and how can I slow down?

- What small, intentional steps can I take today to build momentum?

- How can I embrace the process instead of fixating on the outcome?

The bonsai reminds us that mastery is a journey, not a destination. And it's through the cultivation of patience, intentionality, and a deep respect for the process that we achieve mastery and create lasting momentum. Just as the bonsai gardener dedicates years to shaping the tree's growth, we too must embrace the long-term vision, trusting that our consistent efforts will lead to the fulfillment of our goals and the creation of a legacy worth cherishing. By embracing patience, intentionality, and consistent effort, we can cultivate momentum that leads to lasting transformation. The bonsai's growth is a testament to the power of momentum – not as a sudden burst but as a steady accumulation of small, intentional steps.

The Japanese Appreciation of Slow Progress

In Japanese culture, there is a profound respect for processes that unfold gradually, with care and intention. This reverence for slow progress is deeply ingrained in traditional practices, art forms, and philosophies. Unlike the Western focus on instant results or quick fixes, Japan places value on the journey itself—on the lessons, growth, and beauty that emerge over time.

This cultural mindset manifests in concepts and practices like **kintsugi** and the cultivation of **bonsai trees**, both of which offer valuable lessons for how we approach personal growth and transformation.

Kintsugi: Embracing Imperfection

The art of **kintsugi**—repairing broken pottery with gold—is one of the most famous examples of Japan's appreciation for slow, deliberate progress. Rather than discarding a broken item, kintsugi celebrates its history by filling its cracks with lacquer mixed with powdered gold, silver, or platinum. The result is a piece of pottery that is not only functional again but also more beautiful and valuable than it was before.

Kintsugi teaches that scars are not flaws to be hidden but symbols of resilience and transformation. Each crack tells a story, and the process of repairing the pottery is as important as the final result. This philosophy stands in stark contrast to cultures that prioritize perfection and discard anything perceived as flawed.

Lessons from Kintsugi

1. Growth Takes Time

Repairing broken pottery is a slow, methodical process. Similarly, healing and growth in our own lives cannot be rushed. Whether it's overcoming personal challenges or rebuilding after failure, meaningful progress requires patience.

2. Beauty in Imperfection

Kintsugi embodies the idea of **wabi-sabi**, the beauty of imperfection and impermanence. In our pursuit of personal development, we often aim for unattainable ideals. Kintsugi reminds us that our imperfections and struggles are what make us unique.

3. A Symbol of Resilience

The repaired pottery is stronger at its seams than it was originally. In the same way, the challenges we face and overcome can make us more resilient and capable.

Bonsai: Mastery Through Patience

The cultivation of **bonsai trees** is another practice that highlights Japan's respect for slow progress. A bonsai tree is not grown to reach a certain size quickly or produce immediate results. Instead, it's nurtured over years, sometimes decades, to achieve a perfect balance of form and function.

The Process of Growing Bonsai:

1. **Shaping Over Time**

   Bonsai trees are shaped through careful pruning, wiring, and trimming. Each adjustment is made with foresight, knowing it will take years for the tree to develop its intended form.

2. **Respecting Natural Rhythms**

   Unlike factory farming or mass production, bonsai cultivation honors the natural pace of growth. The tree grows at its own rate, and the gardener works with its natural tendencies rather than against them.

3. **A Lifelong Endeavor**

   Bonsai trees often outlive their caretakers, with some specimens being passed down through generations. This long-term perspective contrasts sharply with the fast-paced, results-driven mindset that dominates much of modern life.

Lessons from Bonsai:

- **Consistency Over Intensity**: True progress comes from small, consistent efforts rather than bursts of activity.

- **Patience Pays Off**: In the same way it takes years to cultivate a bonsai, meaningful personal growth requires patience and persistence.

- **Mindfulness in Action**: The act of tending to a bonsai is a meditative practice that encourages focus, care, and presence in the moment.

The Value of Slow Progress in Personal Growth

Both kintsugi and bonsai reflect the Japanese belief that slow progress is not a weakness but a strength. This mindset is particularly relevant in today's fast-paced world, where instant gratification often takes precedence over long-term growth.

In personal development, slow progress allows us to:

1. **Build Depth and Resilience**

   Like a bonsai tree strengthened by years of care or pottery reinforced with gold seams, the challenges we face and overcome deepen our character.

2. **Appreciate the Journey**

   Rushing toward a goal often leads to burnout or dissatisfaction. Embracing slow progress helps us find joy in the process, making the journey itself as meaningful as the destination.

3. **Align with Natural Rhythms**

   Just as the bonsai tree grows in harmony with its environment, our personal growth is most sustainable when we work with our natural tendencies and cycles, rather than forcing outcomes.

Everyday Examples of Slow Progress

In addition to kintsugi and bonsai, there are many other examples of Japan's appreciation for slow progress:

- **Tea Ceremony**: The intricate rituals of a Japanese tea ceremony are designed to create a moment of mindfulness and connection, reminding participants that beauty and meaning can be found in simplicity.

- **Calligraphy**: Mastering Japanese calligraphy takes years of practice. Each stroke reflects the artist's discipline, focus, and connection to the present moment.

- **Martial Arts**: In disciplines like judo, kendo, and aikido, practitioners spend years honing their skills. The focus is not on quick wins but on the continuous pursuit of mastery.

Applying These Lessons to Your Life

To embrace the value of slow progress in your own life, consider:

1. Where Can You Honor the Process?

Reflect on areas where you've been rushing or expecting instant results. How can you shift your focus from the outcome to the process?

2. What Needs Patient Care?

Identify aspects of your life—whether relationships, skills, or personal goals—that could benefit from a slower, more intentional approach.

3. How Can You Celebrate Small Wins?

Just as each step in bonsai cultivation or kintsugi repair contributes to the final masterpiece, every small step you take toward growth is worth celebrating.

The Japanese appreciation for slow progress challenges us to rethink our approach to personal growth. Whether through the golden seams of kintsugi or the delicate branches of a bonsai, we are reminded that beauty and strength emerge not from speed but from patience, intention, and perseverance. By adopting this mindset, we can cultivate a life of depth, resilience, and lasting transformation.

Tools: Building a "Momentum Map" to Track Your Progress

When embarking on a journey of personal growth, one of the most empowering tools you can use is a **momentum map**. This visual representation helps you track progress, stay motivated, and celebrate small wins along the way. Unlike traditional goal-setting methods, a momentum map emphasizes incremental progress and the continuity of effort rather than perfection or immediate results.

What Is a Momentum Map?

A **momentum map** is a personalized, adaptable plan that tracks your growth over time. It helps you visualize the steps you've taken and the direction you're heading, reinforcing your sense of accomplishment while keeping your goals in focus. Think of it as a dynamic roadmap where each milestone builds on the last, showing the cumulative impact of your efforts.

Why Use a Momentum Map?

1. **Clarity**: It provides a clear, organized way to see how far you've come and what lies ahead.

2. **Motivation**: By highlighting small wins, it keeps you motivated, even when progress feels slow.

3. **Accountability**: It serves as a reminder of your goals and the consistent effort required to achieve them.

4. **Adaptability**: A momentum map evolves with you, allowing flexibility as your priorities and circumstances change.

Creating Your Momentum Map

Step 1: Define Your Big Picture Goal

Start by identifying the **main area of life** you want to focus on. This could be your health, career, relationships, or personal habits. Write a clear, compelling goal that reflects your desired outcome.

Example:

- "I want to improve my physical health by building a consistent exercise habit and eating more nutritious meals."

- "I want to deepen my relationships by spending quality time with loved ones and improving communication skills."

Step 2: Break It Down into Milestones

Big goals can feel overwhelming, so break them into smaller, manageable **milestones**. These are key steps that mark progress toward your overall goal.

Example Milestones for Health Goal:

1. Start walking 15 minutes a day, three times a week.

2. Incorporate one new vegetable into meals each week.

3. Transition from walking to jogging after one month.

4. Replace sugary snacks with healthier alternatives.

5. Commit to a weekly fitness class or activity.

Step 3: Identify Micro-Steps

Under each milestone, list **micro-steps**—specific, actionable tasks that are easy to accomplish. These are the foundation of your momentum map, ensuring that progress feels accessible.

Example Micro-Steps for "Start Walking 15 Minutes a Day":

- Day 1: Find a comfortable pair of walking shoes.

- Day 2: Choose a nearby park or walking route.

- Day 3: Set a reminder on your phone for your walking time.

- Day 4: Walk for 5 minutes to test the route.

- Day 5: Gradually increase to 15 minutes.

Step 4: Create a Visual Framework

Now, translate these milestones and micro-steps into a **visual map**. You can use tools like:

- A **flowchart** to show how each step leads to the next.

- A **timeline** to map out when you'll complete each milestone.

- A **progress tracker** with checkboxes or color coding for completed steps.

Step 5: Include Reflection Points

Every few milestones, build in moments to **pause and reflect**. Ask yourself:

- What have I learned so far?

- What challenges did I overcome?

- How can I adjust my approach to make further progress?

These reflection points ensure that your momentum map remains a living document, evolving with your growth.

Using Your Momentum Map

1. Daily Check-Ins

Spend 5-10 minutes each day reviewing your map. Mark off completed tasks, and plan for the next micro-step.

2. Celebrate Small Wins

Each time you complete a milestone or a set of micro-steps, reward yourself. This could be as simple as acknowledging your effort or treating yourself to something you enjoy.

3. Adapt as Needed

Life is unpredictable, and progress isn't always linear. Use your momentum map as a flexible guide, not a rigid rulebook. If a milestone feels too ambitious, break it into smaller steps.

Example of a Momentum Map

Goal: Build a Consistent Meditation Practice

1. **Milestone 1: Set Up a Meditation Space**

   - Micro-Step: Clear a quiet corner in your room.

   - Micro-Step: Add a cushion or chair for comfort.

   - Micro-Step: Place a calming object like a candle or plant.

2. **Milestone 2: Start with 5-Minute Sessions**

   - Micro-Step: Download a meditation app.

   - Micro-Step: Set a timer for 5 minutes.

   - Micro-Step: Practice deep breathing.

3. **Milestone 3: Increase Duration to 10 Minutes**

   - Micro-Step: Add 1 minute each week.

   - Micro-Step: Explore guided meditations.

   - Micro-Step: Track sessions in a journal.

4. **Milestone 4: Join a Meditation Group**

   - Micro-Step: Research local or online groups.
   - Micro-Step: Attend your first session.
   - Micro-Step: Share your progress with others.

The Long-Term Benefits of Momentum Mapping

1. **Builds Confidence**

   Seeing tangible evidence of your progress boosts your self-belief and reinforces the idea that small steps lead to big results.

2. **Enhances Self-Awareness**

   By tracking your actions and reflecting on your journey, you gain a deeper understanding of what works for you and where you can improve.

3. **Sustains Motivation**

   A momentum map transforms abstract goals into concrete actions, making it easier to stay motivated over the long term.

Your momentum map is more than just a tool—it's a companion on your journey of growth. By breaking down your goals, celebrating small wins, and remaining flexible, you can maintain steady progress while building resilience and discipline. Over time, you'll discover that the process itself is just as rewarding as the results, and your map will serve as a testament to your transformation.

Implementation Intentions and Goal Achievement

The study *Implementation Intentions and Goal Achievement* by Gollwitzer and Sheeran provides compelling evidence on the power of specific plans in driving success. Their research demonstrates that forming detailed "if-then" statements—known as implementation intentions—can increase the likelihood of achieving goals by an impressive 65%. This finding connects directly to the principles of habit formation, emphasizing the importance of creating clear, actionable strategies to bridge the gap between intention and behavior.

In my recovery journey, this concept became a game-changer. Like many people, I often set vague intentions: "I'll do my physical therapy exercises tomorrow" or "I'll focus on getting better." These goals, while well-meaning, lacked the specificity necessary to overcome daily obstacles. The insight from this study helped me understand why these attempts often failed: without a clear plan, it's too easy to defer action or get derailed by distractions.

The brilliance of implementation intentions lies in their simplicity. Instead of vague resolutions, they tie actions to specific cues: *If situation X arises, I will do Y.* For example, during my rehabilitation, I restructured my approach to therapy with concrete statements like, *After breakfast, I will do 10 minutes of stretching exercises.* By attaching the activity to a fixed event in my day, the act became automatic, requiring less mental effort or willpower.

This strategy is supported by the study's findings on how our brains process specific plans. By pre-committing to a course of action, we reduce the cognitive load of decision-making in the moment. Our brains treat these intentions almost like a script, automatically activating the planned behavior when the specified situation occurs. This mechanism not only increases follow-through but also minimizes reliance on motivation, which can be fickle and inconsistent.

One of the most interesting aspects of the study is its applicability across different types of goals. From health-related habits like exercising more regularly to productivity goals like writing or studying, implementation intentions consistently lead to higher success rates. During my recovery, I saw this principle echoed in how Japanese culture approached daily life. Whether it was the orderly routines of hospital staff or the structured approach to community tasks, everything seemed to be guided by clear, actionable steps. This alignment between intention and action created an environment of efficiency and predictability.

A particularly striking moment came when I observed how one nurse implemented this approach. She used a checklist system to ensure patient care was thorough. Each task was tied to specific cues: *If it's 10 a.m., check vital signs. If administering medication, confirm patient identity.* While this might seem procedural, it ensured consistency and drastically reduced errors. It mirrored the *if-then* framework of implementation intentions, demonstrating its power not just for individuals but within structured systems.

For readers seeking to form habits, this study offers a simple but profound takeaway: specificity matters. Instead of saying, "I'll meditate more," try, *After I wake up, I will meditate for five minutes.* Or instead of planning to "eat healthier," say, *When I feel like snacking, I will reach for fruit instead of chips.* These small, intentional shifts create a sense of clarity and purpose, making it easier to follow through even on challenging days.

Reflecting on my journey, I now see how crucial these micro-commitments were in my recovery. By tying actions to predictable moments in my day, I was able to build momentum even when progress felt slow. The study highlights that while motivation can spark change, implementation intentions sustain it, ensuring that small steps lead to meaningful, lasting transformation.

PART V:

COMPASSION – OMOIYARI

CHAPTER THIRTEEN
THE HEART OF GROWTH

Omoiyari, a Japanese term that encapsulates the essence of compassion and empathy, is more than just a feeling—it's a way of being. It's about deeply understanding and sharing the feelings of others, offering support, and showing care without expecting anything in return. Omoiyari is about stepping into someone else's shoes, sensing their needs, and offering the kind of help that respects their dignity and humanity.

During my time in Japan, one moment stands out as an unexpected lesson in growth—not a dramatic event, but a quiet, unassuming act of kindness that spoke volumes about the heart of human connection.

It was in a small, suburban hospital in Tokyo where I first met Ayumi, a nurse with a calm demeanor and a gentle spirit. She didn't speak much English, and I, being still relatively new to the language and culture, struggled to communicate with her. Yet, it wasn't the words that struck me; it was the way she conducted herself and the silent care she gave to her patients.

It was a busy morning in the ward, with patients coming in and out of the room, and the air was filled with the typical sounds of a hospital—beeping machines, rustling sheets, and the low murmur of conversations. But amidst the hustle and bustle, Ayumi seemed to move through the space like a quiet river—steadfast, focused, and serene. Her movements were deliberate, and there was a sense of calmness in everything she did.

One afternoon, an elderly patient—who had been struggling with severe pain and isolation—was in the room when Ayumi walked in.

She immediately noticed that the patient was agitated, fidgeting with the blankets, eyes darting around as if trying to make sense of the discomfort. Instead of addressing the patient with rushed words or the clinical manner I had seen in other hospitals, Ayumi knelt beside the bed and gently took the patient's hand. She didn't say anything at first. She simply sat there, offering silent companionship. After a few minutes, she softly began talking, her voice low and steady, asking the patient about their family and hobbies. Her tone wasn't one of pity or sympathy but of genuine curiosity and warmth. Slowly, the patient began to relax.

It was in this moment, watching Ayumi's approach, that I understood the power of quiet kindness and presence. This wasn't about offering solutions or even solving the problem. It was about showing up, being present, and acknowledging the patient's humanity. Ayumi didn't try to fix the pain—she simply honored the person's experience.

Ayumi's actions highlight a crucial aspect of Omoiyari: the importance of self-compassion. Before we can truly extend compassion to others, we must first learn to be compassionate toward ourselves. This means acknowledging our own struggles, forgiving our mistakes, and treating ourselves with the same kindness and understanding that we would offer to a friend in need. Only when we embrace self-compassion can we authentically connect with and care for others.

It was a small act, seemingly insignificant in the grand scheme of things, but it had a profound impact on the patient, who eventually fell into a peaceful sleep.

What struck me most was how Ayumi's actions reflected a philosophy deeply ingrained in Japanese culture: the idea that growth isn't always about doing more or being louder; sometimes, it's about *being present* and *nurturing* the environment around you. True growth, I realized, wasn't just about striving or achieving—it was about cultivating an environment that allowed others to grow, even in the most subtle ways.

Ayumi's kindness was a reminder that growth can often be found in the quieter, gentler acts—the small moments where we take the time to be fully present with ourselves and others. In a world where we're often told that progress must be marked by loud declarations or tangible outcomes, Ayumi's silent grace taught me that growth can sometimes be the result of just showing up and offering a hand to hold, a listening ear, or a kind word.

This lesson in quiet kindness also led me to reflect on my own life. How often had I rushed through moments, eager to fix or achieve, rather than simply being with people and allowing space for their own growth? How many times had I failed to offer that simple presence in my relationships, thinking I had to offer solutions instead of just my attention and care?

Through Ayumi, I learned that the heart of growth lies not only in striving toward external goals but in nurturing the internal spaces where true connection, healing, and development occur. It's in the quiet moments—the ones we often overlook in our haste to "do"— that we find the seeds of real transformation.

This story, this quiet lesson in kindness, has stayed with me. It serves as a reminder that growth isn't just about the effort we put into our own lives—it's also about the way we show up for others. In every moment of interaction, no matter how small, we have the opportunity to help foster growth by offering kindness, presence, and understanding.

What is Omoiyari? The Science of Compassion

Omoiyari is a Japanese concept that embodies the deep, almost innate sense of compassion and empathy towards others. In its essence, it's not just about feeling sorry for someone or extending a superficial kindness. It's about understanding another person's situation, offering support, and showing care without expecting anything in return. It's about truly stepping into someone else's shoes, sensing their emotional needs, and offering the kind of help that respects their dignity and humanity. Omoiyari is often a guiding force in Japanese culture, shaping relationships in both personal and professional settings. It is a kind of compassion that doesn't just come from a place of charity or pity but from a deep understanding of the shared human experience.

The word "omoiyari" is derived from the Japanese verb "omou," meaning to think or feel, and "yari," a form of "yaru," which means to give or do. So, in the simplest terms, it translates to "to give thought to others," or more beautifully, "to act with compassion and understanding." In Japan, omoiyari is a value that permeates daily life—from the way people interact with each other in public spaces to the subtle, unspoken understanding between close friends and family members.

Omoiyari is often described as one of the core values that underpin the Japanese notion of *wa*—a sense of harmony or balance. It encourages people to put the needs of others before their own, to create an environment where everyone feels seen, heard, and valued. This doesn't mean that individual needs are ignored, but rather that there is a prioritization of communal well-being, making it a profound way to build both social cohesion and personal fulfillment.

While compassion is a universal concept, the Japanese interpretation of omoiyari carries certain distinctive cultural nuances that can offer us valuable insights into the science of compassion itself. In this chapter, we will explore not only the meaning of omoiyari but also the science behind compassion—why it's essential for human connection, how it impacts our mental and physical health, and how we can practice it in our own lives.

The Roots of Omoiyari in Japanese Culture

To understand the full depth of omoiyari, it's important to first look at its roots in Japanese culture. One of the most powerful cultural influences that shape omoiyari is the concept of *giri*—a moral or social obligation. In Japan, there's often a sense of responsibility to others that goes beyond mere politeness. It's a deep-seated understanding that our actions affect not just ourselves but the broader social fabric.

Omoiyari is also closely tied to *wabi-sabi*, the appreciation of imperfection and transience. The Japanese are known for their reverence for the fleeting nature of life, and this awareness often brings with it an openness to others' struggles and pain. Omoiyari acknowledges the impermanence of life, recognizing that everyone goes through hardship at different times. In many ways, it invites us to cherish each other with a sense of urgency and appreciation for the briefness of our connections.

Another key aspect of omoiyari is its relationship with silence. In Japanese culture, actions often speak louder than words, and much of what people do for others is unspoken. It's the little gestures—the quiet cup of tea for a friend going through a tough time, the thoughtful gesture of holding the door open, or the act of listening deeply without offering advice unless it's asked for. These actions are expressions of omoiyari. It's not about grand gestures but the subtle attentiveness to someone else's needs and emotions.

The Science of Compassion: Why Omoiyari Matters

Compassion, as a neurological and psychological phenomenon, has been a subject of increasing interest in the field of behavioral science. Numerous studies have shown that compassion has profound effects on both the giver and the receiver, contributing to emotional well-being, mental resilience, and physical health.

When we engage in acts of compassion, the brain releases oxytocin, sometimes called the "love hormone" or "bonding hormone." This hormone is associated with feelings of warmth and connection, and it plays a critical role in building trust and forming social bonds. Oxytocin also reduces cortisol levels, the stress hormone, which in turn lowers stress and anxiety. It's not just the receiver who benefits from acts of compassion—research has shown that people who give compassion are more likely to experience lower blood pressure, reduced stress, and even increased life satisfaction.

But beyond the immediate physiological benefits, the science of compassion goes deeper. The act of practicing compassion strengthens the brain's capacity for empathy, which is essential for emotional intelligence. Empathy is our ability to understand and share the feelings of others. It's the emotional foundation of omoiyari. When we practice empathy, we're able to connect with others on a deeper level, respond to their emotional needs, and offer support that is truly meaningful.

The concept of empathy is supported by mirror neurons in the brain. These neurons fire not only when we perform an action but also when we observe someone else performing the same action. This is why we can often "feel" what someone else is going through—whether it's their joy, pain, or sadness. By training ourselves to notice and respond to the emotions of others, we can cultivate deeper compassion and connection. This is the essence of omoiyari: noticing and responding to the needs of others in ways that make them feel seen and supported.

Omoiyari and Emotional Intelligence

At its core, omoiyari is a practice in emotional intelligence (EQ). Emotional intelligence refers to the ability to perceive, understand, manage, and regulate emotions in ourselves and others. It involves four key components: self-awareness, self-regulation, social awareness, and relationship management. Omoiyari emphasizes social awareness—the ability to understand the emotions and needs of others—while also practicing relationship management, which involves offering support in ways that foster trust and emotional connection.

In Japanese culture, emotional restraint is often valued, and this is where omoiyari shines as a tool for emotional intelligence. It's not about expressing emotions loudly or overtly but about being attuned to the subtle emotional cues of others. By tuning in to nonverbal signals—body language, tone of voice, facial expressions—we can offer support in ways that feel both appropriate and deeply meaningful.

Moreover, omoiyari challenges us to extend compassion not only to those we love but also to strangers and even adversaries. In many ways, this mirrors the concept of *metta* in Buddhist practice, which encourages loving-kindness toward all beings, regardless of their relationship to us. In a world often divided by differences, practicing omoiyari allows us to transcend these divisions and create a culture of empathy, understanding, and care.

Practical Ways to Cultivate Omoiyari in Daily Life

1. **Listen More, Speak Less**: One of the simplest ways to practice omoiyari is by becoming a better listener. Rather than immediately offering solutions or advice, take the time to listen deeply to what others are saying. Sometimes, the most compassionate thing we can do is simply be present and hear someone out without interruption.

2. **Practice Nonverbal Acts of Kindness**: Small gestures like holding the door open for someone, giving a smile, or offering a helping hand can be powerful expressions of omoiyari. These actions don't need to be grand or noticed—they just need to be genuine.

3. **Offer Help Without Expecting Anything in Return**: One of the hallmarks of omoiyari is the absence of expectation. True compassion doesn't come with strings attached. When you offer help or kindness, do so freely, without expecting any return. This fosters a sense of community and shared humanity.

4. **Develop Empathy for Others**: Make an effort to understand the emotions of others. Try to place yourself in their shoes, not just in moments of distress but in moments of joy as well. This practice can help you become more attuned to the needs and emotions of those around you.

5. **Mindful Acts of Compassion**: Engage in regular acts of mindfulness to tune into the emotional states of others. When you're aware of your own emotional responses, you become better equipped to respond compassionately to others, without judgment or haste.

Omoiyari is more than just a cultural value in Japan; it is a universal human need. The science of compassion shows us that being kind and empathetic doesn't just benefit others—it improves our own mental and physical well-being. By practicing omoiyari, we create an environment of understanding, trust, and care, where both ourselves and others can thrive.

Ultimately, omoiyari teaches us that the heart of growth lies not in personal achievement but in the connections, we cultivate with others. It reminds us that true strength and transformation come not from isolated effort, but from shared humanity, compassion, and the willingness to put the needs of others before our own. It is a mindset that fosters peace, resilience, and emotional depth, making it a vital practice for anyone on the path of personal growth.

Tools: Daily Compassion Practices—Acts of Kindness, Gratitude Letters

Cultivating compassion is not a one-time event but an ongoing practice. It requires mindfulness, intentionality, and the willingness to engage in small, meaningful actions every day. Just as a muscle grows stronger with regular exercise, the practice of compassion deepens with consistent effort. In this section, we'll explore several tools to integrate compassion into your daily routine—tools that are designed not just to benefit others but also to enrich your own life, fostering a sense of emotional connection, resilience, and joy. Two of the most accessible and powerful practices are acts of kindness and writing gratitude letters.

1. Acts of Kindness: Everyday Opportunities to Show Compassion

Small acts of kindness may seem insignificant in isolation, but they accumulate over time, creating an environment of care and

271

connection. These acts not only support others but also activate positive feelings within us, creating a cycle of goodwill. In fact, studies show that engaging in random acts of kindness has measurable benefits on our emotional and physical health. The act of helping others can reduce stress, boost happiness, and even increase longevity.

Everyday Acts of Kindness

1. **Start Your Day with Kindness**: Each morning, commit to performing at least one act of kindness before the day gets too busy. It could be as simple as offering a smile to a colleague or letting someone go ahead of you in line. These small gestures set the tone for a compassionate day ahead.

2. **Give Compliments Freely**: One of the easiest and most effective acts of kindness is offering genuine compliments. Compliment someone's outfit, their work ethic, or their personality. Acknowledge their unique strengths. Compliments create positive energy and foster goodwill.

3. **Offer Help Without Being Asked**: Look for opportunities where you can offer assistance, whether it's holding the door for someone, offering to carry something heavy for a neighbor, or volunteering your time at a local charity. Offering help before it's asked can feel like a gift to the recipient, as it shows attentiveness and care.

4. **Leave Thoughtful Notes**: A written note—whether it's a sticky note on someone's desk, a card for a friend, or a simple message of encouragement—can brighten someone's day and make them feel seen and appreciated. These small, thoughtful gestures are often remembered far beyond the moment.

5. **Practice Active Listening**: In conversations, prioritize active listening. Put away distractions like your phone, focus on the speaker, and give them your undivided attention. Acknowledging someone's words and emotions creates a space for them to feel heard and valued, which is one of the deepest acts of compassion we can offer.

6. **Donate or Volunteer**: Consider giving your time, skills, or resources to a cause that resonates with you. Whether it's volunteering at a shelter, donating clothes you no longer use, or supporting a family in need, giving to others in a tangible way is a powerful form of compassion.

7. **Respond with Patience**: When someone is upset or frustrated, responding with patience and understanding instead of defensiveness is an act of compassion. Take a deep breath, remain calm, and listen to their concerns without rushing to solve the problem. Sometimes, the greatest gift we can offer is the space for someone to express themselves.

The Impact of Acts of Kindness

The beauty of acts of kindness lies in their simplicity. While we often associate grand gestures with compassion, the truth is that small, everyday acts have a profound impact. Not only do they benefit the recipient, but they also have a ripple effect, inspiring others to pay it forward. This cycle of kindness can spread throughout communities, workplaces, and families, creating a culture of care and empathy.

Moreover, the act of giving kindness actually boosts our own well-being. It releases feel-good chemicals in the brain like oxytocin, serotonin, and dopamine, which help reduce stress and anxiety, increase happiness, and even improve immune function. Research has shown that people who regularly engage in acts of kindness experience increased life satisfaction and greater emotional resilience.

2. Gratitude Letters: A Powerful Tool for Expressing Compassion

Writing gratitude letters is another deeply impactful tool for cultivating compassion. A gratitude letter is a simple yet profound expression of thanks to someone who has made a positive impact in your life. Unlike generic "thank you" notes, gratitude letters go deeper, detailing the specific ways the recipient has influenced or supported you. Writing these letters not only benefits the person who receives them but also strengthens your own emotional intelligence and sense of connection.

Why Gratitude Letters Work

Gratitude is a powerful emotion that has been shown to improve mental health, increase happiness, and even boost physical health. Writing gratitude letters taps into the science of positive psychology, helping us focus on the positive aspects of our relationships and life experiences. In fact, studies have shown that people who regularly express gratitude are happier, more optimistic, and less depressed.

Gratitude letters are a way to deepen our connection with others. By reflecting on the specific ways someone has supported or inspired us, we create a sense of mutual appreciation. These letters can serve as a reminder of the positive relationships in our lives, reinforcing the importance of compassion and care in our daily interactions.

Steps for Writing a Gratitude Letter:

1. **Choose the Recipient**: Think about someone in your life who has had a positive influence on you. It could be a family member, friend, colleague, mentor, or even a stranger who made a difference in a small but meaningful way.

274

2. **Reflect on the Impact**: Before you start writing, take a moment to reflect on how this person has influenced your life. Think about specific moments, conversations, or acts of kindness that have had a lasting effect on you. These are the details that will make the letter feel personal and heartfelt.

3. **Write from the Heart**: Begin by expressing your gratitude, but go deeper. Share how their actions made you feel, how it impacted your life, and why it mattered to you. The more specific you can be, the more meaningful the letter will be to both you and the recipient.

4. **Deliver the Letter**: Once you've written your gratitude letter, decide how you want to deliver it. You can hand it to the person in person, mail it, or even send it via email. No matter how it's delivered, the act of sharing your gratitude will undoubtedly deepen your relationship and create a bond of mutual respect and appreciation.

5. **Reflect on the Experience**: After writing the letter, take a moment to reflect on the experience. How did it feel to express your gratitude? Did it shift your perspective on the person or your relationship? By reflecting on the impact of the letter, you'll reinforce the power of gratitude and its role in your life.

The Benefits of Writing Gratitude Letters:

When we express gratitude, we train our brains to focus on the positive aspects of our lives and relationships. Writing gratitude letters helps us acknowledge the value others bring to our lives, enhancing our sense of connection and reinforcing the importance of compassion. Research suggests that gratitude practices like writing letters can reduce feelings of loneliness, increase emotional resilience, and improve overall well-being.

Additionally, gratitude letters are not just about making the recipient feel good—they also benefit the writer. The act of reflecting on the positive impact others have had on our lives helps us develop a greater sense of appreciation for the people around us. It reinforces the importance of nurturing relationships and can even improve our outlook on life.

3. Combining Acts of Kindness and Gratitude

The practice of kindness and gratitude are deeply intertwined. Acts of kindness help us connect with others, and gratitude helps us appreciate those connections. By combining these two practices, we can create a powerful, ongoing cycle of compassion.

You might want to try incorporating acts of kindness into your gratitude letters. For example, after writing a letter, you could follow it up with a small gesture of kindness—like buying the person a coffee, offering a favor, or simply spending quality time together. This combination creates a tangible manifestation of your gratitude and strengthens the bond you share.

Likewise, the more acts of kindness you perform, the more opportunities you'll find to express gratitude. These small moments of connection add up, creating a life that is filled with compassion and appreciation.

Compassion, whether expressed through small acts of kindness or deeply thoughtful gratitude letters, is not just a value to aspire to—it is a practice to embody every day. By incorporating these tools into your routine, you create a life that is not only more connected but also more joyful and fulfilling. Through compassion, we build stronger relationships, foster deeper understanding, and contribute to a culture of care and empathy. Whether you're expressing your appreciation for someone or showing kindness in a quiet, unspoken way, these practices remind us that the act of caring is one of the most powerful tools for growth, connection, and transformation.

By practicing compassion daily, we not only enrich the lives of others but also create a more compassionate and fulfilling life for ourselves. Furthermore, this understanding of Omoiyari—the ability to recognize and honor the needs of those around us—lays the foundation for compassionate leadership. When we cultivate compassion in our personal interactions, we develop the skills and mindset needed to lead with empathy, creating environments where others feel valued, respected, and empowered to thrive. This is how we transform not only our personal relationships but also our professional and community spaces.

Compassion Training Alters Altruism and Neural Responses to Suffering

The study *Compassion Training Alters Altruism and Neural Responses to Suffering* explores how cultivating compassion can transform both behavior and brain function. By practicing compassion-focused techniques, participants demonstrated an increase in prosocial behaviors—acts of kindness and altruism—while also experiencing improved well-being. This research highlights how intentional efforts to develop compassion not only benefit others but also create profound internal shifts in those who practice it.

Reflecting on this during my recovery in Japan, I saw compassion at work daily, not just as a gesture but as a way of life. One moment stands out vividly. A nurse—let's call her Aiko—would always pause, make eye contact, and bow slightly before entering my room. It wasn't just politeness; it was an act of presence, signaling that she genuinely saw me as a person, not just another patient on her list.

Despite the busyness of her day, she took the time to ensure I felt cared for. This small act resonated deeply, especially when I was struggling to adjust to my limitations. It wasn't only her actions that helped—it was the sense that she was fully present, offering care that went beyond routine.

The study explains how such compassion-oriented behaviors emerge through intentional practice. Compassion training involves exercises that help individuals develop empathy while managing emotional distress, enabling them to respond to suffering with genuine care. Neurologically, these practices strengthen connections between the prefrontal cortex (responsible for rational decision-making) and the areas of the brain that process emotions, like the amygdala. This shift allows people to engage with others' pain without becoming overwhelmed, which is crucial for sustainable acts of kindness.

Interestingly, the study revealed that those who practiced compassion training exhibited not only increased altruistic behaviors but also heightened activity in brain regions associated with reward. In other words, helping others became intrinsically fulfilling. I saw this mirrored in Aiko and others at the hospital. Despite their demanding jobs, they didn't show the burnout or fatigue you might expect in such a setting. Instead, their approach to care seemed to energize them. It was as if the act of compassion itself fueled their resilience.

This deeply contrasts with some of my experiences outside of Japan, where acts of kindness often felt transactional or obligatory. In these cases, compassion didn't seem to stem from genuine concern but from societal pressure or a desire for recognition. What the study, and my time in Japan, made clear is that true compassion arises from intention and practice—it's a skill, not just an innate quality.

For me, this understanding transformed how I approached relationships. Compassion isn't about grand gestures or fixing someone's problems. It's about being present, showing empathy, and responding with care, even in small ways. One exercise in compassion training involves imagining someone who is suffering and silently wishing for their relief. While this might seem simple, it rewires how we respond to others' pain, fostering a mindset that prioritizes connection and kindness.

This study also connects to broader themes in Japanese culture. Concepts like *omoiyari*—the ability to anticipate and respond to others' needs—reflect a deeply ingrained value system that prioritizes harmony and collective well-being. In contrast, many Western frameworks emphasize individualism, where compassion often requires deliberate effort rather than being instinctive. Observing this cultural difference during my recovery, I realized how much I had to learn about letting go of self-centered thinking and embracing a more inclusive mindset.

As I began incorporating these lessons into my own life, I noticed subtle but meaningful changes. Whether it was reaching out to a friend in distress or simply listening without judgment, practicing compassion shifted my perspective. The study reinforces that these changes aren't just psychological but biological. When we train ourselves to care deeply and authentically, we align our actions with a sense of purpose and belonging, enhancing not only others' lives but also our own.

Ultimately, this research reminds us that compassion is not just a moral ideal—it's a powerful tool for personal and societal transformation. By intentionally cultivating it, we build connections that enrich our lives and contribute to a kinder, more empathetic world. This lesson, embodied by people like Aiko, became one of the most enduring gifts of my time in Japan.

CHAPTER FOURTEEN

HEALING CONNECTION

Omoiyari, the practice of compassion, is not just about extending kindness and empathy to others—it's also about being open to receiving it. True healing often occurs within the space of connection, where compassion flows freely in both directions. It's in those moments of shared humanity, where we feel seen, heard, and understood, that our wounds begin to mend.

It was a cold, drizzly afternoon when I found myself standing on the edge of exhaustion, both physically and emotionally. The weight of life had never felt heavier. I had recently moved to a new city, overwhelmed by the challenges of adapting to an unfamiliar environment, juggling responsibilities, and carrying an invisible burden of loneliness. On that particular day, a series of small frustrations—the kind that pile up until they feel insurmountable—had pushed me to the edge.

My phone buzzed in my pocket. A text from an old friend: "Thinking of you today. Hope you're doing okay." I smiled briefly, appreciative of the gesture but unable to shake the gnawing sense of isolation. I decided to head to a small café I'd passed a few times, thinking a warm drink might help lift my spirits.

The café was tiny and intimate, its walls lined with shelves of mismatched books and succulents. A soft hum of conversation filled the space. I ordered a cup of tea and settled into a corner, trying to drown my thoughts in the quiet comfort of the place.

Moments later, the barista approached my table—not just to deliver my tea but also with a small plate of cookies. Surprised, I looked up, thinking they'd made a mistake. Before I could say anything, she smiled and said, "These are on us. You seemed like you could use something sweet today."

Her words caught me off guard. I hadn't realized how visible my weariness had become. I thanked her quietly, unsure how to articulate the mix of gratitude and vulnerability I suddenly felt. That small, unexpected gesture—cookies worth only a couple of dollars—did something I hadn't been able to do for myself all day. It cracked open the walls I'd been building around my feelings, offering me a moment of warmth and connection that reminded me I wasn't as alone as I had convinced myself I was.

Later that evening, I reflected on what had happened. That simple act of kindness from a stranger had made me feel seen in a way that no grand gesture ever could. It reminded me of the power of connection, especially during times of struggle. I realized that healing often comes not from monumental changes but from the small, human moments when someone reaches out to remind us of our shared humanity.

Compassion is the cornerstone of healing connections, both in our personal relationships and within our broader communities. When we approach others with empathy and understanding, we create an environment where vulnerability is welcomed, and healing can occur. In personal relationships, compassion fosters deeper bonds, allowing for forgiveness, support, and the rebuilding of trust. Within communities, compassion creates a sense of belonging and shared humanity, enabling collective healing and resilience in the face of adversity.

The story of that day in the café stayed with me, not because of its grandiosity but because of its simplicity. It highlighted a truth that often gets overshadowed in the chaos of modern life: we heal in connection with others. Whether it's the kindness of a stranger, the unwavering support of a loved one, or the shared understanding of someone who has walked a similar path, connection has the power to mend wounds that solitude cannot.

In Japan, there's a term, *omoiyari*, which translates loosely to "empathy" or "thoughtfulness." It reflects a cultural value of anticipating the needs of others and responding with care. This concept is woven deeply into everyday life, from the way public spaces are designed to be inclusive to the unspoken courtesies exchanged between strangers. Acts of *omoiyari* are often subtle and quiet, yet their impact can be profound.

In moments of hardship, it's these connections—built on empathy, kindness, and understanding—that provide the foundation for healing. They remind us that we're not alone, even when the world feels overwhelming.

Kindness as a Catalyst for Healing

When we think of healing, we often imagine it as a solitary process, something that happens in isolation as we work through our pain. While introspection and personal growth are essential, the role of others in our healing journey cannot be understated. Research in behavioral science supports this idea, showing that social connections and acts of kindness significantly impact our mental and emotional well-being.

Kindness, both given and received, activates the brain's reward system, releasing hormones like oxytocin and serotonin that reduce stress and foster feelings of happiness and connection. In times of need, these small gestures can serve as a lifeline, grounding us in the present and reminding us of the good that still exists in the world.

Cultivating Healing Connections

1. **Reach Out in Vulnerability**: Often, the hardest part of connection is being honest about your struggles. But vulnerability is a powerful bridge. Sharing your feelings with someone you trust can create an opportunity for deeper understanding and support.

2. **Offer Small Gestures of Care**: Healing connections aren't built on grand gestures but on consistent, thoughtful actions. A text to check in on a friend, offering a listening ear, or even a warm smile can make a significant difference.

3. **Create Rituals of Connection**: In Japan, rituals often play a role in fostering connection, whether it's through tea ceremonies, communal meals, or festivals. Consider creating your own rituals—like a weekly call with a loved one or a monthly gathering with friends—to nurture relationships.

4. **Listen Without Judging**: One of the greatest gifts you can offer someone is your presence. Practice active listening, focusing fully on the other person without interrupting or offering solutions unless asked.

5. **Be Open to Receiving Kindness**: Sometimes, healing requires letting others care for you. Accepting kindness can feel vulnerable, but it's an essential part of connection.

Healing doesn't happen in isolation. It's through our connections—with friends, family, and even strangers—that we find the strength to navigate life's challenges. The kindness I received that day in the café wasn't monumental, but it was exactly what I needed in that moment. It reminded me of the power we all hold to create healing connections, both for ourselves and for those around us.

In fostering these connections, we not only support others but also create a network of care that sustains us through life's trials. Whether through acts of *omoiyari*, vulnerability, or simply showing up for one another, we weave the threads of resilience and compassion that hold us together.

These experiences of compassion and empathy within our personal connections serve as a powerful training ground for compassionate leadership. By cultivating Omoiyari in our daily interactions, we develop the skills and awareness needed to lead with empathy, creating spaces where others feel valued, respected, and empowered to thrive. The healing power of connection, therefore, extends beyond our personal lives, shaping our ability to create positive change in our workplaces and communities.

Cultural Contrasts: Japanese Collective Thinking vs. Western Individualism

When considering the cultural landscapes of Japan and the West, one of the most striking contrasts lies in the emphasis placed on collective thinking versus individualism. These two paradigms shape how people view themselves, interact with others, and navigate the complexities of life. Both perspectives have unique strengths and weaknesses, and understanding their differences can illuminate paths to deeper connection and personal growth.

The Essence of Collective Thinking in Japan

In Japan, the concept of *wa* (harmony) is a cornerstone of social interaction. Rooted in centuries-old traditions, this value prioritizes group cohesion and the minimization of conflict. Collective thinking, or *shuudan ishiki*, encourages individuals to align their actions and decisions with the needs of the group, whether it's family, workplace, or society at large.

Key Characteristics of Japanese Collective Thinking:

1. **Interdependence Over Independence**

   Japanese culture emphasizes the importance of interdependence, where each person's role contributes to the collective well-being. This mindset is evident in everyday practices, from the punctuality of trains to the seamless cooperation in disaster recovery efforts.

2. **Modesty and Self-Restraint**

   Individuals are encouraged to avoid drawing undue attention to themselves. Success is often viewed as a reflection of group effort rather than individual achievement. For example, when a Japanese team wins a sports event, the players typically emphasize their gratitude to teammates, coaches, and supporters.

3. **Consensus-Building**

   Decision-making in Japan often involves extensive discussion to ensure that everyone feels heard and that consensus is reached. This practice fosters inclusivity and reduces the likelihood of conflict. However, it can sometimes slow progress, as prioritizing harmony may mean delaying tough decisions.

The Western Emphasis on Individualism

In contrast, Western cultures, particularly in countries like the United States, celebrate individualism as a marker of freedom and self-expression. Rooted in Enlightenment ideals, individualism encourages people to pursue their own goals, express their unique identities, and prioritize personal growth.

Key Characteristics of Western Individualism:

1. **Autonomy and Personal Freedom**

   Individualism champions the idea that each person has the right to chart their own path, unencumbered by societal expectations. This value is reflected in everything from career choices to self-help movements that emphasize "finding your true self."

2. **Meritocracy and Competition**

   Success is often attributed to individual effort and talent. In many Western societies, there's a strong focus on personal achievements, such as career milestones, academic accomplishments, or entrepreneurial success.

3. **Direct Communication**

   Western cultures tend to value directness and clarity in communication, even if it means confronting difficult truths. This contrasts with Japan's preference for indirect communication, which aims to preserve harmony.

Bridging the Divide: Lessons from Each Perspective

Both collective thinking and individualism have strengths that can enrich the other. Japanese collective thinking fosters deep connections, resilience in group dynamics, and a sense of shared purpose. Meanwhile, Western individualism encourages creativity, innovation, and the freedom to pursue passions.

The Strengths of Japanese Collective Thinking:

1. **Strong Social Safety Nets**

   In Japan, the emphasis on group well-being creates a strong sense of responsibility toward others. This mindset underpins societal practices like universal healthcare and elder care, ensuring that the vulnerable are not left behind.

2. **Resilience in Crisis**

The 2011 earthquake and tsunami are often cited as examples of Japanese collective thinking at its best. Communities came together to rebuild, showing remarkable discipline and solidarity in the face of devastation.

3. **Subtle Acts of Kindness**

Everyday life in Japan is filled with small, considerate actions—bowing in greeting, offering help without being asked, and maintaining cleanliness in public spaces. These gestures create an environment where people feel cared for, even among strangers.

The Strengths of Western Individualism

1. **Innovation and Creativity**

Individualism nurtures out-of-the-box thinking. The freedom to challenge norms and take risks has led to groundbreaking advancements in technology, art, and science.

2. **Empowerment and Self-Expression**

The emphasis on personal identity allows people to embrace their uniqueness and advocate for change. Social movements for civil rights, gender equality, and environmental activism often find their roots in individual voices uniting for a common cause.

3. **Adaptability in Diverse Settings**

Western individualism thrives in multicultural environments, where different perspectives are encouraged and valued. This adaptability fosters cross-cultural understanding and collaboration.

Tensions Between the Two Perspectives

While each approach has its strengths, the differences between collective thinking and individualism can lead to misunderstandings and conflict:

1. **Workplace Dynamics**

   In Japanese workplaces, the group often takes precedence over the individual, leading to long hours and collective decision-making. In contrast, Western workplaces often prioritize efficiency and reward individual contributions, which may clash with Japan's more patient, consensus-driven approach.

2. **Mental Health Stigmas**

   The emphasis on harmony in Japan can sometimes suppress open discussions about mental health, as admitting personal struggles might disrupt group cohesion. Western cultures, with their focus on individuality, are often more open to seeking therapy and discussing personal challenges.

3. **Approaches to Leadership**

   Japanese leaders are often expected to embody humility and prioritize team success. In Western contexts, charismatic and visionary leadership is frequently celebrated, sometimes overshadowing the contributions of the team.

To navigate the complexities of a globalized world, individuals and societies can benefit from integrating aspects of both collective thinking and individualism:

1. **Adopt Collective Resilience**

   Embrace the Japanese principle of interdependence by cultivating strong support networks in your personal and professional life.

2. **Foster Individual Empowerment**

   Encourage self-expression and personal growth within the context of community well-being. Recognize that individual achievements can inspire collective progress.

3. **Practice Empathy Across Cultures**

   Whether through the Japanese value of *omoiyari* or Western ideals of equality and inclusion, empathy is the bridge that connects seemingly opposing perspectives.

Japanese collective thinking and Western individualism may seem like opposing philosophies, but they are, in fact, complementary. The interconnectedness of the group and the freedom of the individual are both essential for a balanced, fulfilling life. By drawing lessons from both, we can create a world that values both the collective good and the unique contributions of each person.

Exercises: Strengthen One Key Relationship Through Intentional Communication

Building and maintaining meaningful relationships requires effort and intentionality, especially in today's fast-paced world. Strengthening a key relationship doesn't happen by chance—it's the result of conscious communication, understanding, and action. This exercise will guide you through a process of reflection and interaction to fortify a relationship that matters most to you.

Step 1: Reflect on the Relationship

Before engaging in intentional communication, take time to evaluate the current state of the relationship. Ask yourself:

- **What is the foundation of this relationship?**

Is it built on shared history, mutual goals, or a deep sense of care?

- **What's working well?**

Identify positive aspects, like shared trust, support, or enjoyable moments together.

- **Where are the cracks?**

Consider areas that may need attention—unresolved conflicts, miscommunications, or lack of time spent together.

Exercise: Write a Relationship Snapshot

Take 10 minutes to jot down your thoughts about this relationship. Write about what makes it valuable, where you feel connected, and what could be improved. This reflection will serve as a baseline for growth.

Step 2: Clarify Your Intentions

Understanding what you hope to achieve through intentional communication is crucial. Strengthening a relationship doesn't necessarily mean solving every problem or becoming inseparable; it might mean fostering understanding, creating more time for each other, or simply expressing gratitude.

Ask Yourself:

- **What do I want this relationship to feel like?**
- **What specific change am I hoping to see?**

- **How can I contribute to this relationship in a meaningful way?**

Exercise: Set an Intention Statement

Write down your goal for this relationship in one clear sentence. For example:

- "I want to rebuild trust with my best friend after a disagreement."

- "I want to feel closer to my partner by spending more quality time together."

- "I want to support my sibling through a challenging period."

Step 3: Practice Active Listening

Effective communication begins with listening—not just hearing words, but truly understanding the other person's feelings and perspective. Active listening helps to create a safe space where the other person feels valued and understood.

How to Practice Active Listening:

1. **Be Present**: Remove distractions. Put away your phone, turn off notifications, and make eye contact.

2. **Reflect Back**: Paraphrase what the other person says to show you understand. For example: "It sounds like you've been feeling overwhelmed at work."

3. **Validate Feelings**: Acknowledge their emotions without judgment. Saying, "That must have been really hard for you," can go a long way.

4. **Ask Open-Ended Questions**: Encourage them to share more by asking questions like, "Can you tell me more about that?"

Exercise: Active Listening Practice

Set aside time to have a focused conversation with the person you want to strengthen your relationship with. During this conversation, focus solely on listening. Avoid offering advice or solutions unless asked.

Step 4: Communicate with Clarity and Empathy

When it's your turn to share, clarity and empathy are essential. Misunderstandings often arise from vague or emotionally charged communication. Instead, express yourself in a way that fosters understanding and connection.

Strategies for Clear and Empathetic Communication:

1. **Use "I" Statements**: Share your feelings without placing blame. For example:

   o   Instead of: "You never listen to me,"

   o   Say: "I feel unheard when we talk about certain topics."

2. **Focus on Specifics**: Avoid generalizations like "always" or "never." Instead, discuss specific situations and behaviors.

3. **Express Appreciation**: Let the person know what you value about them. For example: "I really appreciate how supportive you've been lately."

4. **Be Open to Feedback**: Invite the other person to share their perspective, even if it's hard to hear.

Exercise: Write a Communication Plan

Draft a script or outline for what you want to say during a meaningful conversation. Include three parts:

- **Gratitude**: "I really value how [specific example]."

- **Concern**: "I've been feeling [specific emotion] about [specific situation]."

- **Request**: "Can we work together to [specific goal]?"

Practice this plan to feel more confident during the actual conversation.

Step 5: Build Rituals of Connection

Strong relationships thrive on consistent, meaningful interactions. These don't have to be grand gestures—they can be simple, intentional rituals that reinforce your bond.

Ideas for Connection Rituals:

1. **Daily Check-Ins**: Spend 10 minutes each day sharing highs and lows.

2. **Weekly Quality Time**: Schedule a regular activity you both enjoy, like cooking dinner together or going for a walk.

3. **Shared Gratitude Practice**: Each week, exchange notes about what you appreciate about each other.

4. **Collaborative Goals**: Work on a shared project, like planning a trip or learning something new together.

Exercise: Create a Connection Ritual

Brainstorm one ritual that feels meaningful and sustainable for your relationship. Write it down and discuss it with the other person. For example:

- "Let's have Sunday morning coffee together, no phones allowed."

- "How about we send each other a quick text each evening about one thing we're grateful for?"

Step 6: Monitor and Adjust

Relationships are dynamic, and what works today might need adjustment tomorrow. Make it a habit to periodically reflect on the progress of your relationship and communicate openly about any evolving needs or concerns.

Exercise: Monthly Relationship Review

Set aside time once a month to review how your intentional communication efforts are going. Ask yourself:

- **What's improved since we started?**

- **Are there any lingering issues that need attention?**

- **What new goals or rituals could we try?**

Use this reflection to celebrate successes and fine-tune your approach.

Strengthening a key relationship isn't about grand gestures or overnight transformations—it's about showing up consistently with intention, empathy, and care. By reflecting on the relationship, practicing active listening, communicating with clarity, and building rituals of connection, you can foster a deeper bond that stands the test of time.

CHAPTER FIFTEEN
COMPASSIONATE LEADERSHIP

L eadership can often conjure images of authority, decisiveness, and unwavering strength. However, in Japan, a different style of leadership—one steeped in empathy and compassion—has quietly demonstrated its enduring power. This is not about weakness or softness but about creating an environment where people feel valued, respected, and inspired to bring their best selves to the table.

In my early career, I had the opportunity to meet Mr. Hiroshi Takeda, a highly respected business leader in Kyoto. He was the CEO of a mid-sized manufacturing company renowned for both its financial success and its exceptional workplace culture. Employees described their workplace as "a second home," which struck me as unusual in a world where work often feels transactional. I wanted to understand what made this company so special, so I reached out to interview Mr. Takeda, expecting to hear strategies focused on efficiency and innovation. What I encountered was a profound lesson in compassionate leadership.

The Morning Ritual

On the day of our meeting, I arrived at the company's headquarters early, eager to make a good impression. The office building was modest, but it exuded a quiet elegance—typical of Japanese aesthetics. Employees were arriving, bowing politely to one another, and there was a sense of calm efficiency in the air.

At precisely 8:00 AM, Mr. Takeda entered the lobby—not in a chauffeur-driven car or with an entourage, but on foot, carrying a simple leather briefcase. His first action surprised me: he stopped to greet every employee he encountered, not with a perfunctory nod but with genuine warmth. He asked about their families, their health, and even small details like how they were adjusting to a recent office renovation.

Later, during our conversation, I asked him why he took the time to personally engage with his employees every morning. His response was both simple and profound:

"A leader is like a gardener. The people in your organization are like plants. They don't thrive because you tell them to grow—they thrive when you nurture them, pay attention to their needs, and provide the right environment."

A Compassionate Turnaround

Mr. Takeda's philosophy wasn't just theoretical; it had tangible results. When he first took over the company, it was struggling financially, and employee morale was at an all-time low. Productivity was declining, and the turnover rate was alarmingly high. Instead of resorting to cost-cutting measures or imposing stricter rules, Mr. Takeda took a different approach: he decided to listen.

He spent weeks holding one-on-one meetings with employees at every level, from senior managers to factory workers. He asked them about their challenges, their aspirations, and their suggestions for improvement. Many were hesitant at first, skeptical of his motives. But over time, his consistent effort to understand and empathize won them over.

One story stood out during these sessions. A factory worker named Yoshiko, who had been with the company for over 20 years, shared her struggles with balancing work and caregiving for her elderly mother. She had been on the verge of quitting, feeling unsupported and overwhelmed. Mr. Takeda didn't just listen—he acted. He implemented flexible work schedules for employees with caregiving responsibilities and introduced an on-site counseling service.

These changes didn't just improve Yoshiko's life; they sent a powerful message to the entire organization: **Your well-being matters.**

Balancing Empathy with Results

Some might wonder: does compassion compromise a leader's ability to make tough decisions? Mr. Takeda's story proves otherwise. While he prioritized empathy, he was also clear about expectations and accountability. His leadership style wasn't about coddling employees but about creating an environment where they felt supported enough to excel.

Under his guidance, the company introduced a profit-sharing program that rewarded employees for their contributions to the company's success. Productivity soared, and the company not only recovered but became a market leader in its niche. Employees didn't just work harder—they worked with a sense of purpose and loyalty that was rare in the industry.

When I asked Mr. Takeda how he balanced compassion with the demands of running a business, he said:

"Compassion and accountability are not opposites; they are partners. When people feel cared for, they are more willing to take ownership of their work. When you lead with empathy, you don't lower standards—you raise them because people want to live up to the trust you've placed in them."

As our interview came to an end, I asked Mr. Takeda what he hoped his legacy would be. He paused for a moment, then said:

"Success is fleeting. What matters is the impact you leave on the people you lead. If they feel stronger, wiser, and more valued because of your leadership, then you have truly succeeded."

That conversation stayed with me, not just as a lesson in leadership but as a blueprint for life. Compassionate leadership isn't about sacrificing performance or indulging in sentimentality. It's about recognizing that at the heart of every organization is a network of human beings—each with their own stories, struggles, and potential.

Mr. Takeda's story reminds us that the most effective leaders are not those who demand loyalty but those who earn it through genuine care and respect. In a world that often prioritizes speed and results, his approach offers a timeless lesson: true leadership begins with compassion.

How Compassion Creates Stronger Teams and Communities

Compassion isn't often the first word that comes to mind when discussing high-performing teams or thriving communities. Yet, when you peel back the layers of what makes groups cohesive, resilient, and successful, compassion emerges as a silent but indispensable force. Compassion—the genuine concern for others' well-being—creates trust, fosters collaboration, and strengthens the bonds that allow people to thrive collectively.

The Science of Compassion in Teams

Research in behavioral science has repeatedly shown that compassion plays a pivotal role in the dynamics of successful teams. A study conducted by the University of California, Berkeley, found that teams demonstrating higher levels of kindness and empathy toward one another consistently outperformed those that didn't. This wasn't because they avoided conflict or challenges; rather, their compassion allowed them to approach disagreements constructively, fostering solutions instead of blame.

Compassion also triggers biological responses that promote collaboration. When individuals feel supported, their brains release oxytocin—the "bonding hormone"—which enhances trust and connection. In turn, these positive emotions reduce stress and increase the likelihood of effective communication.

Trust as the Foundation

Compassion builds trust, and trust is the cornerstone of strong teams and communities. Without trust, collaboration becomes transactional and shallow, leaving little room for genuine creativity or problem-solving. When people know their concerns will be heard and that their well-being matters, they feel safe to take risks, share ideas, and ask for help.

Consider a team where mistakes are met with ridicule or harsh judgment. In such an environment, individuals are more likely to hide errors or avoid innovation altogether, fearing backlash. Now imagine a team where mistakes are viewed as opportunities for growth, and members support each other in finding solutions. Compassion transforms a punitive culture into a growth-oriented one, enabling the group to move forward together.

The Ripple Effect of Compassion in Communities

Communities are not merely aggregates of individuals; they are ecosystems where actions ripple outward. Acts of compassion have a domino effect, inspiring others to follow suit. Sociologists refer to this as **"emotional contagion"**—the phenomenon where emotions spread from one person to another. When compassion is modeled by leaders or influential members of a community, it sets a tone for others to emulate.

For instance, in Japanese culture, the practice of **omotenashi**—a deep-seated philosophy of selfless hospitality—is a prime example of how compassion strengthens communities. This cultural norm extends beyond mere politeness; it is about anticipating others' needs and acting with genuine care. From the small gestures of shopkeepers to large-scale disaster relief efforts, omotenashi illustrates how a compassionate mindset can weave a community tightly together.

Compassion Enhances Collaboration

Teams and communities that prioritize compassion tend to collaborate more effectively. When people feel valued and understood, they are more likely to contribute their talents and ideas without fear of judgment. Compassionate leaders foster this dynamic by encouraging open communication and creating a culture where every voice matters.

An illustrative example comes from a global health organization that implemented a compassionate leadership model. By prioritizing empathy in team interactions, the organization saw a significant increase in both employee retention and project success rates. Employees reported feeling more connected to their work and colleagues, which translated into higher levels of engagement and productivity.

Compassion also builds resilience—both for individuals and the groups they belong to. When setbacks occur, teams with a foundation of compassion are better equipped to navigate challenges. They rally together, pooling resources and emotional support to overcome obstacles.

For example, during the 2011 earthquake and tsunami in Japan, communities exemplified the power of compassion-driven resilience. Strangers shared resources, volunteers traveled long distances to assist, and neighbors checked on one another despite their own struggles. This collective response not only alleviated immediate suffering but also laid the groundwork for long-term recovery.

Practical Ways to Foster Compassion in Teams

1. **Normalize Vulnerability**

   Encourage team members to share their challenges and concerns. By modeling vulnerability, leaders can create an environment where people feel comfortable expressing their needs without fear of judgment.

2. **Practice Active Listening**

   Listening with intent shows others that their voices matter. Avoid interrupting or rushing to solve problems; sometimes, the act of being heard is enough to foster trust.

3. **Celebrate Small Wins**

   Acknowledging individual and collective achievements reinforces the value of each team member's contributions. Gratitude fosters a sense of belonging and shared purpose.

4. **Encourage Peer Support**

   Compassion doesn't have to come solely from leaders. Encourage team members to support one another through mentorship programs, buddy systems, or informal check-ins.

5. **Prioritize Well-Being**

   Create policies and practices that prioritize mental and physical health. Flexible schedules, wellness initiatives, and open-door policies for addressing personal issues all contribute to a compassionate environment.

Compassion as a Competitive Advantage

In a world that often prioritizes speed, efficiency, and individual achievement, compassion may seem like an unlikely strategy for success. Yet, as countless examples and studies show, compassion enhances not only the emotional health of teams and communities but also their overall performance.

Compassionate teams are not only more effective but also more sustainable. People want to stay in environments where they feel seen and valued. In the long term, this reduces turnover, strengthens loyalty, and fosters a sense of collective pride.

Compassion is not a luxury—it is a necessity for creating strong, cohesive, and high-performing teams and communities. It builds trust, enhances collaboration, and fosters resilience, all while creating a sense of purpose and belonging. Whether in a workplace, a neighborhood, or a global movement, compassion has the power to transform groups from mere collections of individuals into unified forces capable of achieving greatness together.

Practical Tips: Applying Omoiyari in Professional and Personal Relationships

Here are practical ways to incorporate omoiyari into your daily interactions.

1. Listen Intently Without Interruptions

Why It Matters

Omoiyari starts with understanding. Listening intently demonstrates that you value the other person's perspective. In professional settings, this can lead to better collaboration, while in personal relationships, it deepens emotional bonds.

How to Practice:

- In conversations, resist the urge to formulate your response while the other person is speaking. Focus entirely on their words.

- Reflect back on what you've heard by summarizing key points or asking clarifying questions.

- Create dedicated moments for listening, such as check-ins with colleagues or uninterrupted time with loved ones.

2. Anticipate Needs Without Being Asked

Why It Matters

Omoiyari shines in its proactive nature. Instead of waiting for someone to voice a need, you observe and act thoughtfully. This practice can alleviate stress and show others that you genuinely care.

How to Practice:

- **At Work:** If you notice a colleague overwhelmed with tasks, offer specific help, such as taking a small assignment off their plate.

- **At Home:** Anticipate emotional or physical needs. If a partner has had a tough day, prepare a favorite meal or create a quiet, relaxing space for them.

3. Express Gratitude Regularly

Why It Matters

Acknowledging others' efforts and kindness is a simple yet powerful way to practice omoiyari. Gratitude reinforces positive behavior and fosters goodwill in both personal and professional relationships.

How to Practice:

- Write a thank-you email or handwritten note to a colleague who has gone above and beyond.

- Tell family members or friends specifically what you appreciate about them. For example: "I really admire how you handled that difficult situation."

- Incorporate daily gratitude practices, like reflecting on three things someone did for you that day.

4. Adapt Communication Styles to the Individual

Why It Matters

Everyone processes information differently. Applying omoiyari involves tailoring your communication to fit the preferences and needs of the person you're engaging with. This reduces misunderstandings and builds rapport.

How to Practice:

- For detail-oriented colleagues, provide comprehensive explanations and follow-up materials.

- For emotionally-driven friends or family, focus on tone and empathy in your conversations.

- Observe and adapt—if someone values brevity, don't overwhelm them with excessive details.

5. Create Space for Others' Emotions

Why It Matters

Emotional awareness is a crucial part of omoiyari. Instead of dismissing or avoiding uncomfortable emotions, allowing space for someone to express their feelings shows genuine care and understanding.

How to Practice:

- **In Professional Settings:** If a teammate appears upset, offer a private space to talk. Say something like, "You seem off today—want to chat about it?"

- **In Personal Relationships:** When a friend or partner expresses frustration, avoid jumping into problem-solving mode. Validate their feelings first: "That sounds really tough. I'm here for you."

6. Give Without Expecting a Return

Why It Matters

The essence of omoiyari lies in selflessness. Offering help, support, or kindness without expecting anything in return builds trust and goodwill.

How to Practice:

- Offer assistance to someone new at work, like showing them the ropes or inviting them to join a lunch group.

- Volunteer your time or resources for a cause meaningful to your community or family.

- Surprise a loved one with a thoughtful gesture, such as flowers or an act of service, "just because."

7. Respect Personal and Professional Boundaries

Why It Matters

Omoiyari isn't about overstepping or smothering; it's about thoughtful consideration of others' space and limits. Respecting boundaries shows you understand and honor their autonomy.

How to Practice:

- **At Work:** Avoid unnecessary interruptions during focused work hours. Instead, schedule a convenient time to connect.

- **At Home:** Respect a partner's need for alone time or personal space, especially after a busy day.

8. Support Growth and Well-Being

Why It Matters

A key aspect of omoiyari is empowering others to thrive. This involves creating opportunities and environments where they can grow and feel supported.

How to Practice:

- **In Professional Settings:** Mentor a junior colleague, share resources, or recommend them for new opportunities that align with their strengths.

- **In Personal Relationships:** Encourage loved ones to pursue their passions or take breaks when needed.

9. Pay Attention to Nonverbal Cues

Why It Matters

Not all needs are verbalized. Being observant allows you to notice when someone might be struggling or in need of support, even if they don't say so outright.

How to Practice:

- Look for signs of stress, such as changes in tone, body language, or energy levels.

- Respond with subtle but meaningful actions, like offering a cup of tea or suggesting a break during a busy day.

10. Lead by Example

Why It Matters

When you practice omoiyari consistently, it inspires others to follow suit. Thoughtfulness can be contagious, creating a ripple effect in your workplace or community.

How to Practice:

- Be the first to extend kindness in group settings, whether it's through gestures of appreciation or acts of service.

- Encourage a culture of care in professional environments by recognizing and rewarding thoughtful actions.

The Role of Compassion in Leadership Effectiveness

The study *The Role of Compassion in Leadership Effectiveness* highlights how compassionate leadership fosters engaged, high-performing teams, with an average 20% improvement in performance. This research challenges traditional notions of authoritative leadership, emphasizing care and empathy as critical for success.

During my recovery, I witnessed this firsthand through Dr. Sato, the hospital's chief administrator. Despite his demanding role, he personally engaged with patients and staff. His genuine inquiries and attentive listening demonstrated a sincere interest in others' well-being. This consistent care fostered a supportive environment, which translated into meticulous and attentive care from the staff.

The study explains how compassionate leadership creates psychological safety, enabling innovation, collaboration, and resilience. When team members feel supported, they're more likely to perform at their best and take calculated risks. Dr. Sato exemplified this, with staff often praising his openness to feedback and commitment to a harmonious environment, which directly improved the quality of care.

The neuroscience of compassion supports these findings. Demonstrating empathy activates oxytocin, a hormone that strengthens trust and belonging. This aligns with the Japanese value of *omoiyari* (consideration for others), emphasizing collective well-being over individual achievement. Contrasting this with assertive Western leadership styles, I saw how transformational a compassionate approach can be.

Compassionate leadership doesn't compromise standards—it empowers individuals by understanding the human factors that drive performance. Leaders like Dr. Sato model care through their actions, inspiring teams to mirror this behavior. Small practices such as active listening and recognizing contributions build trust and engagement, proving that compassion is a strategic advantage.

Dr. Sato's example reshaped my view of leadership. Compassion is not a weakness but a strength that aligns people toward shared goals, blending care and purpose for outcomes that benefit everyone involved.

Cultivating Compassion: The Omoiyari Stage

The **Omoiyari** stage centers on compassion—both for yourself and for others. Rooted in Japanese culture, *omoiyari* translates to "thoughtful consideration" or "empathy," a quiet yet profound way of being that seeks to alleviate suffering and foster connection. This stage teaches that true growth is not complete until it ripples outward, touching the lives of those around you.

Stage Recognition

Recognizing when you're in the Omoiyari stage requires attention to your evolving awareness of relationships and the impact of your actions.

- **Key Indicators:**

    - A desire to be more present and supportive for those around you.

    - Heightened empathy for others' struggles, coupled with a sense of responsibility to help.

    - A growing kindness toward yourself, especially in moments of vulnerability.

- **Behavioral Patterns:**

    - Prioritizing active listening and offering thoughtful responses.

    - Performing small acts of kindness without expecting recognition.

- Reflecting on how your choices affect others emotionally and practically.

- **Relationship Dynamics:**
  - Deepening connections marked by trust, understanding, and mutual respect.
  - A willingness to repair strained relationships by taking accountability or offering forgiveness.

Self-Assessment Exercise:

- Ask yourself:
  - How often do I consider the feelings and needs of others before acting?
  - Do I extend the same compassion to myself that I offer to others?
  - When was the last time I performed an act of kindness simply because I could?

Stage Completion Markers

Completing the Omoiyari stage means integrating compassion into your daily life in ways that feel natural and enduring.

- **Mindset Shifts:**
  - Realizing that compassion is not weakness but strength.
  - Embracing vulnerability as a bridge to authentic connection.

- **Behavioral Changes:**

  - Responding to conflict with empathy instead of defensiveness.

  - Seeking opportunities to uplift and empower others.

- **Emotional Milestones:**

  - Feeling fulfilled by giving and connecting, rather than seeking validation.

  - Developing greater self-compassion, especially during setbacks.

- **Relationship Developments:**

  - Strengthened bonds built on genuine care and mutual support.

  - A sense of community and shared purpose with those around you.

Next Stage Preparation

As you transition from Omoiyari to **Ikigai**, compassion becomes a catalyst for discovering your purpose. This shift happens naturally as you recognize how your unique strengths can serve others.

- **Internal Signals:**

  - A desire to channel your compassion into meaningful action.

  - Clarity about the kind of impact you want to make in the world.

- **Transition Challenges:**
    - Balancing care for others with maintaining your own boundaries and well-being.
    - Avoiding burnout from overextending yourself.
- **Preparation Exercises:**
    - **Purpose Mapping:** Reflect on how your talents and passions align with the needs of others.
    - **Boundaries in Compassion:** Practice saying no to ensure you have energy for what truly matters.

Regression Warnings

While Omoiyari is a deeply rewarding stage, it can be challenging to sustain, particularly during times of stress or personal difficulty.

- **Early Warning Signs:**
    - Feeling resentful or drained from giving too much.
    - Retreating into self-criticism or neglecting your own needs.
- **Common Triggers:**
    - Overcommitting to others at the expense of your well-being.
    - Experiencing rejection or ingratitude after offering help.
- **Stages to Avoid Regressing To:**
    - Returning to self-absorption or isolation (Naikan).

- Focusing solely on personal growth without regard for others (Kaizen).

- **Recovery Practices:**

  - Reevaluate your boundaries and adjust your commitments.

  - Reconnect with supportive people who uplift and inspire you.

Stage Integration

The lessons of Omoiyari don't end when you move to the next stage; they become foundational to your way of being, ensuring that compassion informs your purpose and actions.

- **Building on Progress:**

  - Incorporate compassionate practices into daily routines, such as gratitude journaling or mindfulness.

  - Use your empathy to foster collaboration and unity in your personal and professional relationships.

- **Sustaining Momentum:**

  - Regularly check in with yourself to ensure you're balancing self-care with care for others.

  - Seek out stories, experiences, or role models that inspire deeper compassion.

- **Integration Exercise:**

  - Identify three people you've positively impacted during this stage and reflect on how their lives have changed.

Compassion is not just a feeling—it's a practice, a commitment, and a way of life. By embracing Omoiyari, you create ripples of kindness and understanding that extend far beyond yourself. Whether through small gestures or grand acts, your compassion has the power to transform relationships, communities, and ultimately, the world.

PART VI:
PURPOSE – IKIGAI

CHAPTER SIXTEEN

DISCOVERING YOUR IKIGAI

In a quiet suburban town outside Kyoto, an elderly man named Hiroshi wakes up at dawn every day with a sense of purpose. His routine is simple but deeply fulfilling: he brews his morning tea, reads the newspaper, and prepares for a few hours of volunteer work at the local community center. For the past decade, Hiroshi has been helping children with their homework, repairing old bicycles, and organizing small community events.

What makes Hiroshi's life remarkable isn't the magnitude of his actions but the joy and contentment they bring him. After retiring from a 40-year career as an engineer, Hiroshi could have chosen a life of leisure. Instead, he embraced volunteering as a way to give back to his community.

"I don't do this for recognition," he once said during a community interview. "I do this because it makes me feel alive. The smiles on the children's faces, the gratitude of a struggling mother whose bike I repaired—they remind me every day that I have something to give."

Hiroshi's days are a blend of simplicity and meaning. On weekends, he tends to his garden and practices calligraphy, a hobby he picked up in his 60s. His ikigai, or reason for being, is clear: it lies in serving others, cultivating his passions, and staying connected to his community.

Hiroshi embodies the concept of **ikigai**, a Japanese philosophy that combines what you love, what you're good at, what the world needs, and what you can be rewarded for (financially or otherwise). Unlike Western ideas of success, which often focus on career achievements or material wealth, ikigai is deeply personal. It's about finding harmony between inner fulfillment and external contribution.

In Hiroshi's case, his engineering skills translated into repairing bicycles, a tangible way to help others. His love for learning and teaching found a new outlet in mentoring children. And his passion for calligraphy reminds us that ikigai doesn't have to be grandiose—it can be found in the smallest joys and quietest moments.

The Journey to Ikigai

Many of us struggle to find our ikigai because we're looking for it in the wrong places. We chase external markers of success: promotions, titles, or possessions. But as Hiroshi's story shows, ikigai isn't something you acquire—it's something you cultivate by aligning your passions, talents, and contributions to the world.

What is Ikigai?

At its core, **ikigai** (pronounced *ee-kee-guy*) is a Japanese concept that translates to "reason for being." It represents the sweet spot where four fundamental aspects of life converge:

1. **What you love** (your passions and interests).

2. **What you're good at** (your skills and strengths).

3. **What the world needs** (your contributions to others or society).

4. **What you can be paid for** (your livelihood or financial sustainability).

When these elements align, they create a sense of purpose and fulfillment. It's a compass for living a meaningful life, helping you navigate your career, relationships, and personal growth.

The Four Dimensions of Ikigai

1. What You Love

This dimension encompasses your passions and the activities that bring you joy. It's about identifying what lights you up and energizes you. For some, it's artistic expression like painting or writing. For others, it might be nurturing relationships, solving problems, or exploring nature.

2. What You're Good At

These are your talents and skills—both innate and developed. This dimension isn't just about expertise but also about recognizing the unique strengths you bring to the table. Think about what people often praise you for or seek your help with.

3. What the World Needs

This dimension shifts the focus outward. It's about connecting your abilities and passions with a greater purpose. What problems can you help solve? How can you make a positive impact? This doesn't mean you have to save the world; even small contributions to your community or loved ones count.

4. What You Can Be Paid For

The financial aspect ensures sustainability. While ikigai doesn't have to be tied to money, aligning your passion and purpose with a way to support yourself can bring balance to your life. This dimension acknowledges the practical realities of living in a modern world.

The Ikigai Diagram: A Map of Purpose

Imagine the four dimensions as overlapping circles in a Venn diagram:

- The intersection of **what you love** and **what you're good at** is your **passion.**

- The overlap of **what you're good at** and **what you can be paid for** is your **profession.**

- Where **what you can be paid for** meets **what the world needs** lies your **vocation.**

- Finally, the combination of **what you love** and **what the world needs** creates your **mission.**

Ikigai is the center where all these overlaps meet—a harmonious blend of passion, mission, vocation, and profession.

Cultural Roots of Ikigai

The concept of ikigai has deep roots in Japanese culture, where it's more than just a philosophy—it's a way of life. Unlike Western ideas of success, often tied to individual achievement, ikigai emphasizes interconnectedness and balance. It's not about grandiose ambitions but about finding joy and meaning in the ordinary.

For example, in **Okinawa**, a Japanese island known for its high population of centenarians, ikigai plays a significant role in longevity and happiness. Residents often cite simple things as their ikigai—tending to a garden, caring for grandchildren, or participating in community rituals.

Ikigai in the Modern World

In today's fast-paced and often chaotic environment, finding ikigai can be a grounding practice. The world pushes us to specialize, hustle, and achieve, but ikigai invites us to slow down and reflect on what truly matters. It's a reminder that success isn't just about doing more—it's about doing what aligns with your deepest values.

319

Common Myths About Ikigai

1. **Ikigai is the same as your job**

   While your career can be part of your ikigai, it's not the whole picture. Many people find their ikigai outside of work—in hobbies, relationships, or volunteering.

2. **You must find it immediately**

   Ikigai is a journey, not a destination. It evolves with you as your priorities and circumstances change.

3. **It has to be monumental.**

   Ikigai can be found in small joys and quiet moments, like sharing a meal with loved ones or helping a friend in need.

Why Ikigai Matters

Finding your ikigai isn't just about personal fulfillment—it's about creating a life that benefits others too. When you live with purpose, you inspire those around you and contribute to a better world. Ikigai encourages us to move beyond self-interest, fostering compassion and connection.

The pursuit of ikigai is both an inward and outward journey. It asks us to explore our passions and talents while considering how we can make a difference. In doing so, we create a life of meaning, resilience, and joy.

Exercises: Mapping Your Own Ikigai

Finding your ikigai is a deeply personal process, one that requires reflection, honesty, and a willingness to explore your true desires and abilities. This exercise isn't about forcing an answer but about creating clarity over time. Let's guide you step by step toward uncovering your ikigai.

Step 1: Reflect on What You Love

Start by asking yourself: *What activities bring me joy?* Think about moments when you feel most alive. These could be simple pleasures or lifelong passions.

- Is there a hobby you lose track of time doing?

- What kinds of problems do you enjoy solving?

- Are there topics you could talk about endlessly with others?

Spend time journaling about these questions. If nothing comes to mind immediately, observe your day-to-day life for clues. When do you feel happiest or most fulfilled?

Step 2: Identify What You're Good At

Next, take stock of your strengths. These might include technical skills, interpersonal abilities, or even qualities like patience or creativity.

- What do others often ask for your help with?

- What tasks feel effortless yet rewarding for you?

- Have you ever received compliments about specific abilities?

Don't just think about formal skills. Soft skills, like listening, problem-solving, or organizing, are equally valuable. Write down as many as you can, even if they seem small or unrelated.

Step 3: Explore What the World Needs

This step involves looking outward. How can you use what you love and are good at to make a positive impact? Start by considering:

- What challenges or needs resonate with you on a personal level?

- Are there causes or issues you feel strongly about?

- What kind of support do people around you seem to lack?

You don't need to focus on solving massive global problems. Small contributions—helping a neighbor, mentoring someone, or creating something meaningful—can be just as powerful.

Step 4: Consider What You Can Be Paid For

Financial sustainability is an important part of ikigai, but it doesn't mean your passion must always turn into a job. Instead, think about how your skills or interests might intersect with practical opportunities.

- What skills or services are people willing to pay for?

- Are there ways to monetize something you already enjoy doing?

- Could your current job align more closely with your passions by shifting roles or responsibilities?

If this part feels challenging, don't worry. Your ikigai might exist outside of your profession, and that's perfectly fine.

Step 5: Look for Overlaps

Now, review your answers from each step. Where do they intersect?

- Are there activities you love and are good at that could also meet a need in the world?

- Do any of your passions align with opportunities to earn a living?

- Can you see connections between what fulfills you personally and what benefits others?

If the answers don't immediately align, that's okay. Sometimes ikigai reveals itself gradually through experimentation and exploration.

Step 6: Test and Adjust

Your ikigai isn't a fixed destination—it's a living process that evolves as you grow. Start small by integrating one or two of your insights into daily life. For example:

- If you love teaching and are good at explaining complex ideas, offer to mentor someone or create an online tutorial.

- If you're passionate about fitness and the world's need for better health, consider hosting free community workouts or starting a fitness blog.

Pay attention to how these actions make you feel. Are they energizing or draining? Use this feedback to refine your path.

An Example of Mapping Ikigai

Let's say you're passionate about art, skilled at storytelling, moved by the lack of creative opportunities for underprivileged youth, and capable of earning through workshops. Your ikigai might be to create an art mentorship program, combining your love for creativity, your skills, and the ability to make a difference while sustaining yourself financially.

As you map your ikigai, give yourself permission to explore without judgment. Purpose isn't something you "find" overnight—it's something you uncover by living intentionally and staying curious. Reflect often and remain open to where the journey leads.

By taking these steps, you'll not only move closer to discovering your ikigai but also start living a more meaningful, aligned life.

Discovering Purpose: The Ikigai Stage

The **Ikigai** stage is the culmination of your journey through transformation—where the lessons learned in the previous stages converge into a clear sense of purpose. In Japanese culture, *Ikigai* is often described as the "reason for being." It represents that sweet spot where your passions, skills, values, and the needs of the world intersect. It's not just about finding what you love—it's about finding what you were meant to do and how that can contribute meaningfully to the lives of others.

Stage Recognition

When you're in the Ikigai stage, your life takes on a new sense of direction. You're no longer driven by external validation or a desire to achieve for the sake of achievement. Instead, you move with intention, deeply connected to the reasons behind your actions.

- **Key Indicators:**
  - A sense of fulfillment that comes not from external recognition, but from the work itself.
  - Feeling aligned with both your internal values and external actions.

- An overwhelming sense of peace, knowing that you are contributing in a way that is meaningful to you and others.

- **Behavioral Patterns:**
  - Pursuing activities that feel intrinsically rewarding, regardless of monetary gain or praise.
  - Demonstrating a commitment to your passions and values, even in the face of obstacles.
  - Engaging in work that serves both personal growth and the greater good.

- **Relationship Dynamics:**
  - Building relationships with others who share similar values or who are inspired by your sense of purpose.
  - Fostering environments where collaboration is driven by a common goal rather than competition.

Self-Assessment Exercise:

- Ask yourself:
  - What am I most passionate about, and how does it serve the world around me?
  - How do I feel when I engage in the work I love?
  - Do my actions align with my core values, and how do they reflect in my relationships and community?

Stage Completion Markers

Completing the Ikigai stage doesn't mean you've reached a destination—it means that you're fully immersed in the journey of living with purpose. You know what you're meant to do, and you're doing it with a deep sense of fulfillment.

- **Mindset Shifts:**

    - Moving from the pursuit of success to the pursuit of meaning.

    - A shift from "what I can achieve" to "how I can serve" or "how I can contribute."

- **Behavioral Changes:**

    - Embracing work that aligns with your values, even if it requires sacrifice.

    - Focusing on long-term impact rather than short-term gratification.

- **Emotional Milestones:**

    - A profound sense of contentment that doesn't depend on external success or failures.

    - Peace in knowing that you're living a life true to who you are.

- **Relationship Developments:**

    - Relationships become deeply rooted in shared values and mutual respect.

    - There is less dependency on others for validation, as you are already self-validated by your purpose.

Next Stage Preparation

The Ikigai stage is not an end but rather a continuous journey of refinement and evolution. As you continue to grow, you'll find that your purpose may evolve or expand, leading you to new opportunities and challenges.

- **Internal Signals:**

  - A desire to expand your purpose and impact, reaching new areas of your life or community.

  - A willingness to learn and grow through new experiences that align with your purpose.

- **Transition Challenges:**

  - Avoiding the temptation to become complacent, as the search for meaning is an ongoing process.

  - Staying open to evolving your purpose as you encounter new phases in life.

- **Preparation Exercises:**

  - **Purpose Expansion:** Reflect on areas of your life that are currently not in alignment with your Ikigai and identify how you can integrate your purpose into them.

  - **Adaptation to Change:** Practice staying flexible by embracing new opportunities that align with your evolving purpose.

Regression Warnings

While the Ikigai stage is a powerful and fulfilling place, there are still potential pitfalls that can cause you to lose your way. It's important to stay aware of signs of regression and take steps to maintain your connection to your purpose.

- **Early Warning Signs:**

- A sense of being "lost" or disconnected from the work you once found fulfilling.

- Feeling overwhelmed by external pressures to conform to societal expectations rather than following your own path.

- **Common Triggers:**

  - Letting distractions or external success criteria take precedence over your inner calling.

  - Comparing your journey to others, leading to self-doubt or a loss of clarity.

- **Stages to Avoid Regressing To:**

  - Falling back into the survival-driven mindset of Genki.

  - Losing sight of your values, slipping into excessive people-pleasing, or letting others dictate your actions.

- **Recovery Practices:**

  - Revisit your core values and passions, and assess how they've changed or been compromised.

  - Refocus on the intrinsic joy and fulfillment of living with purpose, rather than external rewards.

Stage Integration

To maintain your sense of purpose and prevent burnout, integrating your Ikigai into the fabric of your daily life is essential.

- **Building on Progress:**

  - Regularly check in with yourself to ensure your actions align with your core purpose.

  - Reinforce your Ikigai by seeking opportunities to teach, inspire, or mentor others who may be searching for their own sense of purpose.

- **Sustaining Momentum:**

  - Develop routines or rituals that support and celebrate your purpose, such as journaling, community service, or creative expression.

  - Embrace new challenges that align with your purpose and expand your capacity to contribute.

- **Integration Exercise:**

  - Identify areas of your life where your purpose is either not present or underdeveloped and create a plan for integrating your Ikigai into these areas.

Living in the **Ikigai** stage is the epitome of authentic strength. It's where your personal growth merges with your contribution to the world, creating a life full of meaning, joy, and fulfillment. The journey doesn't end here; it evolves, deepens, and spreads out, touching every corner of your life. Embrace it fully—your purpose is your greatest legacy.

CHAPTER SEVENTEEN
LIVING WITH ALIGNMENT

A few years ago, I found myself at a crossroads. On the surface, everything seemed to be in order. My career was stable, and I had achieved many of the goals I once thought defined success. But deep down, I felt an unsettling disconnection—like I was moving forward on a path that wasn't truly mine.

The realization hit me one evening during a long commute home. I had just wrapped up another exhausting day, having spent hours in meetings and chasing deadlines that felt increasingly meaningless. As I sat on the train, staring at the blur of city lights, I asked myself a question I hadn't dared to confront before: *Is this really the life I want?*

At first, the answer was a mix of fear and confusion. I had spent years building this version of success, one that ticked all the boxes society deemed important—financial stability, recognition, and a comfortable routine. Yet, I couldn't escape the nagging sense that I was living someone else's dream.

This question haunted me for weeks. I began noticing all the small signs of misalignment I had ignored: the dread I felt every Monday morning, the lack of joy in my accomplishments, and the growing sense that my true passions had been buried beneath practicality and expectations.

The Moment of Clarity

One weekend, I decided to take a break from the noise of daily life. I packed a small bag and traveled to a quiet retreat center nestled in the mountains. There, surrounded by stillness and nature, I finally allowed myself the space to reflect deeply.

It was during a guided meditation session that the clarity I had been seeking began to surface. The facilitator asked us to visualize our lives as a flowing river. We were encouraged to notice whether we felt like we were moving with the current or struggling against it.

In my mind's eye, I saw myself swimming upstream—exerting tremendous effort to go somewhere I didn't even want to be. The image was so vivid it brought tears to my eyes. It became clear that I wasn't living in alignment with my values, passions, or sense of purpose.

The Decision to Realign

Returning from that retreat, I knew I couldn't continue down the same path. But I also understood that change wouldn't happen overnight. Realignment, I realized, is a gradual process of small, intentional shifts.

The first step was identifying what truly mattered to me. I revisited my childhood passions, remembered moments of pure joy, and reflected on the kinds of work that felt meaningful. I also considered the relationships and activities that energized me versus those that drained me.

One by one, I began making changes. I set boundaries at work to create more space for personal projects I was passionate about. I reconnected with friends who shared similar values and distanced myself from relationships that felt transactional. Over time, I even transitioned into a career path that allowed me to combine my skills with a deeper sense of purpose.

The Power of Alignment

Realigning my life wasn't easy. It required confronting fears, letting go of old definitions of success, and embracing uncertainty. But with each step, I felt lighter and more connected to who I truly was.

Now, when I reflect on that period of transition, I'm grateful for the discomfort that pushed me to reevaluate. Living with alignment doesn't mean life is free from challenges. Instead, it means those challenges feel purposeful, like part of a journey that's authentically mine.

This personal story taught me that alignment isn't about perfection or having all the answers. It's about listening to your inner voice, trusting your instincts, and having the courage to pivot when something feels off. Alignment is a dynamic process, one that evolves as we grow—but the rewards are undeniable. Life feels richer, more fulfilling, and deeply meaningful when we move in harmony with our true selves.

Tools for Aligning Daily Actions with Long-Term Purpose

Living in alignment with your purpose doesn't happen by accident. It requires intentionality, introspection, and practical adjustments to ensure that your everyday actions reflect your values and long-term goals. This process isn't about overhauling your entire life overnight—it's about creating a steady, conscious rhythm that keeps you connected to what truly matters.

Begin with a Clear Vision

Alignment starts with knowing what you're aligning to. Take the time to articulate your long-term purpose. What drives you? What impact do you want to have in the world? Consider reflecting on the following:

- **What brings you joy?** Think of moments when you've felt most alive and fulfilled.

- **What are your core values?** Identify the principles that guide your decisions and make you feel authentic.

- **What legacy do you want to leave?** Imagine looking back on your life—what would make you proud?

These reflections form the foundation of alignment. Without clarity, daily actions can easily drift into routines disconnected from your true aspirations.

Prioritize Through Reflection

Once you have a vision, the next step is to audit your daily life. Where are your actions aligned with your purpose, and where are they not?

One effective approach is to review your week with two questions in mind:

1. Which activities felt meaningful and energizing?

2. Which activities felt draining or purposeless?

This exercise isn't about labeling every task as "good" or "bad." It's about noticing patterns. For example, if spending time mentoring a colleague felt fulfilling, that's a sign that teaching or supporting others may be part of your purpose. On the other hand, if excessive time spent on social media left you feeling empty, it's worth reconsidering how you allocate that time.

Align Through Micro-Actions

Big goals can feel overwhelming, especially when they require significant changes. That's why alignment often begins with micro-actions—small, manageable steps that create momentum over time.

For instance:

- If your purpose involves creativity, set aside 15 minutes a day to write, draw, or brainstorm ideas.

- If it's about nurturing relationships, start with one intentional conversation a week.

- If your purpose is health-related, begin by adding one healthy meal or a short daily walk.

The key is consistency. These small actions, when repeated, create habits that align your life with your deeper intentions.

Use Your Calendar as a Compass

A calendar isn't just a tool for managing appointments; it's a reflection of your priorities. To ensure your daily actions align with your purpose, look at how you allocate your time.

Start by scheduling "purposeful blocks" in your calendar. These are dedicated periods for activities that connect to your long-term goals, whether that's personal development, creative pursuits, or spending time with loved ones.

For example:

- Block an hour every Sunday for self-reflection or planning.

- Dedicate a morning each week to learning a new skill.

- Set aside evenings for family dinners or meaningful conversations.

By intentionally carving out time, you signal to yourself (and others) that these priorities matter.

Create Alignment Rituals

Rituals are powerful tools for maintaining alignment because they ground you in intentionality. Unlike routines, which can become mechanical, rituals are imbued with meaning.

For example:

- **Morning Ritual:** Begin each day by revisiting your purpose. Spend five minutes journaling about how today's actions can bring you closer to your goals.

- **Closing Ritual:** End your day by reflecting on moments when you felt aligned and identify small adjustments for tomorrow.

- **Weekly Reset:** Set aside time each week to review your calendar, evaluate your progress, and make intentional plans for the days ahead.

Rituals act as touchpoints, helping you course-correct when life pulls you off track.

Embrace the Power of Saying No

One of the biggest obstacles to alignment is overcommitment. When your schedule is filled with obligations that don't reflect your purpose, it's nearly impossible to stay on course.

Learning to say no—graciously but firmly—is a vital skill for alignment. Before agreeing to a new task or commitment, ask yourself:

- Does this align with my values and goals?

- Will this bring me closer to my purpose, or is it a distraction?

By saying no to what doesn't serve you, you create space for what truly matters.

Accountability and Feedback

Alignment isn't a solitary journey. Sharing your goals with a trusted friend, mentor, or coach can provide the accountability needed to stay consistent.

Consider creating a system where you regularly check in with someone about your progress. They can offer encouragement, constructive feedback, and an outside perspective to help you stay aligned.

For example, you might:

- Share your weekly or monthly goals with an accountability partner.

- Join a group or community that shares your values and purpose.

- Seek mentorship from someone who embodies the kind of alignment you're striving for.

The Importance of Flexibility

While consistency is crucial, so is adaptability. Alignment isn't about rigidly sticking to a plan—it's about staying true to your purpose even when circumstances change.

For example, if a family emergency disrupts your schedule, your alignment might shift from pursuing personal goals to providing support and care. Recognizing this flexibility as part of your purpose allows you to navigate life's unpredictability with grace.

Building Alignment Over Time

Alignment isn't a destination; it's a lifelong process. There will be moments when you feel completely in sync with your purpose and others when you drift off course. The key is to view misalignment not as failure, but as an opportunity to reflect, recalibrate, and grow.

By consistently aligning your daily actions with your long-term purpose, you create a life that feels authentic, meaningful, and deeply fulfilling. Every small step you take brings you closer to living in harmony with your true self.

Action Steps: Developing a "Purpose Compass" for Decision-Making

In a world full of distractions and competing priorities, it's easy to lose sight of what truly matters. A **purpose compass** is a mental or physical tool that helps you stay aligned with your values and long-term goals when making decisions. Like a traveler navigating unknown terrain, this compass provides direction, clarity, and confidence, especially in moments of uncertainty.

Step 1: Define Your True North

Your "true north" is the core of your purpose—the guiding principle that defines what success and fulfillment mean to you. To identify it, reflect on the following:

- **What energizes you?** Think about activities or moments that leave you feeling alive and engaged.

- **What values drive your decisions?** Examples might include integrity, creativity, compassion, or growth.

- **What impact do you want to have on others or the world?**

Write down your answers and distill them into a single, concise statement. For instance:

- "My true north is to inspire and empower others to reach their potential."

- "My true north is to create meaningful connections and foster compassion."

This statement becomes the anchor of your purpose compass.

Step 2: Establish Core Compass Points

A compass doesn't just have one direction—it's divided into key points that guide navigation. Similarly, your purpose compass can have **four core points** representing essential areas of your life. These might include:

1. **Health:** Maintaining physical and mental well-being.

2. **Relationships:** Nurturing meaningful connections.

3. **Growth:** Pursuing personal or professional development.

4. **Contribution:** Making a positive impact on your community or the world.

For each point, define specific values or principles that guide your actions in that area. For example:

- **Health:** "I prioritize balance and consistency over extremes."

- **Relationships:** "I value quality time and honest communication."

Having these points ensures that your decisions reflect a well-rounded, purposeful life.

Step 3: Create a Decision-Check Framework

When faced with a decision, use your purpose compass to evaluate options. Ask yourself:

1. **Does this align with my true north?** Will this action bring me closer to or farther from my purpose?

2. **Which compass points does it support?** For example, if an opportunity nurtures your growth but compromises your health, is it worth pursuing?

3. **What are the trade-offs?** Consider the resources—time, energy, and attention—required.

For decisions that feel especially complex, try assigning a score (1-5) to each compass point to assess how well the choice aligns with your values.

Step 4: Build Reflection into Your Routine

Your purpose compass will only be effective if you regularly check its direction. Build reflection into your routine to ensure you're staying on course.

- **Daily Reflection:** Spend a few minutes each evening asking, "Did my actions today align with my purpose?"

- **Weekly Review:** Set aside time to evaluate key decisions and whether they supported your compass points.

- **Quarterly Alignment Check:** Revisit your true north and compass points to see if they still resonate or need adjustment based on new experiences or goals.

Step 5: Practice Decision-Making with Small Choices

Using your purpose compass doesn't have to start with life-altering decisions. Begin by applying it to smaller, everyday choices. For example:

- **Choosing how to spend your free time:** "Does scrolling social media align with my growth or relationships?"

- **Deciding what to say yes or no to:** "Does this request honor my health or contribution?"

By practicing with smaller decisions, you build the habit of purposeful alignment, making it easier to apply the compass to bigger life choices.

Step 6: Visualize Your Compass

While the purpose compass can be a mental framework, creating a tangible version can enhance its effectiveness. Consider:

- **Drawing a literal compass:** Place your true north at the center and write your compass points around it.

- **Keeping a digital version:** Use a notes app or goal-tracking tool to remind yourself of your values.

- **Creating a mantra:** A short phrase like, "True to my purpose, steady in my actions," can reinforce your alignment in moments of doubt.

Having a physical or digital representation of your compass ensures it's always within reach when you need guidance.

Step 7: Trust the Process

Remember, your purpose compass isn't a tool for achieving perfection—it's a guide for making intentional, values-driven decisions. There will be times when you stray off course, and that's okay. The beauty of the compass is its ability to bring you back to your true north whenever you feel lost.

By developing and using your purpose compass, you create a life that not only feels aligned but also allows you to navigate challenges and opportunities with clarity and confidence.

Purpose in Life and Reduced Risk of Myocardial Infarction

Compassionate leadership fosters engaged, high-performing teams. Studies like *The Role of Compassion in Leadership Effectiveness* reveal that leaders who integrate empathy into their management see measurable improvements, including a 20% increase in team performance. This approach challenges traditional notions of leadership as authoritative or detached, highlighting compassion as a critical element of success.

During my recovery, I experienced the impact of compassionate leadership firsthand through Dr. Sato, the hospital's chief administrator. Despite his responsibilities, he engaged personally with patients and staff. His genuine inquiries and active listening created a sense of value and psychological safety, which translated into meticulous care from the team. This mirrors findings from the study: when individuals feel seen and supported, innovation, collaboration, and resilience thrive. Compassionate leaders inspire trust and loyalty, fostering a culture where people perform at their best.

Compassion activates oxytocin, a hormone that strengthens bonds, creating a sense of belonging. This aligns with the Japanese value of *omoiyari* (consideration for others), emphasizing collective well-being. In contrast to Western models focused on assertiveness, compassionate leadership exemplifies strength through care. Leaders like Dr. Sato model this by example, inspiring their teams to mirror their behavior, proving that compassion is a strategic advantage.

The Purpose-Health Connection

Purpose is not just an abstract concept but a vital factor for longevity and quality of life. The study *Purpose in Life and Reduced Risk of*

Myocardial Infarction found that individuals with a strong sense of purpose experience a 15% reduced risk of heart attack. Purpose serves as a stabilizing force, helping people navigate challenges with resilience and reducing the physical and emotional effects of stress.

During my recovery, the Japanese concept of *ikigai* (a reason for being) reshaped my understanding of purpose. Immobilized and stripped of my routines, I reflected deeply on what truly mattered. Nurses, doctors, and even patients demonstrated a calmness rooted in their sense of purpose. For example, Takako, a nurse of 30 years, saw her work not just as a duty but as a vocation. Her alignment with what she loved, was good at, and found meaningful gave her emotional energy and fulfillment.

Ikigai emphasizes the intersection of passion, skill, need, and reward, forming a foundation for a balanced and meaningful life. Purpose aligns actions with values, creating coherence and satisfaction. This sense of alignment reduces stress, preventing burnout and chronic ailments. For me, recovery became an opportunity to reorient my life toward internal sources of fulfillment—relationships, personal growth, and being present.

The integration of compassion and purpose demonstrated their profound influence on physical and mental health. As I embraced *ikigai*, my rehabilitation turned into a journey of transformation, proving that leadership and life are most impactful when guided by care and purpose.

CHAPTER EIGHTEEN
THE LEGACY OF A
WELL-FORGED BLADE

In the quiet halls of a Japanese museum, sunlight glints off the blade of a centuries-old katana. Its surface, gleaming and unblemished, carries a story of its own—a story of fire, resilience, and purpose. As I stood there, captivated by the weapon's beauty, I couldn't help but think about the lives it had touched. Not just the warriors who wielded it, but the craftsmen who poured their spirit into its creation, the families it protected, and the cultural legacy it preserved. The katana is more than steel; it's a testament to enduring strength and intention.

This moment of reflection wasn't just about the sword. It was about what it represented: the journey of transformation and the lasting impact we leave behind when we live with purpose and authenticity. The katana is a reminder that life's challenges, like the forging process, shape us into something both beautiful and resilient.

The Katana's Symbolism: More Than a Weapon

For centuries, the katana has stood as a cultural and spiritual icon in Japan. Its creation process, steeped in tradition, symbolizes the harmony of art, craftsmanship, and function. Every step in its making—from heating the blade in fire to folding it repeatedly and tempering it in water—represents transformation through hardship.

Unlike other weapons, a katana is revered not just for its sharpness but for the spirit it embodies. Samurai believed their swords carried part of their soul, serving as an extension of their values: loyalty, honor, and courage. This reverence transforms the katana from a mere tool into a legacy, a piece of history imbued with meaning that endures long after the individual who wielded it.

The Parallel to Our Lives

Our lives, like the katana, are shaped by fire and friction. The challenges we face—whether personal failures, external adversities, or deep moments of self-doubt—act as the flames that heat and soften us, making us malleable enough to grow. The folds of the steel, akin to the repetition of difficult experiences, may seem redundant or even punishing, but they add strength and depth. Finally, the cooling and tempering bring balance—a reminder that resilience isn't just about enduring hardship but also about finding equilibrium.

When we approach life as a craftsman approaches a katana, with patience, intention, and a respect for the process, we create a legacy worth leaving behind. The key is understanding that our legacy isn't built in grand gestures or singular achievements but in the steady, intentional forging of our character.

What Legacy Will You Leave?

In considering the legacy of a well-forged blade, it's natural to turn inward and ask: *What will I leave behind?* Legacy isn't about fame or fortune. It's about the small, meaningful ways we touch the lives of others. Just as a katana carries the spirit of its maker, our actions, relationships, and choices carry our essence into the world.

Think about the people you admire most. Chances are, their legacy isn't defined by material success but by the values they lived by: kindness, perseverance, wisdom, or integrity. They've left an imprint on your heart, not because they were perfect, but because they allowed themselves to be shaped into something extraordinary through life's trials.

Living Intentionally for a Lasting Legacy

Leaving a meaningful legacy starts with living intentionally. Consider these principles:

1. **Focus on Impact:** Reflect on the ways your actions influence those around you. Are you leaving people better than you found them?

2. **Live Your Values:** Like the samurai who honored their code, align your actions with the principles you hold dear.

3. **Embrace Imperfection:** A katana isn't flawless; it's purposeful. Likewise, your life doesn't need to be free of mistakes—it needs to be authentic.

4. **Invest in Relationships:** Our greatest legacies often lie in the lives we touch. Nurture connections with empathy and generosity.

A Legacy of Resilience

As I stood before that katana, I couldn't help but think about its creator. The swordsmith likely never imagined their work would be admired centuries later, but they poured their heart into it regardless. That's the thing about legacy—it often takes shape in ways we'll never see.

What we can control is how we live now. Are we crafting a life of resilience, depth, and authenticity? Are we allowing ourselves to be shaped by life's challenges rather than shattered by them? Like the katana, our legacy will reflect the care, intention, and spirit we put into our journey.

When we live with the awareness that each moment contributes to the blade of our legacy, we approach life with greater purpose. We embrace challenges as part of the forging process, knowing that the fire doesn't destroy us—it transforms us.

The katana's beauty lies not only in its craftsmanship but in its timelessness. Long after the fire has died and the hammer has been laid to rest, the blade continues to inspire. It's a reminder that strength isn't about avoiding hardship but about embracing it with grace and intention.

Your life, like a well-forged blade, can leave an enduring legacy. By living with purpose, resilience, and compassion, you create something far greater than yourself—a lasting symbol of what it means to grow, adapt, and thrive.

As you move forward, ask yourself: *What legacy am I forging?* The answer lies in the fire, the folds, and the balance you bring to your own life's journey. Just as the katana leaves a legacy of strength and purpose, we too can forge a lasting impact through our actions and values.

How to Leave a Legacy Rooted in Authenticity, Resilience, and Compassion

Legacy isn't defined by achievements but by the impact of your character, values, and actions on others. To create a meaningful legacy, embrace **authenticity, resilience, and compassion. Authenticity** means living true to yourself. Define your core values, align actions with beliefs, and share your story. Authenticity builds trust and strengthens relationships.

Resilience is thriving through challenges. Shift perspectives, build a support system, and adopt a growth mindset. Resilience inspires others to overcome adversity. **Compassion** connects us to others. Practice empathy, perform small acts of kindness, and forgive freely.

Compassion creates a ripple effect of kindness. When combined, these values build a multidimensional legacy—honest, strong, and deeply human. Your legacy starts today in the choices you make and the lives you touch.

The Role of Purpose in Life Course Development

The study *The Role of Purpose in Life Course Development* delves into the significant role that purpose plays in shaping how individuals make decisions and experience satisfaction throughout their lives. The researchers found that having a clear sense of purpose not only improves decision-making but also fosters a greater sense of life satisfaction. Individuals who were able to articulate their purpose experienced more fulfilling lives, marked by a greater sense of control and direction.

This finding is particularly relevant when considering the concept of legacy. A person with a clear purpose tends to live with intention, making decisions that align with their values and long-term goals. This alignment enables individuals to build a life that feels cohesive and meaningful, ensuring that their actions leave a positive, lasting impact on others. In contrast, without a defined purpose, decisions can feel scattered or reactive, and satisfaction may be fleeting. The sense of direction that comes from knowing one's purpose acts as a compass, helping to navigate the complexities of life with greater confidence and clarity.

The study suggests that purpose is not only about grand ambitions but also about having a vision that aligns with one's deepest values. This alignment is what shapes the legacy that one leaves behind—whether it's through personal achievements, the influence we have on others, or the contributions we make to the world. Purpose-driven decision-making leads to actions that reflect our true selves, ensuring that the

347

legacy we build is not just a collection of accomplishments, but a reflection of our deepest values.

In the context of building a legacy, this study provides valuable insight: living with purpose encourages us to make choices that align with the legacy we want to leave. Whether we seek to influence our families, communities, or larger society, a clear sense of purpose ensures that our contributions have meaning and endurance. When we understand our "why," we make decisions that resonate with that core purpose, allowing us to create a legacy that's not only impactful but also fulfilling.

This connection between purpose and legacy is an important theme, showing how the clarity of our life's direction directly impacts the lasting effects of our choices. The study affirms that a life well-lived, guided by purpose, leads to both personal satisfaction and a legacy worth leaving behind.

Exercises: Define Your Legacy Statement

A legacy statement is a declaration of the values, principles, and impact you wish to leave behind. It goes beyond what you accomplish in your lifetime; it's about how you show up in the world and the mark you leave on others. To craft a legacy statement, you need to reflect deeply on what matters most to you and what you want to stand for.

Start by thinking about the end of your life. What do you hope people will say about you when you're no longer around? What qualities or actions do you want to be remembered for? Is it your kindness? Your resilience? The way you lifted others up? Defining your legacy is an act of clarity, allowing you to focus on the things that will truly matter to you in the long run.

In this exercise, take a moment to reflect on the impact you want to have in your relationships, work, and community. Imagine that someone is speaking at your memorial or writing about your life. What would you want them to say? What kind of person do you want to have been? In order to define your legacy statement, ask yourself these reflective questions:

- What values define who I am?

- What have I learned from the challenges I've faced?

- How do I want to be remembered by the people I've loved and worked with?

- What positive impact have I made on others' lives?

Once you have spent some time reflecting on these questions, it's time to translate that into a coherent statement. Your legacy statement doesn't need to be long or overly complex; it should simply capture the essence of your values and the lasting impact you want to have on the world around you.

For example, a legacy statement could be: *"I want to be remembered as someone who always tried to see the good in people, someone who believed in resilience, and who left the world a little better than I found it."* Or, perhaps: *"I want my legacy to be one of compassion and service, making the lives of others easier, whether by offering a listening ear or lending a helping hand."*

The key is to stay authentic to who you are and what resonates most deeply with you. Once you've written your legacy statement, read it aloud and see if it aligns with how you want to live moving forward. Does it inspire you? Does it remind you of the impact you want to have in your day-to-day life? If it doesn't, continue to refine it until it feels true.

Your legacy doesn't come from a single moment, but from the cumulative effect of how you choose to live each day. By defining your legacy statement, you're planting a seed that can help guide you toward meaningful, intentional actions.

CONCLUSION

L ife is a constant process of refinement, like forging a katana. True strength is shaped by adversity, not avoidance. Each stage of transformation—stability, acceptance, reflection, growth, compassion, and purpose—builds upon the last. The Ikigai stage reminds us that living with meaning comes from aligning passions and values with the world's needs.

Your journey is not a destination but an ongoing act of crafting resilience and authenticity. Each step sharpens your purpose, like a blade honed by fire. Embrace the process, knowing your legacy is defined not by achievements but by how you live and contribute.

Printed in Dunstable, United Kingdom